UNDERSTANDING SUICIDE IN THE UNITED STATES

T0373800

By integrating sociological, psychological, and biological perspectives, this book aims to demystify and destigmatize a challenging and taboo topic – suicide. It weaves current theories and statistics on suicide into a larger message of how suicide can affect almost anyone, and how urgent prevention needs are. Written in an accessible manner, it assumes no preexisting knowledge of suicide. The broad nontechnical overview will appeal to general readers and a wide range of disciplines, including politics and policy, biology, psychology, sociology, and psychiatry. It concludes on a positive note, focused on recovery, resilience, and hope. It considers not only how these factors may play a role in suicide prevention but also how, despite persistent suicide rates, we can proceed optimistically and take concrete action to support loved ones or promote suicide prevention efforts.

MEAGHAN STACY is a licensed clinical psychologist and Associate Professor of Psychiatry at Yale School of Medicine, Yale University. She has over 15 years of experience in healthcare system change and improvement, and she has authored more than 40 articles and 100 presentations in national and international settings. She is co-editor of *Recovering the US Mental Healthcare System: The Past, Present, and Future of Psychosocial Interventions for Psychosis* (2022).

JAY SCHULKIN was Research Professor at the University of Washington and a prolific researcher with over 500 papers and nearly 40 books to his name. His broad philosophical and scientific interests ranged such topics as behavioral neuroscience, naturalistic philosophy, feeding behavior, homeostasis, and the evolution of the human brain.

UNDERSTANDING SUICIDE IN THE UNITED STATES

A Social, Biological, and Psychological Perspective

MEAGHAN STACY

Yale University

JAY SCHULKIN

University of Washington

CAMBRIDGE
UNIVERSITY PRESS

Shaftesbury Road, Cambridge CB2 8EA, United Kingdom

One Liberty Plaza, 20th Floor, New York, NY 10006, USA

477 Williamstown Road, Port Melbourne, VIC 3207, Australia

314–321, 3rd Floor, Plot 3, Splendor Forum, Jasola District Centre, New Delhi – 110025, India

103 Penang Road, #05–06/07, Visioncrest Commercial, Singapore 238467

Cambridge University Press is part of Cambridge University Press & Assessment, a department of the University of Cambridge.

We share the University's mission to contribute to society through the pursuit of education, learning and research at the highest international levels of excellence.

www.cambridge.org
Information on this title: www.cambridge.org/9781009386920

DOI: 10.1017/9781009386937

First published 2024

A catalogue record for this publication is available from the British Library

A Cataloging-in-Publication data record for this book is available from the Library of Congress

ISBN 978-1-009-38692-0 Hardback
ISBN 978-1-009-38690-6 Paperback

My dear friend, Jay, thank you for everything. – MS
For Angie, her loss, and her dignity. – JS

Contents

Figures

Tables

Boxes

x

Preface

Suicide is a challenging, heavy, and potentially uncomfortable topic. Unfortunately, it is also a phenomenon that impacts nearly everyone. In fact, it has been suggested that for every suicide death, 135 individuals are impacted (Cerel et al., 2019). The current technology and rapid news transmission can further this impact by increasing the dissemination of news about celebrity suicides. Almost all of us have heard reports of the suicide deaths of Kurt Cobain, Robin Williams, and others. Celebrity deaths drive home the fact that almost anyone can be at risk for suicide despite appearances, income, success, and reasons to live. Indeed, it is some of these stories that help people begin to wrap their heads around the severity and scope of suicide as a national problem. The first question following a suicide, is often "Why?" Speculation abounds: depression, anxiety, trauma history, medical diagnoses, and addiction. And there are stigmatizing and stereotypical explanations that perpetuate misunderstanding: instability, weakness, and selfishness. Thus, this seemingly ubiquitous experience warrants discussion and understanding, despite it potentially being uncomfortable and stigmatized.

Authors with lived experiences of suicidality have similarly brought the topic of suicide to wide audiences. For example, by weaving personal experience, historical information, and scientific research, Kay Redfield Jamison (2011) humanizes suicide and provides evidence-based information that demystifies and destigmatizes the topic. Elyn Saks' memoir, *The Center Cannot Hold* (2007), elucidates the fear and confusion that accompany suicidality and mental illness. They and others (Bering, 2018; Hammond, 2018) destigmatize mental illness and suicidality, increase empathy, and offer a heartening perspective about the possibility of recovery. These memoirs are particularly powerful given that they are written by individuals with objectively high levels of success (e.g., professor, public health consultant, psychologist, and physician) and highlight suicide as a significant problem that can affect anyone.

We, as individuals, have not been unscathed by suicide. As academics in healthcare fields, we've encountered discussions of suicide, its causes, and its prevention. As a psychologist, one of us (MS) has worked with clients and clinical programs to promote recovery-oriented care and suicide prevention. And while we have worked together for sixteen years on numerous projects regarding mental health, what forged our partnership on this book were recent, and seemingly increasing, personal experiences with suicide. In the aftermath, we began asking that inevitable question, "Why!?" and listing the reasons people appeared to have for living. In making sense of our experience, we discussed potential, often invisible and undisclosed, causes. We read. We shared news stories and journal articles. And in an effort to turn our feelings of futility toward positive action, Jay said: "Let's write a book." And here we are.

The intention of this book is twofold: (1) to integrate social, psychological, and biological perspectives on the etiology, prevention, and treatment of suicide ideation and behavior (e.g., attempts, deaths) and (2) to independently serve as a public health intervention to increase awareness about and destigmatize suicide. Chapter 1 provides historical context, followed by a discussion of key psychological and social theories on suicide and the various forms of pain and suffering that contribute to suicide (Chapter 2). Chapter 3 describes biological features that may contribute to suicide via allostatic load, followed by a description of the demographics of suicide (Chapter 4). With this foundation, the book then orients toward action, namely clinical and community interventions (Chapter 5). We conclude on an optimistic note, with Chapters 6 and 7 focusing on building resilience and hope, respectively. Our intention is to provide insight into a problem that will impact many of our lives and instill hope for a future when that isn't a tragic fact.

CHAPTER I

A Brief View on the Social History of Suicide

There has been a long history of suicide discourse, and although there are discrepant reports on the first documented suicide (e.g., Ramses II, Lucretia, Periander, Empedocles), this phenomenon has been present worldwide for millennia. Writings touching on suicide can be found from cultures in ancient Greece and Rome, sub-Saharan Africa, China, Russia, Indigenous cultures in North, Central, and South America, and others (see Battin, 2015 for a robust overview).

In some cultures, suicide is part of legend, with the memory of the deceased revered. For example, Cleopatra, queen of Egypt, died by suicide after her army's defeat at Alexandria. Rather than be a trophy, she took her own life. The story of Lucretia, who died by suicide to protect her honor and speak out against Etruscan rule, is credited as the origins of the Roman Republic (Ruff, 1974). As a result, Lucretia was venerated for centuries and her story recounted in many pieces of art and literature (e.g., Canterbury Tales, Dante's Inferno, Rembrandt's *Lucretia*). Other ancient Romans and Greeks (e.g., Empedocles, Cato) endured similar fates, dying by suicide to achieve transformation or preserve their honor or legacy (Chitwood, 1986; Drogula, 2019). It is in dying by suicide that these individuals cemented their names in history. Suicide after defeat in war as a means to preserve honor can be seen across time and geography. In Japan, seppuku (or hara-kiri) is a ritualistic suicide in which the samurai died by self-disembowelment to preserve their family's honor. In these examples, the underlying philosophy is death before dishonor (Pierre, 2015).

The Stoics (e.g., Marcus Aurelius, Seneca, Epictetus, Cato, Musonius) taught that virtue is the only good, and if there was a potential to behave virtuously, then suicide is not rational (Englert, 1990). However, they acknowledged circumstances under which it may be acceptable, honorable, or an expression of freedom (Falkowski, 2016). While they argued that suicide based on life dissatisfaction was wrong, they acknowledged benefits of suicide as a means to avoid oppression, colonization, or subjugation.

Seneca was unique in that he emphasized the freedom suicide offers in the absolution of fear, pain, and embarrassment. Some argued that dying for friends or country was acceptable, and Musonius argued that if suicide would benefit others more than would remaining alive, then suicide could be virtuous (Burton, 2022).

Many religions, mostly monotheistic (Judaism, Christianity, Islam), condemn suicide (Barry, 1995; Gearing & Alonzo, 2018). For Christians, particularly Catholics, views have shifted over time. Initially, martyrdom was viewed as a way to prove loyalty to God, but following the writings of St. Augustine and Thomas Aquinas, the view transitioned to disapproval. For example, Thomas Aquinas makes several arguments against suicide, including that the commandment "Thou shalt not kill" includes oneself and life is a gift from God that must not be rejected. As such, the Church ultimately labeled suicide a mortal sin resulting in an eternity in hell (Torgler & Schaltegger, 2012). In the Middle Ages, the Church would inflict further punishment: denying burial, punishing the corpses, or appropriating their estate, leaving survivors without resources (Torgler & Schaltegger, 2012).

In the Enlightenment, the Church's strict doctrine came under question. Writings from David Hume (Frey, 1999) and others argued that some suicides can be viewed as moral and universal condemnation is unwarranted. Hume also highlighted the irony that the person experiencing misery has the God-given power to end his suffering, but do not for fear of offending God. This more secularist view argues that a person is their own master, free to kill themselves if they wish, and in some scenarios it is a positive, honorable, and emancipating endeavor (Beauchamp, 1989; d'Holbach, 1770; Hume, 1777).

Darwin's (1859) theories caused further debate as many grappled with reconciling religious, secular, and evolutionary perspectives, which influenced philosophers like Friedrich Nietzsche. As a result, Nietzsche's writings emphasized the importance of finding value in life, regardless of the existence of Heaven. The focus on the present moment, the current life, is reinforced by his view that if value and meaning cannot be found in one's current existence, then it must be created for oneself, rather than anticipating an afterlife. This also informs his view that death should be an experience and decision that falls under one's own control, a voluntary death and respectable act (Nietzsche, 1964).

These views of suicide and its morality have evolved and pendulated over time, as informed by the zeitgeist. Currently, suicide is viewed as a significant public health issue worldwide (see Figure 1.1; Knox, 2014;

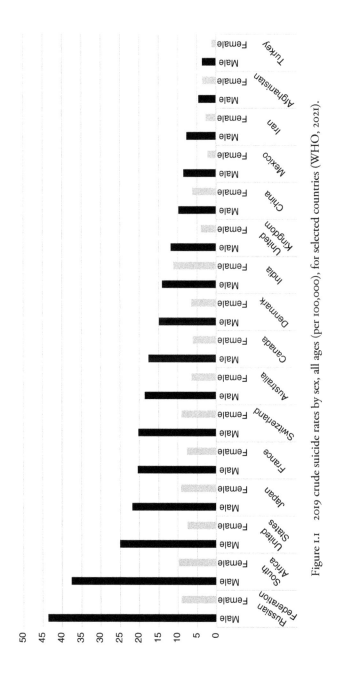

Figure 1.1 2019 crude suicide rates by sex, all ages (per 100,000), for selected countries (WHO, 2021).

World Health Organization, 2014), with someone dying by suicide every *40 seconds* (World Health Organization, 2019). Suicide contributes to premature mortality, morbidity, lost productivity, and healthcare costs (U.S. Office of the Surgeon General and National Action Alliance for Suicide Prevention, 2012; World Health Organization, 2014), and has wide-ranging consequences for survivors and society as a whole (Barman & Kablinger, 2021; Cerel, 2008; Jordan & McIntosh, 2010; McDaid et al., 2010; Ruskin et al., 2004). As a result, numerous organizations have set suicide prevention as a top priority (Carroll, Kearney, & Miller, 2020; Stone et al., 2017).

Suicide has traditionally been addressed with a focus on the individual and clinical interventions (Bryan & Rozek, 2018; Isacsson et al., 1997; Jobes, Au, & Siegelman, 2015; Linehan et al., 2015). However, many who die by suicide have not received mental healthcare in their last year (Miller & Druss, 2001), limiting the impact clinical interventions can have. Further, suicide is the result of diverse biological, genetic, social, cultural, psychological, and behavioral factors that may not be addressed by clinical interventions (De Leo, 2004; Qin et al., 2003; Turecki et al., 2019). As such, suicide prevention requires integrated approaches to address upstream risk factors and public health approaches to reduce risk in the whole population (Center for Mental Health Services & Office of the Surgeon General, 2001; Knox, 2014; Knox et al., 2004; Lytle, Silenzio, & Caine, 2016).

Public health approaches incorporate clinical- *and* community-based interventions to address the health status and needs of a population in addition to focusing on at-risk individuals. These efforts focus on prevention strategies and the implementation of high-quality services at the population level (World Health Organization, 2012). The public health approach to suicide prevention includes: reducing stigma; increasing help-seeking; increasing lethal means safety; providing access to crisis lines and effective treatment; prevention strategies for the general population, at-risk groups, and individuals; community-based programs; and others (Knox et al., 2004; Lytle et al., 2016; Parcover et al., 2015; World Health Organization, 2012).

However, despite years of significant suicide prevention efforts, suicide rates in the United States have continued to rise (Hedegaard, Curtin, & Warner, 2018; Perlis & Fihn, 2020) until very recently (Curtin, Hedegaard, & Ahmad, 2021). Increasing deaths of despair, including suicide, have contributed to greater mortality rates in the United States than sixteen other industrialized countries, a discrepancy that has been growing for two decades (National Academy of Sciences, 2021). Several hypotheses as to why these types of deaths are rising have been proposed and potential interventions suggested. Sterling and Platt (2022) highlight how the sixteen countries with decreasing deaths of despair offer more support for their residents, such as through prenatal and maternal care, maternity leave, preschool provision, school equity, no or low tuition for universities, lower cost medical care, and significant vacation time. Given the range of potential interventions, it is unlikely that a single approach will reduce suicide rates (Lytle et al., 2016). Thus, our current understanding is that *integrated* efforts that blend cutting-edge clinical advances with community-based policies and resources will likely be more fruitful to destigmatize, address, and prevent suicide.

CHAPTER 2

Pain, Suffering, and Buffering

Beyond the early writings and philosophies on the morality of suicide, the current focus has been on explaining *why* suicidal behavior occurs (Klonsky & May, 2015; Klonsky, Saffer, & Bryan, 2018; Van Orden et al., 2010). This chapter first summarizes several theories of suicide, with a focus on the eighteenth century to the present, and how they uniquely frame various aspects of pain and suffering that lead to suicide. We high-light how these theories evolved over time, with varying foci on individual and societal pathology, and how earlier theories are evident in present day views. We then conclude with a discussion of the known factors that con-fer and buffer against risk for suicide.

Suicide Theories

We can see the underpinnings of our current understanding of suicide as far back as the French psychiatrist Jean-Etienne Dominique Esquirol (1845). He viewed suicide as an involuntary behavior, the result of genetic, psychological, and social factors outside of one's control. His view is one of the earliest indications of the shift from perceiving suicide as a sinful, volitional behavior within an individual to an understanding of it as a result of various biopsychosocial forces. These views are later reflected in the work of Emile Durkheim (see below) and have influenced our current understandings of suicide, which highlight the impact of complex biopsy-chosocial factors.

Early understandings of suicide also grappled with cognitive components of the phenomenon. Arthur Schopenhauer (1893), a German philosopher, suggested that the mind constructs one's understanding of everything; therefore, suicide is due to distress resulting from cognitive errors that lead to the conclusion that one's existence is the problem. Here, the fear of life outweighs the fear of death. Schopenhauer highlights that emotion-ally distressing events can remove objectivity, distorting one's perceptions.

6

Schopenhauer's focus on cognitive errors and distortions can be seen in contemporary theories emphasizing the importance of believing oneself is a burden or does not belong (see Interpersonal Theory below), as well as cognitive interventions for suicide prevention. And with Schopenhauer's focus on the events that can impair objectivity, he begins the discussion of *external* factors that can contribute to suicidogenic cognitions and drive suicide.

Similarly, Emile Durkheim (2005), the founder of French sociology, also focused on external drivers, suggesting that suicide is the result of the society in which one lives. Durkheim's philosophies were steeped in the idea of collective consciousness, the view that a shared set of beliefs and knowledge within a group influences our sense of self, belonging, and behavior. As such, the social environment, as opposed to individual psychology, was the key construct in his understanding of suicide. Durkheim suggested that a society's acceptance of suicide as an alternative is a symptom of larger societal dysfunction and theorized that suicide is a symptom of societal breakdown. With suicide reflecting the nature of a society's social relationships, he created a typology categorizing suicide into four groups (altruistic, egoistic, anomic, and fatalistic; see Figure 2.1), each varying in degree of social integration and social regulation, with suicide risk increasing at the extremes of the continua.

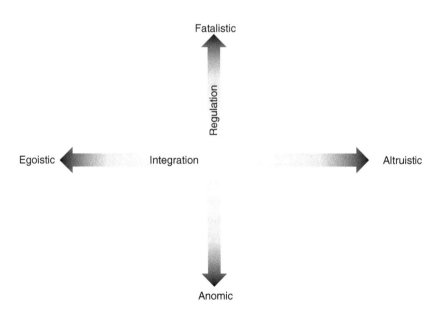

Figure 2.1   Durkheim's four types of suicide (adapted from Pope, 1976).

Egoistic suicide occurs in a society with little sense of belonging, social integration, and connectedness. Excessive individuation results in hopelessness, meaninglessness, apathy, and negative mood. On the other hand, altruistic suicide is characterized by too much integration into society, with individual needs outweighed by those of society. Here, individual identity is lost or meaningless. Anomic suicide occurs in societies that lack social or moral regulation, most commonly during social, political, or economic unrest that leave people grappling with uncertainty and instability. At the high end of social regulation is fatalistic suicide, occurring when society is excessively regulated. Here, there is almost no change in social environment or role expectations, generating monotony and hopelessness. While Durkheim designated this a theoretical category, it may occur in oppressive regimes, where people would rather die than persevere.

Per Durkheim, the decreasing importance of state, religion, marriage, and family has resulted in a regulation deficit in modern society. These formerly core institutions no longer provide social structure and organization, resulting in a growing sense of alienation and social issues that have negative health consequences and increased suicide rates. He posited that, instead, work has become the central institution within modern society, so investing in corporations, workplaces, and occupational groups is a potential pathway for reinstating a collective consciousness. Although Durkheim's theory is not without limitations (Mueller et al., 2021), it remains a key foundational theory for understanding suicide.

Psychodynamic theories diminished the role that society plays in suicide and reflected the general understanding of human behavior as the result of psychological forces. The specific forces varied depending on the theory but were largely seated within the individual (Bowlby, 1973; Hendin, 1991; Menninger, 1938). For example, Sigmund Freud (1938, 1957) emphasized the role of unconscious drives, particularly the death drive, *Thanatos*, as the underlying impetus for aggression, self-destructive behavior, and suicide. From his perspective, suicide can serve as a punishment or fulfillment of a wish. The latter suggests that suicide occurs when the person has identified so strongly with an object (another person, such as a parent), and they turn the wish of death for that object against themselves, indirectly fulfilling that wish.

Collaborators of Freud's, who later fell out of favor with the psychodynamic leader, added their own perspective to the psychodynamic view of suicide. Alfred Adler (1964), for example, was one of the earliest to view suicide from a social psychology perspective, emphasizing roles for both individual characteristics and situational factors in the development of suicidality. This more holistic perspective aligned with the evolution of psychiatry and psychology at the time and also his theory of individual psychology where social and human contexts are essential to understanding and treating psychiatric concerns. In regard to suicide, Adler highlighted the role of social interest, a person's connection with others and a sense of belonging in the community. As such, suicide is something that could be intervened upon by increasing social connectedness and relationships (Adler, 1964; Ansbacher, 1969), a foreshadowing of later theories that incorporate aspects of belonging.

Edwin Shneidman (1981, 1993), the founder of the American Association of Suicidology, identified intense psychological pain, which he called psychache, as the most significant contributor to suicide. Psychache is an overwhelming amount of emotional pain that, when it exceeds the individual's capacity to cope with it, results in suicide. While his theory was influenced by his predecessors in that it is individually focused, it can be paired with interpersonal and sociological explanations and thus helped move psychology out of its focus on psychoanalytic explanations. Shneidman's movement away from psychodynamic explanations and his emphasis on overwhelming psychological pain has influenced later researchers and theorists, particularly those emphasizing the role of escape. This can be seen with Baumeister (1990) describing suicide as a means of escape from an aversive state of mind or self-awareness, Linehan (1993) highlighting the role of escaping difficult emotions, Williams (2001) suggesting suicide as an escape from defeat or entrapment (similar to arrested flight per Gilbert & Allan, 1998), and Beck et al. (1975) and Abramson et al. (2002) adding to this by highlighting the role of hopelessness. Indeed, significant effort has been spent to characterize the various aspects of intense psychological pain.

Shortcomings of the preceding theories include the limited differentiation of suicide ideation and behavior, emphasis on single variables, and no clear mechanism by which ideation transitions to behavior. More recent theories addressed these gaps by embracing an ideation-to-action framework (Klonsky, Saffer, & Bryan, 2018). These theories include the Interpersonal-Psychological Theory – also called the Interpersonal Theory – of Suicide (Joiner, 2005; Van Orden et al., 2010), the Integrated Motivational–Volitional (IMV; O'Connor & Kirtley, 2018) Model, the Three-Step Theory (3ST; Klonsky & May, 2015), and the Fluid Vulnerability Theory (FVT) (Rudd, 2006). These models explore pathways to suicide ideation and ultimately behavior. This is important considering a larger proportion of the population experiences ideation than

Table 2.1 *Interpersonal theory of suicide constructs (Joiner, 2005; Van Orden et al., 2010)*

Construct	Occurs when	Representative cognitions
Thwarted belongingness	Unmet need for social connectedness	"I am all alone." "I don't fit in here."
Perceived burdensomeness	Unmet need for social competence (e.g., relationship problems, unemployment)	"I am such a drain on other people." "It would be better for everyone else if I were gone."

behavior; these groups are likely qualitatively different, and it is necessary to understand the overlapping and unique processes that result in suicidal thoughts, actions, and deaths.

Interpersonal Theory (Joiner, 2005; Van Orden et al., 2010) is one of the most influential and empirically supported theories of suicide. This theory indicates that suicide is the result of a combination of both the desire and the ability to kill oneself. The desire to die by suicide is a function of self-perceptions related to others, specifically social cognitions about thwarted belongingness and perceived burdensomeness (see Table 2.1). When thwarted belongingness and perceived burdensomeness persist and one begins to feel hopeless, desire for suicide will emerge.

This desire transforms into suicide behavior when the person develops the capability to overcome their natural instincts to avoid pain, injury, and death (Joiner, 2005; Smith et al., 2016; Van Orden et al., 2010). Suicide capability fluctuates over time (Law & Anestis, 2021) and is largely developed through an opponent process and habituation. The more the person experiences pain- or fear-inducing events, the less the events affect them. When such events occur repeatedly, the initial aversive response is suppressed. Indeed, capability for suicide is increased among those with previous suicide attempts, self-harm, familiarity with the idea of suicide and death, and a high pain threshold. Capability for suicide behavior can be acquired through life experiences that are known risk factors for suicide, such as sexual trauma, violence, and intravenous drug use (Joiner, 2005). Thus, the mechanism by which these risk factors contribute to suicide may be by increasing suicide capability. There is strong empirical support for Interpersonal Theory, its constructs, and their relationships, though some have highlighted a need for further clarification of constructs and better measurement tools (Klonsky, Saffer, & Bryan, 2018; Ma et al., 2016; Stewart et al., 2017).

Another ideation-to-action theory, the Integrated Motivational–Volitional (IMV; O'Connor & Kirtley, 2018) Model of suicidal behavior is heavily influenced by the Cry of Pain Theory (Williams, 2001), which suggests that suicide is a response to circumstances with three components: defeat, no escape, and no rescue. The IMV model breaks suicide into three phases that highlight the roles of and relationship between defeat, humiliation, and entrapment (O'Connor & Kirtley, 2018). The Pre-Motivational Phase describes the biopsychosocial context in which suicide ideation and behavior emerge. Then, in the Motivational Phase, negative feelings of defeat and their interaction with poor coping and problem-solving skills ultimately contribute to feeling trapped. This experience, feeling trapped, contributes to viewing suicide as an alternative to negative life experiences and drives suicidal intent (O'Connor & Kirtley, 2018). When there is an increased capacity for suicide, impulsivity, planning, imitation/contagion, access to lethal means, and other facilitating factors, intent transforms into suicide behavior in the Volitional Phase. There is support for the IMV model, with evidence that defeat and entrapment are strongly associated with suicide ideation (SI) and that variables broader than just acquired capability differentiate those with ideation vs. attempts (Dhingra et al., 2015). However, further validation of this model and adaptations for certain groups may be necessary (Pollak et al., 2021).

Klonsky and May's (2015) 3ST defines the pain that can generate SI more broadly than other ideation-to-action theories and does not limit this to psychological pain. This theory suggests that suicide behavior is explained by four components (pain, hopelessness, connection, and capability for suicide), and both pain *and* hopelessness must be present for suicide desire to emerge. In the absence of hopelessness, energy would instead be diverted to coping rather than toward escape or avoidance. As pain and hopelessness intensify or persist, they erode the buffering effects of connectedness (i.e., social support, roles, and purpose) that make life worth living. The extent to which pain and suffering overwhelm an individual's connectedness determines the intensity of suicide desire. Similar to other ideation-to-action theories, 3ST suggests that suicidal desire leads to a suicide attempt when suicide capability exists. Here, suicide capability is determined by factors that go beyond acquired capability, and includes broader experiences that reduce fear of pain, injury, and death, dispositional factors (e.g., temperament, genetics), and practical factors (e.g., access to means). Klonsky and May's (2015) preliminary research on this model demonstrated that pain and hopelessness combine to account for a large proportion of the variance in SI and may predict SI to a greater extent than just thwarted belongingness and perceived burdensomeness, as proposed by Interpersonal Theory. Further, the model's broader variables related to suicide capability each predicted suicide attempt history beyond what was predicted by current and lifetime SI (Klonsky & May, 2015). Additional support for the 3ST model comes from studies in the UK (Dhingra, Klonsky, & Tapola, 2019), China (Yang, Liu, Chen, & Li, 2019), and Canada (Tsai et al., 2021).

A final ideation-to-action framework, the FVT (Rudd, 2006), is based on a cognitive-behavioral framework suggesting people may be vulnerable to suicide as a stress response, a "suicidal mode" (Rudd, 2000). FVT also uniquely addresses temporal dynamics and periods of ambivalence around suicide. The model assumes that suicide risk operates in a nonlinear fashion, has both stable and dynamic aspects, and is resolved when multiple components of the "suicidal mode" are addressed. Like other models, FVT posits that cognitions can drive suicide but is less restrictive in terms of which cognitions are suicidogenic. This model does not focus on burdensomeness or belongingness but rather highlights a suicidal belief system, comprised of many thoughts that can contribute, singly or in combination, to suicide. The model also highlights the role that mechanisms like cognitive inflexibility and emotion regulation deficits can play in fostering such a belief system. There is support for this theory, showing that a wider range of cognitions better discriminate those with SI vs. attempts vs. non-suicidal self-injury (Bryan et al., 2014; Klonsky, Saffer, & Bryan, 2018). Further, measures that assess a wider range of cognitions (e.g., unlovability, unbearability) better predict suicide attempts and crisis intensity relative to more narrow measures of thwarted belonginess or perceived burdensomeness and hopelessness (Bryan et al., 2014). This is not to say that burdensomeness or thwarted belonging are *not* suicidogenic but are likely among numerous cognitive pathways that lead to suicide.

More recently, Macintyre and colleagues (2021) have applied Perceptual Control Theory (PCT; Powers, 1973), a transdiagnostic framework of well-being and distress, to suicide, specifically focusing on crisis periods. The authors argue that although hopelessness, entrapment, thwarted belonginess, and burdensomeness are integral to suicide, these cognitive–affective states result from chronic, unresolved, distressing goal conflict (e.g., increasing belonging without feeling like they are burdening others). As the conflict goes unresolved and the person becomes aware of this incompatibility, there can be a perceived loss of control great enough to generate a crisis. It is at this point that suicide is viewed as way to regain control and achieve a goal, such as ending emotional pain. Macintyre and colleagues

(2021) further argue that because individuals experiencing SI often experience cognitive constriction, with a bias toward suicide-related stimuli and rumination (Cha et al., 2010; Rogers, Gallyer, & Joiner, 2021), they may lose sight of how suicide impacts the attainment of other goals. The authors suggest that this limited awareness is the common mechanism underlying suicide attempts, regardless of the constellation of specific risk factors present. Thus, they suggest that treatment target this mechanism rather than the cognitive–affective states that emerge from it (e.g., burdensomeness) and focus on increasing awareness of higher-order goals and identifying effective ways to achieve these goals.

There is no shortage of theories on the underpinnings of suicide. All of these theories highlight various painful aspects of the human experience (albeit at times with overlapping and poorly defined constructs; Millner, Robinaugh, & Nock, 2020; see Figure 2.2) that overwhelm coping skills, emotion regulation, and biological systems to transition into suffering, and ultimately suicide. In the next section, we highlight briefly what is known about the specific risk factors that contribute to this process.

Risk Factors for Suicide

As theories of suicide are developed and evaluated, they must be able to accommodate each of the many known suicide risk factors. Risk factors are categorized into either static or dynamic risk factors. Static risk factors are stable characteristics (e.g., age, sex, and race) that confer a foundational risk for suicide, whereas dynamic risk factors vacillate over an individual's life and can be targeted in treatment (e.g., alcohol use and relationship conflict) (Steele et al., 2017). Figure 2.3 depicts how risk (and protective) factors can be categorized across ecological levels (individual, interpersonal, community, and societal), capturing the broader context of factors that drive suicide.

Individual-Level Risk Factors

At the individual level, within-person risk factors, such as clinical characteristics or family history, are critical to addressing suicide risk. For example, significant research has demonstrated that a history of suicide attempts increases risk of future attempts (Beghi & Rosenbaum, 2010; Hawton et al., 2005; Nanayakkara et al., 2013). Further, those who make *multiple* attempts have significantly greater odds of making subsequent attempts compared to those with ideation or a single attempt

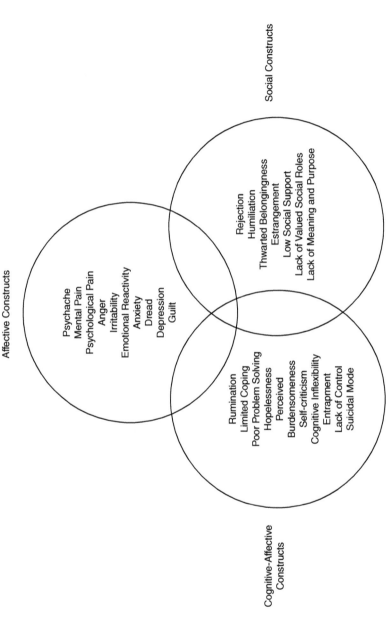

Figure 2.2   The overlapping vague constructs historically used in suicide theories. Figure adapted from Millner, Robinaugh, and Nock (2020).

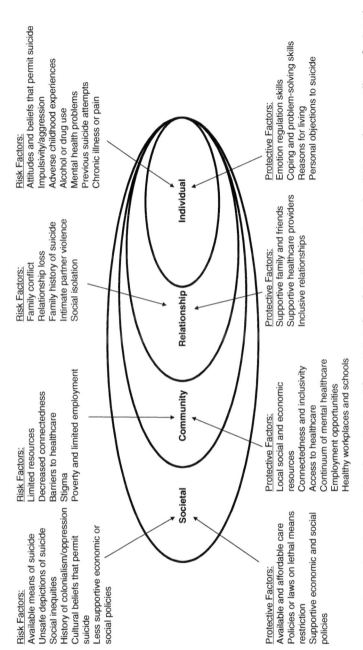

Risk Factors:
Attitudes and beliefs that permit suicide
Impulsivity/aggression
Adverse childhood experiences
Alcohol or drug use
Mental health problems
Previous suicide attempts
Chronic illness or pain

Risk Factors:
Family conflict
Relationship loss
Family history of suicide
Intimate partner violence
Social isolation

Risk Factors:
Limited resources
Decreased connectedness
Barriers to healthcare
Stigma
Poverty and limited employment

Risk Factors:
Available means of suicide
Unsafe depictions of suicide
Social inequities
History of colonialism/oppression
Cultural beliefs that permit suicide
Less supportive economic or social policies

Protective Factors:
Emotion regulation skills
Coping and problem-solving skills
Reasons for living
Personal objections to suicide

Protective Factors:
Supportive family and friends
Supportive healthcare providers
Inclusive relationships

Protective Factors:
Local social and economic resources
Connectedness and inclusivity
Access to healthcare
Continuum of mental healthcare
Employment opportunities
Healthy workplaces and schools

Protective Factors:
Available and affordable care
Policies or laws on lethal means restriction
Supportive economic and social policies

Individual
Relationship
Community
Societal

Figure 2.3   The social–ecological model of suicide adapted from U.S. Office of the Surgeon General and National Action Alliance for Suicide Prevention (2012).

(Miranda et al., 2008), and having multiple attempts increases the odds of eventual suicide death (Reid, 2009). It should be noted, though, that most individuals who attempt to die by suicide will not actually go on to die by suicide (Owens, 2002).

Many, but not all, individuals who die by suicide have mental health diagnoses. While mental illness is common among people who die by suicide (Bertolote et al., 2004; Ferrari et al., 2014), most people with a mental illness do not attempt suicide (Van Orden et al., 2010). Some diagnoses are known to confer greater risk. For example, individuals with bipolar disorder are at – twenty to thirty times greater suicide risk than the general population. Indeed, bipolar disorder has the highest suicide rate of all psychiatric diagnoses, and up to one-half of individuals with bipolar disorder make one or more suicide attempts (Miller & Black, 2020). However, Stone et al. (2018) reported that over half of those in twenty-seven U.S. states who died by suicide between 1999 and 2016 had no known mental illness. Similarly, Ahmedani et al. (2014) showed only about half of those who died by suicide had mental health diagnoses in the year before their death. This shows the complex relationship between mental health and suicide and that addressing only a clinical population (i.e., those with a psychiatric diagnosis) will overlook a proportion of people who die by suicide.

Alcohol and substance use can increase the risk of suicidal behavior by impairing judgment, reducing impulse control, and compounding negative life events and problems (Esang & Ahmed, 2018). In addition to increasing suicide risk, numerous suicides take place during intoxication. Esang and Ahmed (2018) reported notable proportions of suicide deaths involve alcohol (22%), opiates (20%), marijuana (10%), cocaine (5%), and amphetamines (3%). Co-occurring mental health and substance use disorders further amplify risk, often in a cycle where mental health symptoms and substance use exacerbate one another (Carra et al., 2014; Effinger & Stewart, 2012). Understanding how substance use and psychiatric disorders increase risk independently and in combination is essential to evaluating suicide risk.

Suicide also occurs more frequently among those with a history of violence, aggressive behavior, and impulsivity (Gvion & Apter, 2011). Numerous studies have documented that individuals with greater impulsivity are more likely to experience SI or engage in suicide behavior (Conner, Meldrum, Wieczorek, Duberstein, & Welte, 2004; Hull-Blanks, Kerr, & Robinson Kurpius, 2004; Maser et al., 2002; Neufeld & O'Rourke, 2009). Impulsivity is associated with the lethality and number of past attempts (Chesin, Jeglic, & Stanley, 2010) and may increase suicide risk beyond the risk associated with mental health diagnoses (Chesin, Jeglic, & Stanley, 2010; Dumais et al., 2005), particularly among those lacking social support (Kleiman et al., 2012).

Beyond their own clinical characteristics, an individual's family history of suicide is a particularly strong risk factor. Studies of twins and adopted children suggest that suicide is genetically transmitted (Glowinski et al., 2001; Statham et al., 1998), with an early study (Roy et al., 1991) reporting that 11.3% of monozygotic twin pairs were concordant for suicide compared with 1.8% of dizygotic twin pairs. While some have suggested that these findings may be driven by the genetic predisposition for mental health problems, evidence suggests that the genetic contribution to suicide is independent of the genetic transmission of psychiatric disorders (Mann et al., 1999; Powell et al., 2000; Qin et al., 2003; Runeson & Åsberg 2003). Thus, assessment of family history of psychiatric diagnoses and suicide is necessary.

Serious medical diagnoses and chronic illnesses can also increase suicide risk (Ferro et al., 2017; Greydanus, Patel, & Pratt, 2010; Gürhan et al., 2019). One meta-analysis demonstrated that the risk of suicide is 100 times greater among people living with HIV/AIDS than in the general population (Pelton et al., 2021). Another meta-analysis (Du et al., 2020) found that individuals with cancer had a high incidence of suicide. Similarly, severe heart diseases, such as heart failure, are associated with increased suicide risk (Liu et al., 2018). This risk is particularly elevated within six months of diagnosis (Du et al., 2020; Liu et al., 2018), and appointments where individuals receive or recently received a diagnosis are an opportunity for screening.

Personal circumstances (e.g., legal, financial) are individual-level factors that can drive suicide risk. Elevated risk has been reported among individuals with legal issues, particularly criminal offenses (Fazel et al., 2008; Pratt et al., 2006). Suicide risk is also greater among those who are unemployed (Cunningham et al., 2021; Milner, Page, & LaMontagne, 2013), and a meta-analysis reported that individuals with debt are almost eight times more likely to die by suicide (Richardson, Elliott, & Roberts, 2013). Thorough assessment of financial and legal concerns is important, and suicide risk screening may be warranted in settings that come in contact with those experiencing legal and financial problems.

While there are many risk factors for suicide identified in the general population, more specific risk factors may exist among certain populations. For example, there have been efforts to identify risk factors in different phases of life (Steele et al., 2018), individuals with psychiatric diagnoses (Bhatt et al., 2018), certain groups of Veterans (Lee et al., 2018), and women (Chaudron & Caine, 2004), among others. Such specificity for risk factors among specific groups, and their intersections, would likely be beneficial to person-centered prevention.

Interpersonal-Level Risk Factors

In line with many of aforementioned theories (Durkheim, 2005; Joiner, 2005), research has demonstrated that suicide risk is impacted by interpersonal factors. Indeed, social factors (e.g., social isolation, loneliness, and low social support) have consistently been identified as risk factors for suicide ideation and behaviors across the lifespan and cultures (Calati et al., 2019; Draper, 2014; King and Merchant, 2008). Relationship loss, conflict, and dissolution are associated with suicide risk (Bridge et al., 2006; Séguin et al., 2014), and divorce can be a precipitating factor in suicide (Kposowa, 2003; Yip et al., 2015). Individuals who are separated, divorced, widowed, or never married are at increased suicide risk compared to married people (Jamison et al., 2017, 2019), with certain groups more greatly impacted by separation and divorce (Wyder, Ward, & De Leo, 2009). A narrative review of the literature (Calati et al., 2019) found that the social constructs associated with suicidal outcomes were marital status, living alone, social isolation, loneliness, alienation, and belongingness. Interestingly, both living alone and the perception of being lonely are associated with suicide ideation and attempts (Calati et al., 2019).

Beyond relationship status, interpersonal *dynamics* can also confer suicide risk. Child abuse and adverse childhood experiences (ACEs) are particularly strong risk factors for suicide. Increased risk for suicidality among those who experience child abuse or neglect has been reported in numerous populations (Devries et al., 2014; Dube et al., 2001; Jardim et al., 2018; Ng et al., 2018; Thompson et al., 2019). Childhood experiences appear to be particularly impactful, with one study reporting that childhood physical, sexual, and emotional abuse were associated with recent suicide attempts, whereas adult sexual or physical assaults were not (Briere, Madni, & Godbout, 2016). One larger, retrospective cohort study found that those who reported having experienced emotional, physical, or sexual abuse were two to five times more likely to have attempted suicide at some point in their lives (Dube et al., 2001). Further, ACEs may have a dose–response relationship with suicide; the number of ACEs is associated with increased odds of suicide ideation and attempts (Bhatta et al., 2014; Liu & Tien, 2005; Serafini et al., 2015; Thompson et al., 2019).

Violence in adulthood may also be associated with suicide (Devries et al., 2011), both indirectly via mental health consequences and as an independent risk factor (Currier et al., 2014; Lambert et al., 2008). This particularly impacts women, for whom physical and sexual violence are prevalent worldwide (García-Moreno et al., 2013). Lifetime prevalence estimates of violence against women reach as high as 50% (Alhabib, Nur, & Jones, 2010). Intimate partner violence (IPV) is associated with suicide behavior and death by suicide (Brown & Seals, 2019; Randle & Graham, 2011; Wolford-Clevenger, 2016), particularly for women (MacIsaac, Bugeja, & Jelinek, 2017), especially Black women (Taft et al., 2009). IPV and recent altercations with significant others have been associated with the suicide risk for pregnant and postpartum women (Adu et al., 2019). More than half of pregnancy-associated suicides involved intimate partner conflict (Palladino et al., 2011), and experiencing IPV was associated with more than nine times great odds of SI among low-income pregnant women (Alhusen et al., 2015). Assessing for abuse and violence exposure is critical to understanding an individual's suicide risk, and assessing for SI in settings that encounter individuals with abuse histories (e.g., shelters) may be beneficial.

The structure of a person's social network matters in terms of suicide risk and suicide contagion (Bearman & Moody, 2004; Mueller & Abrutyn, 2016). For example, adolescent and early adulthood exposure to friends who died by suicide increases the likelihood of suicide ideation and behavior (Bearman & Moody, 2004; Mueller, Abrutyn, & Stockton, 2015). The impact of social networks can be broad, as evidenced by the fact that knowledge of *friends of friends* who attempted suicide was associated with more seriously considering suicide (Baller & Richardson, 2009). Interestingly, the impact of networks appears to have gendered effects, with adolescent girls having specific social structures (i.e., very small networks, or intransitive networks where friends are not friends with each other) being at increased risk of suicidality (Bearman & Moody, 2004). Interpersonal loss, status, dynamics, and structure all impact suicide risk, directly and indirectly, and should be assessed thoroughly. These interpersonal dynamics also likely interact with community- and societal-level variables that warrant attention.

Community- and Societal-Level Risk Factors

At the next ecological level, suicide risk is impacted by societal beliefs, norms, and messaging about mental health and suicide. For example, stigmatizing views of people who experience SI (e.g., weak, unable to cope) have been reported in many groups and countries (e.g., Nicholas et al., 2022). Greater anticipated stigma is associated with increased suicidality, and this is partially mediated by secrecy (Mayer et al., 2020). Stigma can contribute to suicide by preventing help seeking during a crisis (Batterham, Calear, & Chistensen, 2013; Ben-Zeev et al., 2012; Niederkrotenthaler et al., 2014; Van Sickle et al., 2016). Thus, interventions to increase literacy about suicide and reduce stigma have been suggested (Batterham, Calear, & Christensen, 2013; Carpiniello & Pinna, 2017), such as targeting sources of stigmatizing messages, such as communities, healthcare providers, or media portrayals (Carpiniello, Girau, & Orrù, 2007; Frey et al., 2016; Van Sickle et al., 2016).

Media portrayals of suicide play a significant role in suicide risk. The media (i.e., newspapers, television, movies, Internet) contribute to socio-cultural beliefs of suicide that drive stigma and can provide information about suicide (e.g., how to access means, lethality of means). Frighteningly, over three-quarters of a sample of individuals who attempted suicide obtained logistical information about suicide from media sources (Stack & Bowman, 2017). Media can also contribute to suicide behavior and contagion (Gould, 2001), particularly if the story is about a real person, the audience closely identifies with them, is a celebrity, or is covered extensively (Fink et al., 2018; Gould, 2001; Stack, 2003, 2005). Celebrity suicides often garner significant media attention, and a large review found that the suicide of a political or entertainment celebrity were 5.27 times more likely to be associated with a contagion than non-celebrity suicides (Stack, 2005). One meta-analysis estimated that suicide risk increased by 13% after media reports of celebrity suicide (Niederkrotenthaler et al., 2020). Beyond news reporting, television shows can increase suicide. In the first three months of the airing of "13 Reasons Why," which focused on the suicide of a 17-year-old girl with significant social stressors, suicide increased by 21.7% among teenaged females (compared to 12.4% of males) (Niederkrotenthaler et al., 2019). As such, there are recommendations for media portrayals of suicide (e.g., providing crisis line numbers, not disclosing suicide means; see www.reportingonsuicide.org for more information).

Another societal-level issue that is strongly related to suicide is access to lethal means, particularly firearms. Firearm access can be influenced at local (e.g., gun storage within the home) and national (e.g., gun laws) levels, and is hotly debated in the United States. Firearm availability is associated with suicide risk (Andres & Hempstead, 2011; Anglemyer et al.,

2014; Fleegler et al., 2013; Kposowa, Hamilton, & Wang, 2016), and one meta-analysis found that firearm availability increased the odds of suicide by 3.24 times (Anglemyer et al., 2014). Groups and communities differ in the value placed on firearms (Parker et al., 2017), and regions with greater access to firearms have higher suicide rates (Anestis & Houtsma, 2018). However, some have found no relationship between gun availability and suicide rates (Kleck, 2019, 2022; though see Lane, 2022), highlighting that the relationship between firearm availability and suicide may be more complex at the societal than individual level (Stack, 2021).

Financial issues may also be more complicated at higher ecological levels. Just as financial problems increase individual suicide risk, economic recessions are associated with increased suicides (Barr et al., 2012; Chang et al., 2013; Haw et al., 2015; Oyesanya et al., 2015), possibly due to unemployment (Barr et al., 2012; Chang et al., 2009) and debt (Reeves et al., 2015). Trends in bankruptcies have been linked to national suicide rates, with one study suggesting that a 1% increase in company liquidations was associated with a 0.08% increase in suicide (Altinanahtar & Halicioglu, 2009). Increasing minimum wage may slow suicide rate growth (Gertner et al., 2019) and may reduce suicide disparities between socioeconomic groups (Kaufman et al., 2020). Particularly relevant in 2023 is inflation, an economic issue associated with increased suicidality. Oksak et al. (2021) reported that a 1% increase in inflation was associated with a 0.09% increase in suicide. Thus, the economy is particularly important to understanding larger contexts that may foster suicide.

Sociopolitical contexts and changes are also important. Wars and presidential elections may be related to suicide rates (Page et al., 2002; Stack, 2002; Tomlinson, 2012), though effects may depend on the level of local social integration (Classen & Dunn, 2010), and some have failed to find an association (Wasserman, 1983). Societal conflict and oppression can also contribute to suicide. Kyriopoulos and colleagues (2022) demonstrated that in months with at least one killing of a Black person by police, there was a slight increase in suicides among Black Americans in the same census division. Social policies and laws can also have an effect, with suicide rates impacted by government levels of social welfare spending (Flavin & Radcliff, 2009; Minoiu and Andres, 2008; Rambotti, 2020; Tuttle, 2018; Yur'yev et al., 2012) and laws regarding lethal means and alcohol availability (Carpenter, 2004; Kivisto and Phalen, 2018; Markowitz et al., 2003; Xuan et al., 2016). Lawmakers might consider the impact of proposed laws on their constituents with increased suicide rates attended to as a potential risk.

Protective Factors

In one sense, suicide is the result of the presence of risk factors that outweigh or overwhelm protective factors that buffer against suicide. There is less research about protective factors than about risk factors, but identifying and understanding them is essential in efforts to mitigate suicide risk. Factors that are characterized as protective against suicide have included strong coping skills, problem-solving ability, adherence to cultural or religious beliefs that discourage suicide, social support, and limited access to lethal means (CDC, 2022). Many of these listed here are the inverse of identified risk factors (e.g., social support vs. social isolation, lethal means access vs. restriction). Thus, it is important to not only lack a risk factor but to build up skills and resources in the opposing direction.

Coping and problem-solving skills are essential to navigating challenges, and the role of coping in suicide has been explored in various populations (Gould et al., 2004; Horwitz et al., 2011; Li and Zhang, 2012; Liu et al., 2009; Nrugham et al., 2012; Speckens & Hawton, 2005). Many studies (Li & Zhang, 2012; Liu et al., 2009; Nrugham et al., 2012) have demonstrated that productive, problem-focused coping strategies are negatively associated with depression and/or suicide behavior, with some suggestion that emotion-oriented coping (e.g., trying to control distress via avoidance) may be harmful (Mirkovic et al., 2015). Adolescents with past suicide behavior have greater deficits in problem-solving (Speckens & Hawton, 2005) and are less likely to adopt a problem-solving coping strategy (Evans et al., 2005; Nrugham et al., 2012) than those without such a history. Although coping deficits are associated with depression, the association between coping deficits and suicide may exist independently of depressive symptoms (Labelle et al., 2013; Li & Zhang, 2012;). One French study of adolescents hospitalized for attempting suicide showed that individuals who no longer had suicidal thoughts had made greater use of productive coping strategies (Mirkovic et al., 2015). Thus, improving coping skills, particularly for adolescents, may offer protection against suicide. Suicide-related coping (Stanley et al., 2017), coping that is applied specifically in response to suicidal urges (Interian et al., 2021), is also important. Individuals who report some ability to control their suicidal thoughts are less likely to make a first suicide attempt (Nock et al., 2018), and individuals at high risk for suicide are less likely to experience a suicidal event within 90 days if they endorsed greater suicide-related coping (Interian et al., 2021). Bolstering productive coping skills broadly, and specifically regarding suicide, can be an important component of individual suicide prevention.

Culture and religion can be protective in that they affect the types of stressors that lead to suicide, the meaning linked to stressors and suicide, and emotional and suicidal expression (Chu et al., 2010). Indeed, one study of people hospitalized with depression found that individuals who had not attempted suicide reported greater moral objections to suicide, fears of social disapproval if they attempted suicide, fear of suicide, and sense of responsibility for their family, compared to those who had a suicide attempt (Malone et al., 2000). Many of these factors can be driven by cultural beliefs and norms. These findings have been borne out elsewhere, with moral and religious objections being identified as protective against suicide (Dervic et al., 2004; Koenig et al., 2001; Lizardi et al., 2008; Rieger et al., 2015) and attendance at religious services being associated with decreased suicide risk (Chen et al., 2020; VanderWeele et al., 2020). Further, suicide rates in more religious countries are lower than rates in secular countries (Gearing & Lizardi, 2009), and a cross-national analysis found that individuals who are religiously committed, engaged with their religious community, and/or living in countries with high levels of religiosity are less accepting of suicide (Dervic et al., 2004; Neeleman et al., 1997).

Religion may reduce suicide risk through several mechanisms. Many religions condemn suicide and violence (Gearing & Alonzo, 2018), so it follows that those committed to their religion do not view suicide as an option, or incorporate these values or the perceived consequences into their contemplation of suicide. Religion may also provide coping strategies during a crisis, such as prayer or social support via the congregation and clergy (Gearing & Alonzo, 2018; Krause et al., 2001; Robins & Fiske, 2009). Religion may also instill meaning and purpose, with those with stronger religious views endorsing more reasons for living (Caribé et al., 2012; Dervic et al., 2011; Rieger et al., 2015). Religiosity may also indirectly buffer against suicide by reducing risk factors by prohibiting aggressive behavior and substance use (Dervic et al., 2004, 2011). Indeed, religiosity is inversely associated with risk factors for suicide, including depression, hopelessness, alcoholism and substance abuse, and anxiety (Bonelli et al., 2012; Koenig, 2012; Koenig et al., 2012).

While religiosity has been associated with reduced suicide (Caribé et al., 2012; Chen et al., 2020; Dervic et al., 2004; Gearing & Lizardi, 2008; Koenig et al., 2001; Lizardi et al., 2008; Neeleman et al., 1997; Rieger et al., 2015; VanderWeele et al., 2020), there have been some discrepant findings (Koenig, 2012). It has been suggested that religiosity is associated with reduced suicide behavior, but not ideation (Burshtein et al., 2016), and some have reported that religiosity is a suicide *risk* factor (Jia & Zhang, 2012; Sidhartha & Jena, 2006). This may be due, in part, to different definitions of religiosity (e.g., attendance at services vs. religious orientation vs. personal practices), which differentially impact suicide (Robins & Fiske, 2009). Further, the influence of religiosity on suicide may vary by sex, age, ethnicity, country/culture studied, and type of religious coping used (Gearing & Alonzo, 2018; McKenzie et al., 2003; Rosmarin et al., 2013; Sisask et al., 2010). Thus, this protective factor must be assessed and understood in context with other risk and protective factors.

Social support and connection can reduce suicide ideation and risk, particularly for individuals with high pain and high hopelessness (Klonsky & May, 2015). Social support can be broadly defined as the availability of friends and family who provide psychological, emotional, and material resources (Hutchison, 1999). One landmark study found that social support has a direct, positive effect on health and well-being, and indirect effects by providing resources and buffering against stress (Cohen & Wills, 1985). Social support is associated with lower likelihood of a lifetime suicide attempt, even after controlling for diverse clinical and demographic variables (Kleiman & Liu, 2013). Even the *perception* that social support is available may reduce suicide ideation or behavior, though the protective effects of perceived social support may be influenced by whether or not the support is accessed (Chioqueta & Stiles, 2007; Kleiman & Riskind, 2013; You, Van Orden, & Conner, 2011). Supportive and collaborative connections with healthcare providers can also reduce suicide risk and ideation (Gysin-Maillart et al., 2016; Ilgen et al., 2009; Simon et al., 2016), placing clinicians and other providers in a key role to bolster social support and the utilization of such networks.

Accessible mental healthcare is an essential piece of suicide prevention. There are low and inequitable rates of mental health treatment engagement, in part driven by lack of access (Wang et al., 2005). Treatment designed to be efficiently and effectively delivered can increase utilization (Coffey, 2007). The Henry Ford Health System, a large health maintenance organization, implemented a program focused on eliminating suicide among its members via core tenets of effectiveness, safety, patient centeredness, timeliness, efficiency, and equity. Their system of screening and follow-up care resulted in an 82% reduction in suicide between baseline and intervention (Coffey, 2006; Coffey & Coffey, 2013; Coffey et al., 2015). Further, visible and accessible mental healthcare can normalize help – seeking, decrease stigma, and increase service utilization. Indeed, states where mental health parity laws have been implemented have seen

Table 2.2 *Suicide risk and protective factors*

Risk factors	Protective factors
Current suicide ideation	Safe environments
Current suicidal intent	Coping skills
Current suicidal plan	Problem-solving skills
Preparatory behaviors	Meaning and purpose in life
Current mental health symptoms	Reasons for living
Current alcohol or substance abuse	Social support and connectedness
Personal history of suicide attempts	Moral, cultural, or religious beliefs against suicide
Family history	Trusting relationship with healthcare provider
Caucasian or White race	Access to high-quality healthcare
Unmarried	Employment
Living alone	
Loneliness or lack of social support	
Interpersonal loss	
Medical illness	
Unemployment	

significant increases in self-reported mental health service utilization (Harris, Carpenter, & Bao, 2006), and about a 5% reduction in suicide rates (Lang, 2013). Thus, focusing on increased mental healthcare access can be critical to fostering protective factors.

Over the past centuries, the various aspects of pain and suffering that lead to suicide have varied in title, measurement, and construction, but we have learned that there must be sufficient pain, suffering, or distress that overwhelms the existing internal and external resources available to a person. Beyond the models that explain how a person begins to contemplate suicide, or propels from SI into action and behavior, we have also learned about evidence-based risk factors that contribute to this trajectory and variables that may buffer against risk. Beyond addressing risk factors, we must bear in mind the available and modifiable resources within an individual and in society that can be bolstered to protect against overwhelming the system and suicide (see Table 2.2).

Chapter 3 similarly focuses on the cumulative impacts of stressors and the need for balance and buffering within a system to avoid it being overwhelmed, but from a biological perspective. With the foundational understanding of sociological and psychological perspectives toward suicide, we now transition to how these events, experiences, and perceptions can impact, and at times break down, biological systems and contribute to suicide.

CHAPTER 3

Allostasis
The Biology and Neuroscience of Suicide

A key challenge in preventing suicide is that no single risk factor accurately predicts suicide (Franklin et al., 2017). It is critical to understand how genetics, biology, adverse events, psychosocial and other factors dynamically contribute independently, and via interaction with each other, to suicide ideation and behavior. However, one limitation of many existing psychological and sociological theories is that they fail to capture the biological context in which suicidality and suicide occur. More recent models incorporate the widely held view that suicide is the result of interrelated biological, social, and psychological factors (Mann & Currier, 2007; Nugent et al., 2019; Stone et al., 2018), but often allude broadly to the fact that biological predispositions and changes can drive suicide risk without delving into the biological processes, mechanisms, or pathophysiology that may contribute to such risk.

One construct beneficial to our comprehension of how biological, social, and psychological factors coalesce to confer risk and precipitate suicide is allostasis (Schulkin, 2003; Sterling & Eyer, 1988). Allostasis is the adaptive physiological response to stress (Power, 2004; Schulkin, 2003), enabling adaptation to, compensation for, and anticipation of adverse events (Schulkin, McEwen, & Gold, 1994; Sterling, 2020). This active process is beneficial when experiencing acute stressors but can be detrimental and lead to pathophysiology in the long term. This may be the case in the setting of chronic stressors, environmental challenges, or unhealthy behaviors (de Kloet, Joëls, & Holsboer, 2005; McEwen, 1998, 2017). Chronic stress, in any form, contributes to the repeated or over-activation of compensatory biological regulatory mechanisms, which generates allostatic load (AL; McEwen & Stellar, 1993).

AL, an objective measure of the pathophysiological impact of chronic stress, indicates the level of "wear and tear" on the brain and body (McEwen & Stellar, 1993). AL can accumulate as a result of exposure to frequent stressors that generate chronic stress and repeated arousal, poor adaptation to repeated stress, poor inhibition of the stress response post-stressor, or an insufficient allostatic response to the stressor such that the stressor perpetuates. Figure 3.1 depicts the various contexts that contribute to AL. As AL accumulates, it can reach a state of allostatic *over*load, a pathological state where the wear and tear overwhelm the organism's ability to cope. It is at this severe end of the spectrum where the organism can no longer adapt to or cope with challenges (Fava et al., 2019; McEwen, 2004; McEwen & Wingfield, 2003) and is at risk for stress-related disease, morbidity, and mortality (Fava et al., 2019; see Figure 3.2).

Several biological systems are central to allostasis, AL, and allostatic overload, including the hypothalamic–pituitary–adrenal (HPA) axis, the autonomic nervous system, the inflammatory system, and their various biochemical components and substrates (e.g., neurotransmitters, inflammatory cytokines, glucocorticoids) (McEwen, 2016, 2017; Schulkin, 2011). The HPA axis figures centrally into this process as it controls the release of cortisol, a steroid often called the body's stress hormone. Cortisol is linked to energy regulation, circadian rhythm, and decreasing inflammation, among other processes, and thus is critical to allostasis.

When we experience stress, the HPA axis is activated and releases corticotropin-releasing hormone (CRH; also called corticotropin-releasing factor) from the hypothalamus. This triggers the release of adrenocorticotropin hormone (ACTH), which initiates the adrenal cortex releasing glucocorticoids, such as cortisol, into the blood. Once released, cortisol increases access to energy stores, promotes the mobilization of protein and fat, and regulates inflammatory responses (Sapolsky et al., 2000; Schulkin, 2011). Imbalance at any part of this cascade will impact other components of the HPA axis and other systems. Such imbalance is evident with increased AL, in the form of increased neurotransmission of CRH and arginine vasopressin, which trigger the release of ACTH and cortisol (Müller et al., 2003; Nemeroff et al., 1984; Purba et al., 1996; Timpl et al., 1998). One mechanism by which this HPA dysregulation occurs may be via attenuated feedback mechanisms within the HPA system; glucocorticoid receptors (GRs) have specifically been suggested as playing a role in this process given their role in inhibiting CRH release (Herman et al., 2012).

There have been efforts to operationalize AL and better understand its causes and effects. One such approach is to use biomarkers (see Box 3.1) or a combination of them in an AL index, as a reflection of multisystemic pathophysiology (Juster, McEwen, & Lupien, 2010).

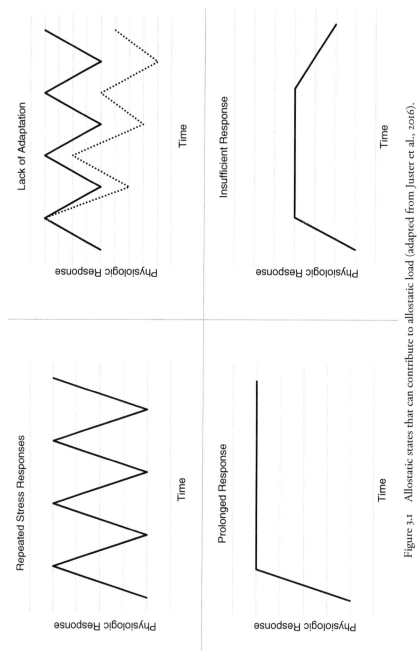

Figure 3.1   Allostatic states that can contribute to allostatic load (adapted from Juster et al., 2016).

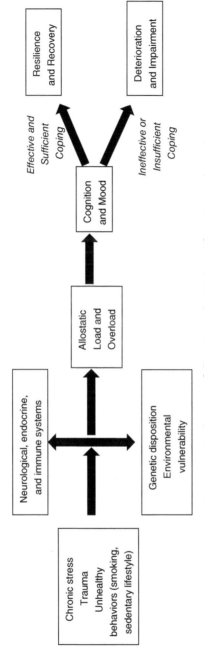

Figure 3.2   Development of allostatic overload (adapted from Fava et al., 2019).

Box 3.1 Measures used as allostatic load biomarkers
(Rosemberg et al., 2020)

- HbA1c
- High-density lipoprotein
- C-reactive protein
- Cortisol
- Diastolic blood pressure
- Systolic blood pressure
- Epinephrine/metanephrine
- Waist-to-hip ratio
- Body mass index
- Total cholesterol
- DHEA-S
- Norepinephrine/normetanephrine
- Heart rate
- Interleukin-6
- Triglycerides
- Low-density lipoprotein
- Fasting glucose
- Insulin
- Waist circumference
- enRAGE
- CD4+/CD8+
- Red blood cell count
- White blood cell count
- E-selectin
- TNFα
- Serotonin
- Copeptin
- Hemoglobin
- Standard deviation of R-R interval
- Fibrinogen
- Creatinine kinase

Another is a clinimetric method involving the measure of clinical symptoms that are the downstream effects of AL (Fava et al., 2019). Both methods have limitations. The use of biomarkers omits psychosocial context and their perceived impact, and a monolithic AL index may obscure more nuanced impacts of the various components of AL or typologies that exist (Carbone, 2021; Gallagher et al., 2021). The clinimetric method is limited in that the symptoms proposed by this method overlap with criteria for some psychiatric disorders (see Box 3.2; American Psychiatric Association,

Box 3.2 Overlap of clinimetric criteria and diagnostic criteria for mental health diagnoses

SUGGESTED CRITERIA FOR ALLOSTATIC OVERLOAD
(FAVA ET AL., 2019)

- Current identifiable source of distress, such as recent life events and/or chronic stress; the stressor is judged to tax or exceed coping skills when its full nature and circumstances are evaluated
- The stressor is associated with one or more of the following within six months of the stressor's onset:
  ○ Psychiatric symptoms
  ○ Psychosomatic symptoms
  ○ Significant impairment in social/occupational functioning
  ○ Significant impairment in psychological well-being

DIAGNOSTIC CRITERIA FOR POST-TRAUMATIC STRESS
DISORDER (APA, 2022)

- Exposure to actual or threatened death, serious injury, or sexual violence
- Presence of one or more intrusion symptoms (e.g., physiological arousal at reminders; memories; dreams) associated with the event, beginning after the event occurred
- Persistent avoidance of stimuli associated with the traumatic event(s), beginning after the traumatic event(s) occurred
- Negative alterations in cognitions and mood associated with the traumatic event(s), beginning or worsening after the event(s)
- Marked alterations in arousal and reactivity associated with the traumatic event(s), beginning or worsening after the traumatic event(s) occurred
- Duration is more than one month.
- Causes clinically significant distress or impairment in social, occupational, or other functioning.
- The disturbance is not attributable to physiological effects of a substance or medical condition.

DIAGNOSTIC CRITERIA FOR ADJUSTMENT DISORDER (APA, 2022)

- The development of emotional or behavioral symptoms in response to an identifiable stressor(s) within three months of the onset of the stressor(s).
- Symptoms or behaviors are clinically significant, as evidenced by marked distress that is out of proportion to the severity or intensity of the stressor, taking into account external context and cultural factors that might influence presentation, and/or significant impairment in social, occupational, or other functioning.

Box 3.2 (cont.)

- The stress-related disturbance does not meet criteria for another mental disorder and is not merely an exacerbation of a preexisting mental disorder.
- Symptoms do not represent normal bereavement.
- Once the stressor or its consequences end, the symptoms do not persist for more than six months.

2022; Fava et al., 2019), posing a challenge unique to evaluations of AL and suicide.

Due to the multiple components of AL and its operationalization, AL studies use different methods and biomarkers, variation that makes it difficult to compare and interpret results across studies. However, many studies have used an AL index that integrates diverse biomarkers including cardiovascular, immune, anthropometric (e.g., BMI), neuroendocrine, and metabolic indicators of AL (Juster et al., 2010). AL indices are associated with low social support (e.g., low belongingness, disconnection), stress, unhealthy behaviors, socioeconomic disadvantage, and genetic predispositions (Juster et al., 2017; McEwen, 1998; Memiah et al., 2022; Miller et al., 2021; Seeman et al., 2010). Readers will note that many of these factors that increase AL are also associated with suicide. Indeed, AL predicts numerous stress-related health outcomes, including mental health problems, cognitive deficits, all-cause mortality, and suicide (Fava et al., 2019; Giudi et al., 2021; Hwang et al., 2014; Juster et al., 2010; McEwen, 1998, 2000, 2003; Seeman et al., 1997).

Allostatic Load and Mental Health

Markers of AL, particularly HPA axis dysfunction, have been documented as antecedents and consequences of mental health problems (de Kloet et al., 2005; Juster et al., 2018; Kobrosly et al., 2014; McEwen, 2000, 2003). For example, individuals with clinimetrically determined allostatic overload have significantly greater self-reported stress levels and psychological distress (Offidani & Ruini, 2012; Tomba & Offidani, 2012), and individuals experiencing psychiatric emergencies have elevated AL indices (Juster et al., 2018). Further, dysregulated cortisol and its resultant downstream pathophysiology may exacerbate depressive symptoms (McEwen, 2003; Sachar et al., 1970). Indeed, Kobrosly et al. (2014) demonstrated that AL index had a similarly sized effect on depression to that of antidepressant medication, but in the opposite direction. Although several studies have reported significant associations between depression, anxiety, and AL (Juster et al., 2011; Kobrosly et al., 2014; Kuhn et al., 2016), this is not universally so (Adynski et al., 2019; Finlay et al., 2021) and may differ based on demographics (Bey et al., 2018).

Beyond depression and anxiety, AL has been associated with other mental health diagnoses. It has been hypothesized that a combination of subclinical mood symptoms and stressful life events may contribute to AL that leads to bulimia nervosa, with further symptoms and AL accumulating as the person experiences additional illness-related stressors (e.g., negative comments about weight or eating habits; Fava et al., 2001). AL is associated with post-traumatic stress disorder (PTSD) and may also have a dose–response relationship with traumatic events and symptoms. For example, AL is greater among women with a greater number of sexual assaults (Beckie et al., 2016) and among women with more PTSD symptoms (Glover, 2006; Glover, Stuber, & Poland, 2006).

Similarly, stress and AL biomarkers (measured by AL summary scores or salivary cortisol) have been implicated in the onset and exacerbation of schizophrenia and bipolar disorders (Kapczinski et al., 2008; Nugent et al., 2015; Ostiguy et al., 2011; Savransky et al., 2018). Increased HPA axis activity (i.e., increased cortisol levels, increased pituitary volume, and reduced hippocampal volume) may lead to the development of psychosis (Aiello et al., 2012; Walker et al., 2010), and the severity of recent-onset positive psychotic symptoms is associated with elevated AL (Savransky et al., 2018). Misiak et al. (2018) found that individuals with first episode psychosis (FEP) had greater AL and were less likely to use active and task-focused coping than controls. Lower odds of using these types of coping were related to greater AL in individuals with FEP, but not controls. Individuals with schizophrenia have greater AL index scores than controls (Savransky et al., 2018), early on and after chronic illness (Misiak et al., 2018; Nugent et al., 2015). Over time, there is a cumulative impairment that results from repeated psychotic and/or mood episodes, which has been partially attributed to AL. These impairments can further increase susceptibility to additional stressors (e.g., poverty, homelessness) and subsequent mood or psychotic episodes (Kapczinski et al., 2008). This has its own implications downstream, given that individuals with greater AL have poorer functioning in several domains (Berger et al., 2018; Piotrowski et al., 2019) and may have worse treatment outcomes (Finlay et al., 2021; c.f. Berger et al., 2018).

Allostatic Load and the Brain

AL can contribute to functional and structural changes in the brain that may both harm mental health and contribute to suicide. Much research in this area has been done in animals, though some translational research has provided evidence of these changes in humans. A key example of this is the negative impact of AL on neuroplasticity, particularly hippocampal neurogenesis (de Kloet et al., 2005), which has largely been demonstrated in animal models. However, decreased hippocampal volume has been consistently documented in patients with major depression, anxiety, and PTSD (McEwen, 2003; Sheline et al., 1999; Treadway et al., 2015; Yehuda, 2006). These diagnoses are also associated with increased AL, suggesting an inverse relationship between AL and neurogenesis, such that neurogenesis may be reduced in people with these conditions. Hippocampal damage or atrophy can impair HPA axis regulation and increase cortisol, which has downstream effects on learning, memory, and subsequent associations between stimuli and the stress response. Thus, this pathophysiology contributes to continued or over-activation of stress responses (McEwen, 2003; Sapolsky et al., 2000), further compounding AL. This pattern is evident in individuals with PTSD (Friedman & McEwen, 2004; Lohr et al., 2020; McEwen, 2003), who have increased AL and heightened arousal symptoms (APA, 2022).

The hippocampus served as the initial gateway to understanding the relationship between stress and brain plasticity. This initial focus has since extended to different, but related, brain regions, most notably the prefrontal cortex (PFC) and the amygdala. Part of the limbic system, the amygdala is key in memory, decision-making, and emotional responses (including fear, aggression), particularly responses to stress and threat (Rosen & Schulkin, 1998, 2022; Schulkin, McEwen, & Gold, 1994). Like the hippocampus, the amygdala is altered by chronic stress and AL, and demonstrates changes in the context of mental health problems (McEwen, 2003; Sheline et al., 1999). During stress, the amygdala is over-activated and increases in size (Lupien et al., 2009; Rosen & Schulkin, 1998, 2022), which feeds back on the HPA axis to increase activity. This pattern has been reported among individuals with anxiety, depression, and PTSD (Cannistraro & Rauch, 2003; McEwen, 2003; Shin et al., 2004). Further, AL can alter neurotransmission within the amygdala (e.g., GABAergic inhibition, synaptic transmission), which fosters susceptibility to stress-related mental health problems (Braga et al., 2004; Zhang et al., 2018).

The PFC is responsible for diverse cognitive abilities, such as complex planning, attention, and prediction. Its connection to other brain regions (e.g., subcortical nuclei) is uniquely involved in the inhibition of responses. The PFC is negatively impacted by stress, both structurally and functionally (McEwen & Morrison, 2013). Even mild uncontrollable stress can result in functional changes in the PFC (Arnsten & Goldman-Rakic, 1998;

Brown, Henning, & Wellman, 2005). In humans, stress impacts activity within the PFC, cognitive tasks that are dependent upon the PFC, and functional connectivity of the PFC with other regions (Liston, McEwen, and Casey, 2009; Luethi et al., 2009; Qin et al., 2009; Sinha et al., 2004). In the PFC, stress contributes to dendritic spine loss, weakened connectivity, and decreased mass. This results in a shift of responsibility for behavioral and emotional responses from the top-down regulation of the PFC to the conditioned, automatic responses of the amygdala (Luethi et al., 2009). Thus, under stress, PFC impairment may lead to disorganized thinking, disinhibition, and cognitive impairments. These stress- and AL-related brain alterations can contribute to further changes in cognition, decision-making, behavior, and impulsivity, suggesting that AL may also play a role in suicide.

Allostatic Load and Suicide

AL is indeed associated with suicide (Jokinen, Ouda, & Nordstrom, 2010; Steinberg & Mann, 2020; van Heeringen & Mann, 2014). HPA axis hyperactivity is associated with increased suicide risk (Coryell & Schlesser, 2001), and inflammation is associated with depression, aggression, and impulsivity, which contribute to suicide behavior (Beurel & Jope, 2014). Further, AL is related to variables that may independently contribute to suicide risk, including ACEs, chronic pain, social isolation, legal and financial problems, sleep disturbance, mental health problems, treatment resistance, and others (Fava et al., 2019; Lund & Sieberg, 2020; Tunnard et al., 2014).

There are numerous studies investigating the link between pathophysiology and suicide, though the biomarkers and samples of interest vary across studies. Dumser, Barocka, and Schubert (1998) demonstrated that individuals who died by suicide had larger adrenal glands than a comparison group, potentially the result of increased CRH and ACTH. Merali and colleagues (2004) reported that individuals who died by suicide had greater concentrations of CRH and fewer CRH type 1 receptors in the PFC. Adrenal steroids can increase CRH gene expression in the amygdala and elsewhere (Schulkin, Morgan, & Rosen, 2005), while decreasing CRH in the paraventricular nucleus (PVN) of the hypothalamus. This is very much in contrast to the restraint of adrenal steroids in the PVN of the hypothalamus (Schulkin, Gold, & McEwen, 1998). Moreover, adrenal steroids can increase CRH in several other areas, including regions of the bed nucleus of the stria terminalis, nucleus accumbens, and regions of the PFC

(Gray et al., 2016). Thus, there are two systems interacting: one, a negative restraint system focused on PVN of the hypothalamus and, the other, a feed-forward system amplifying the signal and stimulating the amygdala and other neural sites.

Postmortem studies of individuals who died by suicide suggest that stress may impair hippocampal neurogenesis and neuroplasticity, given evidence of reduced nerve growth factor (NGF), tyrosine kinases, and brain-derived neurotrophic factor (BDNF) (Banerjee et al., 2013; Dwivedi et al., 2003, 2009; Pandey et al., 2008). Reduced BDNF may contribute to impaired 5-hydroxytryptamine (5-HT; serotonin) turnover, given that these two signaling systems co-regulate one another and have been implicated in synaptic plasticity, neurogenesis, and neuronal survival (Mattson, Maudsley, & Martin, 2004). Further, impairments in 5-HT and BDNF signaling are a core issue in depression and anxiety, and serotonergic dysfunction has been implicated in suicide (Arango et al., 1990; Lopez et al., 1997; Mann et al., 1986; Pandey et al., 2002; Pompili et al., 2010). Telomere length, which is impacted by stress and inflammation, has also been investigated in relation to AL and suicide. A recent study demonstrated that among patients with affective disorders, a greater number of suicide attempts were associated with shorter telomere length (Birkenæs et al., 2021). Thus, a number of biological indicators suggest a link between AL and suicide.

One of the most common biomarkers used to evaluate the role of AL-related pathophysiology in suicide is dexamethasone resistance (Brunner et al., 2001; Coryell & Schlesser, 2001; Mann & Currier, 2007). In humans, dexamethasone binds to GRs, inhibits pituitary ACTH release, and subsequently decreases cortisol secretion. The dexamethasone suppression test (DST) measures whether ACTH and downstream cortisol secretion can be suppressed. Those who do not demonstrate suppression are presumed to have a diminished GR response, possibly the result of genetics or GR desensitization due to increased ACTH and cortisol (Hageman, Andersen, & Jorgensen, 2001; Parker, Schatzberg, & Lyons, 2003; Sher & Mann, 2003). One meta-analysis showed that dexamethasone resistance was associated with >4.5 times increased suicide risk among people with mood disorders (Mann et al., 2006). One fifteen-year study (Coryell & Schlesser, 2001) followed individuals with major depression or schizoaffective disorder and found that those who failed to suppress DST had a fourteen times greater suicide risk when compared to DST suppressors, even when considering sex and age. In fact, in this study DST non-suppression was the strongest predictor of suicide.

While HPA over-activity is implicated in suicide risk (Berardelli et al., 2020), there are less conclusive findings about the role of cortisol. Some have shown that suicide intent and behavior are associated with *lower* cortisol levels (Keilp et al., 2016; Lindqvist et al., 2008; Melhem et al., 2016), while others report *elevated* cortisol in association with suicide (Chatzittofis et al., 2013; O'Connor et al., 2017; Westrin et al., 1999). Further, O'Connor and colleagues (2017) found that, for individuals who had previously engaged in suicide behavior, cortisol levels during a stress task were inversely correlated with suicide ideation one month later. The relationship between cortisol levels and suicide is not straightforward.

One variable that may contribute to discrepant findings about cortisol and suicide may be the time since the stressor occurred and/or the age of the individual. Cortisol levels increase as a natural part of aging, but this pattern is moderated by stress (O'Connor et al., 2016), and older adults with stress-related disorders (e.g., PTSD) have *lower* cortisol levels (Fries et al., 2005; Yehuda, 2005). A meta-analysis (O'Connor et al., 2016) suggests that age may impact the relationship between cortisol and suicide based on findings that in samples less than 40 years old suicide attempts were associated with higher cortisol levels, whereas older groups had lower cortisol levels. The time since the onset of a stressor has also been shown to be inversely associated with cortisol (Miller, Chen, & Zhou, 2007). This suggests that the HPA axis may be activated upon initial stress and cortisol is secreted, but after chronic stress, compensatory downregulation results in lower cortisol. These and other findings of hypocortisolism following chronic stress-related HPA axis hyperactivity (Fries et al., 2005) may indicate a "burnt-out" HPA axis.

One factor that can contribute to long-term, chronic stress and is particularly relevant to suicide are ACEs (e.g., physical or sexual abuse). Maltreated children often exhibit elevated basal cortisol (Cicchetti & Rogosch, 2001; Tarullo & Gunnar, 2006) and a hyperreactive cortisol response to stress (Harkness, Stewart, & Wynne-Edwards, 2011), which can negatively impact cognition, behavior, learning, mood regulation, emotional processing, and decision-making (Lupien et al., 2009; van Heeringen & Mann, 2014), all of which play a role in suicide (Kiosses, Szanto, & Alexopoulos, 2014; van Heeringen & Mann, 2014). ACEs are associated with increased AL, mental health problems, treatment resistance, and suicide (Alfonso & Schulze, 2021; Choi et al., 2017; Tunnard et al., 2014; Widom et al., 2015). The number of ACEs experienced is impactful later in life, with the number of ACEs associated with earlier and repeated suicide attempts (Choi et al., 2017). Blosnich et al. (2021) found that, among Veteran men, the strongest correlate of an adulthood suicide attempt was having experienced more than six ACEs. Further, ACEs impart enduring effects on the brain (Carpenter et al., 2011; Chaney et al., 2014; Price et al., 2021; Tomoda et al., 2011, 2012) and epigenetic changes that have been associated with suicide. For example, the regulation of hippocampal GR expression, histone modifications, DNA methylation, and non-coding RNA interference and silencing have all been associated with ACEs and suicide (Alfonso & Schulze, 2021; Ernst et al., 2009; Fiori et al., 2010; Keller et al., 2010; Maussion et al., 2012; McGowan et al., 2009; Poulter et al., 2008).

Given that ACEs and the childhood environment figure prominently in the development of suicide risk, it may behoove us to conceptualize adolescence as critical period for understanding suicide risk. Developmentally, there is a change in the relationship between stressors and predisposing vulnerability due to maturing regulatory systems (Lupien et al., 2009). Adolescents experience significant physical, cognitive, and emotional changes, and are particularly susceptible to stress due to underdeveloped regulation of hormonal responses and greater stress sensitivity of certain brain regions (Gunnar et al., 2009; Lupien et al., 2009; Perlman et al., 2007; Romeo, 2017). Further, stressful adolescent experiences may change brain function and structure (Eiland & Romeo, 2013; Isgor et al., 2004; Romeo, 2017; Swartz, Williamson, & Hariri, 2015). Adolescents are also prone to compounding stressors due to dependent events and ineffective coping. For example, family conflict may distress a teen, who copes by using drugs, which ultimately causes further family, school, and legal problems (Notredame et al., 2020; Stone et al., 2014). Thus, interventions prior to and during adolescence may be important, particularly those that address impulsivity and bolster effective coping and problem-solving skills. Indeed, Notredame and colleagues (2020) highlighted the critical period that adolescence plays in AL trajectories and age of suicide. This group demonstrated that life-long AL patterns differed between individuals who died by suicide before and after age 30. Individuals who died by suicide in their late adolescence had continuous accumulation of AL, whereas those who died by suicide in middle age experienced a temporary plateau of AL during early adolescence; however, later on AL increased again and worsened until death by suicide (Notredame et al., 2020). As such, early adolescence may be a key period for intervention to minimize or reverse AL in order to prevent suicide.

The combination of genetic, epigenetic, and psychosocial effects on suicide risk highlights the relevance of the diathesis-stress model, which

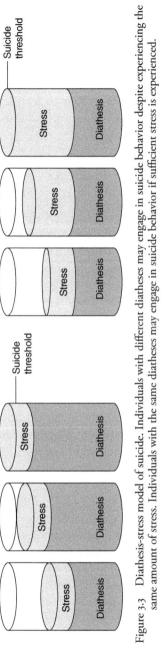

Figure 3.3 Diathesis-stress model of suicide. Individuals with different diatheses may engage in suicide behavior despite experiencing the same amount of stress. Individuals with the same diatheses may engage in suicide behavior if sufficient stress is experienced.

suggests that some individuals are predisposed to a disorder or behavior, such as suicide as a result of genetic, cognitive, social vulnerabilities (i.e., diathesis; van Heeringen, 2012). This diathesis can be activated by adverse experiences and stressors (van Heeringen & Mann, 2014). AL is one way a diathesis for suicide may transition from vulnerability to actuality. In this conceptualization, a combination of predisposition, exposure to stress, AL, and multisystem pathophysiology have overwhelmed biologic regulatory and adaptive processes, and allostatic overload is manifested as suicide (see Figure 3.3).

Resilience

Research suggests that AL can be reduced, and epigenetic effects and negative health outcomes can be reversed (McEwen, 2004). For example, Karlamangla, Singer, and Seeman (2006) measured AL biomarkers in older adults and found that a reduction in AL was associated with lower mortality risk 4.5 years after the study concluded. The brain has also demonstrated resilience, which is promising given that the brain is the central actor in stress and adaptation, and regulates health behaviors (e.g., eating, sleeping) that impact AL (McEwen, 2007). In the human brain, such resilience has been demonstrated in the hippocampus, amygdala, and PFC, the regions previously highlighted as being impacted by AL (Erickson et al., 2011; Leaver et al., 2018; McEwen, Gray, & Nasca, 2015). One marker of resilience, neurogenesis, can be fostered in the hippocampus, possibly by oxytocin via HPA axis suppression (Lin et al., 2017). Reducing AL can decrease amygdalar size and oxytocin can decrease amygdalar activation (Kirsch et al., 2005). These brain changes are associated with improvements in brain function as well. For example, increases in the anterior hippocampus has been associated with improved memory (Erickson et al., 2011).

One may note the multiple mentions of oxytocin in the reversal of impacts of stress. Oxytocin, a natural hormone produced in the hypothalamus and released into the bloodstream by the pituitary gland, is primarily involved in childbirth but is also important in social behavior and bonding. Decreased oxytocin levels have been demonstrated in the cerebrospinal fluid (CSF) of individuals who have attempted suicide (Jokinen et al., 2012), and oxytocin has been implicated in allostasis, resilience, and anxiety suppression. Animal models have demonstrated that endogenous oxytocin reduces HPA axis activity during stress and promotes fear extinction (Takayanagi & Onaka, 2022). Human research has similarly found

Figure 3.4 Resilience and recovery, in which oxytocin is implicated, counteract the effects of stress and challenge in the development of allostatic load/overload and its sequelae (adapted from Takayanagi & Onaka, 2022).

that oxytocin administration decreases anxiety (Janeček & Dabrowska, 2019) and amygdala activity (Kanat et al., 2015; Labuschagne et al., 2010), and that social interactions bolster oxytocin and reduce cortisol and anxiety (Takayanagi & Onaka, 2022). Thus, oxytocin may attenuate stress responses, though some have reported detrimental effects of chronic oxytocin and effects that vary by sex, context, and administration method (McDonald & Feifel, 2014; Winter et al., 2021). A recent review (Takayanagi & Onaka, 2022) concluded that oxytocin maintains homeostasis, plays a role in the inhibition of AL and overload, and contributes to recovery by activating coping responses to stress, and this oxytocin-facilitated resilience further inhibits stress responses and AL (see Figure 3.4, adapted from Takayanagi & Onaka, 2022). Oxytocin's involvement in adaptation to environments and social relationships suggests that it plays a role in buffering against negative emotions, attenuating the stress response, and building resilience (Feldman, 2020), which has been associated with reduced HPA axis activity and positive health outcomes (Babic et al., 2020).

Given its role in resilience and its low risk profile, oxytocin is receiving attention as a potential treatment for numerous stress-related and mental health disorders, though with conflicting results (Takayanagi & Onaka, 2022). Research on resilience and oxytocin in humans is in the early stages and thus further clarification of its role, its interaction with other biologic factors (e.g., vasopressin and vasopressin 1a receptors), and the various individual factors that impact its effectiveness (e.g., sex, age, genetics, social context, early life adversity, etc.) is needed. Research clarifying these questions can inform subsequent treatment to reduce the impact of AL and prevent or reverse its effects. If AL is malleable via oxytocin or other mechanisms, and its sequelae are reversible or preventable, this implies that AL interventions may reverse the impact of trauma, adverse events, and chronic stress (McEwen, 2004), and provides hope that interventions to reduce AL may also reduce suicide risk.

Interventions

Both pharmacological and non-pharmacological interventions have been suggested as a means by which to reduce AL, promoting neuroplasticity and fostering resilience. With regard to pharmacological interventions, medications traditionally used to treat mental health concerns have received attention. For example, low doses of alprazolam, a benzodiazepine often used to treat anxiety, have been shown to not only decrease anxiety but also salivary 3-methoxy-4-hydroxyphenylglycol (a metabolite of norepinephrine), systolic blood pressure, and the AL index (Soria et al., 2018). Antidepressants have been shown to reduce AL, normalize HPA axis activity by modulating GRs (Anacker et al., 2011), inhibit neuronal cell death, and promote neurogenesis and volumetric increases in the hippocampus (Boldrini et al., 2009; Colla et al., 2007; Frodl et al., 2008; Malberg et al., 2000). Mood stabilizers may also diminish AL biomarkers (Kapczinski et al., 2008) and treatment with second-generation antipsychotics can reduce AL index scores among those with schizophrenia or first-episode psychosis (Berger et al., 2018).

The ideal intervention may depend on individual factors, such as which biomarkers are elevated, sex, and social context. As such, identifying a single pharmacologic approach to broadly reduce AL across diverse populations may prove challenging given that: individuals may have different increased biomarkers regardless of diagnosis; different medications impact different physiological contributors to AL; pharmacological interventions do not always have their intended impact; and multiple systems contribute to and are impacted by AL. Cannabinoids have been suggested as a potential universal treatment to address AL-related multi-system pathology (Lohr et al., 2020). Exogenous activation of Type I cannabinoid receptors (CB1Rs) can reverse stress-related cognitive impairments (Hill et al., 2005), and cannabinoids can reduce many measures of AL (Lohr et al., 2020). Further, postmortem studies show increased CB1R protein concentrations and signaling in the frontal cortex of those who died by suicide (Mato et al., 2018). Thus, pharmacological intervention targeting the endogenous cannabinoid signaling system may be applicable across multiple biomarkers and diverse groups, which could benefit suicide prevention efforts.

Another means by which to impact multiple physiological systems and AL-related targets may be non-pharmacological interventions and behavioral changes, which have been shown to improve many AL measures, both independently and in conjunction with other treatments (D'Alessio et al., 2020; Tan et al., 2019). Lifestyle changes (e.g., improving diet, sleep, and physical health, decreasing substance use) may reduce allostatic load (Seeman et al., 2002; Tan et al., 2019). Enhancing social support and connectedness may bolster well-being via oxytocin (Kirsch et al., 2005; Lin et al., 2017; Stevenson et al., 2019), and promoting healthy work–life balance, meaning, and purpose can reduce AL (Juster, McEwen, & Lupien, 2010). Non-pharmacological interventions that instill positive feelings in general can be beneficial (Schenk et al., 2017; Seeman et al., 2002) and can create a reinforcing cycle to compound positive effects on AL.

Exercise and physical activity have been associated with reduced depression and improved regulation in the HPA axis and the sympathetic nervous system (Morres et al., 2019; Pascoe, Thompson, & Ski, 2017). Animal and human studies have shown that exercise can offset the effects of chronic stress and AL, and may promote hippocampal neuroplasticity, greater synaptic plasticity, enhanced contextual and spatial memory, increased cerebral blood flow, and higher levels of BDNF (Kandola et al., 2016; Lucassen et al., 2010; Vaynman, Ying, & Gomez-Pinilla, 2004). This exercise-induced resilience, specifically neurogenesis and reduced AL, has been a hypothesized mechanism by which exercise improves mood, stress responses, and functioning (Sylvia, Ametrano, & Nierenberg, 2010). Yoga may promote parasympathetic activity and reduce AL biomarkers, such as cortisol, blood pressure, heart rate, and cytokine levels (Pascoe, Thompson, & Ski, 2017). Such improvements have been associated with lower perceived stress, and improved mood and cognition (Gothe, Keswani, & McAuley, 2016; West et al., 2004). Yoga may also promote neurogenesis, neuroplasticity, and greater hippocampal volume (Garner et al., 2019; Hariprasad et al., 2013; van Aalst et al., 2020; Villemure et al., 2015; Yang et al., 2016). Similarly, Tai Chi (Carroll et al., 2015) and osteopathic manipulative treatment (Nuño et al., 2019) may reduce AL, though studies on these interventions and their impact on AL are small or noncontrolled, so more rigorous research is needed.

Psychotherapy may be another means by which to broadly reduce AL. Cognitive behavioral therapy (CBT) can reduce AL among older individuals with insomnia (Carroll et al., 2015), and mindfulness-based interventions may have an impact on AL via increased hippocampal gray matter, as well as changes in the amygdala and other structures implicated in learning, memory, cognition, and emotion regulation (Hölzel et al., 2011). Peer support may also be a potential avenue of intervention, with one randomized controlled trial (RCT) showing that weekly peer support and education decreased AL among women with breast cancer (Ye et al., 2017). Family psychotherapy can have positive impacts on AL for children and adolescents. For example, family interventions have been shown to help normalize cortisol levels among children who had experienced maltreatment (Cicchetti et al., 2011; Fisher et al., 2007) or parental bereavement (Luecken et al., 2010). At a minimum, interrupting and preventing ongoing maltreatment or abuse is essential to prevent trauma-induced pathophysiology and other neurobiological and psychological sequelae of trauma/adversity, including suicide (Beauchaine, Hinshaw, & Bridge, 2019). Offering psychosocial interventions, either as stand-alone treatments or augmenting pharmacological treatment, may reduce AL and promote resilience without stigma or additional side effects (D'Alessio et al., 2020; Kandola et al., 2016; Sylvia, Ametrano, & Nierenberg, 2010). However, larger, longitudinal RCTs investigating their effects on AL and suicide are needed.

Given that structural factors (e.g., sociopolitical and physical environment, income, housing, access to healthcare, educational opportunities, transportation, safety) can contribute to stress and AL (Carlson & Chamberlain, 2005; Memiah et al., 2022; Miller et al., 2021; Saxbe et al., 2020), the potential for societal-level interventions to prevent suicide should not be underestimated. Beginning in early childhood, social circumstances, economic resources, and neighborhood or household dynamics can impact levels of adversity, which can result in toxic stress and AL, particularly if strong, positive social supports are absent (McEwen, 2022). Thus, macro-level interventions are likely necessary to maximally address AL.

AL has contributed to the understanding of how social and environmental stressors impact physiological functioning and health disparities (Juster et al., 2017; Miller et al., 2021; Seeman et al., 2010), and there are best practices evident from other countries with reduced rates of suicide and other deaths of despair (Sterling & Platt, 2022). Sterling and Platt (2022) highlight that suicide and other deaths of despair are likely caused by modifiable societal factors, and suggest that the lower mortality rates in other industrialized countries are due to supports like prenatal and maternal care, paid parental leave, subsidized preschool, nationally supported public school systems, improved living conditions for single parents (e.g., decreased poverty risk, housing stability, child benefits, tax deductions), no- or low-cost college tuition, lower medical costs, and mandated vacation time. As such, these authors suggest that U.S. policymakers focus on implementing these best practices in the United States and shift the focus of causes of mortality from an individual level to a societal one. We would also posit that interventions that target social inequities, increase educational opportunities, promote empowerment, and address issues such as pollution, isolation, polarization, poverty, and other stressors may help mitigate AL and offset its consequences (Juster, McEwen, & Lupien, 2010). Given that health disparities reflect institutionalized oppression (Williams et al., 2001), inequality and discrimination (e.g., racism, homophobia, misogyny) must be addressed at the societal level to reduce AL within marginalized or at-risk populations.

This chapter highlights AL as a framework to detail one potential biological pathway to suicide. And while it is largely understood that biological vulnerability, psychological factors, and social variables can converge to result in suicide (Alfonso & Schulze, 2021; van Heeringen & Mann, 2014), models that equally attend to all three aspects are rare. Sociological and psychological models of suicide could benefit from incorporating AL, and further research about AL's role, if any, in the transition from suicide ideation to behavior could inform ideation-to-action models. McEwen and McEwen (2017) developed a view of the sociological and biological processes that underlie pathology in general. They emphasize how social forces drive biological processes of growth and development, and later how biological and sociological processes have reciprocating roles that result in individual life trajectories and larger health disparities (McEwen, 2022; McEwen & McEwen, 2017). Similar approaches and understandings within the field of suicide prevention may be beneficial.

Although several AL biomarkers have been proposed, to date, none has been established to predict suicidal behavior, and some are not clinically practical (Alfonso & Schulze, 2021). Research to identify the biological correlates of suicide behavior (particularly those independent of mental illness biomarkers), specific biomarkers or cutoffs for suicide risk, and how these readily available and clinically practical indicators of AL may be used to inform suicide risk assessment or monitor treatment outcomes would be beneficial. Further investigation into AL profiles or typologies (Carbone, 2021; Gallagher et al., 2021) and their associations, if any, with suicide could be pivotal. Identifying what single or combined indicators of AL are most strongly associated with risk, are amenable to change, and what interventions (at either clinical or societal levels) are effective at changing them are essential next steps.

CHAPTER 4

Suicide Demographics in the United States

Now – equipped with knowledge about theories of suicide, factors that increase risk and buffer against it, and how these experiences drive pathophysiology that contributes to suicide – we turn to the discussion of epidemiology of suicide. People of any age, race, ethnicity, sex, and other demographic variables can experience SI or die by suicide, but it is well established that, in the United States, certain groups have substantially higher rates of suicide than the general population. This chapter highlights what is known about suicide generally in the United States and specifically among various demographic groups.

Suicide has been a leading cause of death in the United States, with 45,979 deaths in 2020 (Ehlman et al., 2022), or about one death every 11 minutes (Drapeau & McIntosh, 2023). In 2020, the most common method of suicide death was firearms, accounting for a little more than half of all suicide deaths, followed by suffocation (including hangings) and poisoning (including drug overdose) (American Foundation for Suicide Prevention [AFSP], 2022). In the United States, suicide rates increased by 30% between 2000 and 2018, recently declined in 2019 and 2020, and then again increased in 2021 (Curtin, Garnett, & Ahmad, 2022). While it is difficult to make cross-national comparisons due to regional variations, different definitions, and measurement, among other factors, it should be noted that global suicide rates *decreased* between 1990 and 2016, and a recent review identified increasing suicide trends in only 8 out of 195 countries studied (~4%), of which the United States was one. Other countries with increasing suicide rates included Cameroon, Jamaica, Liberia, Mexico, Paraguay, Uganda, and Zimbabwe (Martinez-Ales, 2020; Naghavi, 2019). However, despite some optimism that there had been decreases in recent years in the U.S. suicide rate, there are certain groups for whom the rates are stagnant or even increasing, as we will describe in the following text.

It should be noted that while this chapter focuses on what is known about suicide among various demographic groups, it is likely that suicide risk and their trends over time differ for individuals with various intersecting identities (e.g., those who identify as Black, Christian, woman, and lesbian), and it is impossible to fully capture all possible combinations in a single chapter. Understanding individuals by a single demographic characteristic ignores the complex interplay of intersecting identities and the potential impact of multiple marginalization (e.g., Wiglesworth et al., 2022). Likewise, much remains to be learned about specific groups, given limitations of methods and data available. For example, small sample sizes often restrict subgroup analyses that could elucidate various aspects of intersectionality as they relate to suicide. Further, researchers emphasize that the reported rates are likely an undercount of the true suicide toll, and that discrepancy may not be equally distributed across racial and ethnic groups. For example, data show that Black individuals who die by suicide are less likely than Whites to leave a suicide note or have documented mental health conditions due to poorer access to care (Novak, 2022). Thus, suicide deaths among certain groups may not be identified as a suicide, obscuring true rates of suicide deaths. Despite these challenges and limitations, there are some established facts about the demographics of suicide, which are summarized in the following sections.

Age

In the general U.S. population, suicide rates peak at ages 45 to 54, start a decline until age 74, and then incline again starting at age 75 through age 85+ (SPRC, 2022). In 2020, suicide was a top 10 cause of death for most age groups, from ages 5–9 through ages 55–64 (see Table 4.1, based on data from CDC Web-based Injury Statistics Query and Reporting System).

Table 4.1 *Suicide's ranking as a leading cause of death varies by age group (CDC Web-based Injury Statistics Query and Reporting System)*

Age group	Suicide's 2020 ranking as cause of death	Number of deaths
5–9	10th	20
10–14	2nd	581
15–24	3rd	6,062
25–34	2nd	8,454
35–44	4th	7,314
45–54	7th	7,249
55–64	9th	7,160

Youth and Young Adults

Although younger people generally have a suicide rate lower than the national rate, suicide is a leading cause of death for this group given that younger people are less likely to die of other causes (e.g., heart disease, cancer). For example, suicide is the second leading cause of death for those 10–14 years old (CDC Web-based Injury Statistics Query and Reporting System). Young people aged 10–24 make up about 14% of all suicides in the United States and are more likely to have emergency department (ED) visits for self-harm than older groups (CDC, 2022b). Certain subgroups of young people are particularly at risk for suicide, such as those who are non-Hispanic American Indian (AI)/Alaska Native (AN) and those who identify as lesbian, gay, bisexual, or transgender (LGBT; CDC, 2022b). In fact, sexual minority youth are over three times as likely to attempt suicide as their heterosexual peers (Raifman et al., 2020).

Suicidal thoughts and behaviors emerge and rise exponentially during adolescence (Nock et al., 2013), and rates of both SI and suicide attempts have recently increased among this group (Miron et al., 2019). One study reported that 17.2% of adolescents reported SI and 13.6% made a suicide plan in the previous year (Kann et al., 2018). The COVID-19 pandemic had harmful effects on adolescent mental health (Nearchou et al., 2020), and ED visits for suspected suicide attempts increased by 31% among adolescents (largely driven by females) from before to during the pandemic (Yard et al., 2021). Given that early-life suicide attempts are associated with poorer health outcomes later in life (Goldman-Mellor et al., 2014), and that suicide attempts are a risk factor for subsequent attempts (Beghi & Rosenbaum, 2010; Hawton et al., 2005; Nanayakkara et al., 2013), these findings are particularly concerning.

Middle Age (35–64 Years Old)

Suicide research has focused on the extremes of age, the young and the old, with less attention paid to adults in middle age. However, those in middle age experience unique risk factors such as economic and employment challenges, dual caregiver responsibilities for children and ageing parents, and the onset of physical ailments and chronic illnesses. Indeed, midlife has been identified as a key crossroads and pivotal transition point in the life course (Infurna et al., 2020; Lachman, Teshale, & Agrigoroaei, 2015). Although adolescents and young adults may be at higher risk for suicidal thoughts and attempts than other age groups, those in middle age, particularly those aged 45–64, have historically had higher rates of suicide than other age groups (Piscopo, 2017).

In recent decades, suicide rates have been increasing over time among those in middle age and growing at a rate faster than other groups (Hempstead & Phillips, 2015; Piscopo, 2017; Sullivan et al., 2013). In 2020, middle-aged adults accounted for just under half of suicides in the United States (CDC, 2022b). The greatest suicide rates among those in middle age were among non-Hispanic AI/AN and non-Hispanic White individuals, though the rates differ by sex. For example, suicide rates were highest for non-Hispanic AI/AN middle-aged males, followed by non-Hispanic White men. For similarly aged women, suicide rates were highest among White women, followed by non-Hispanic AI/AN women (CDC, 2022b), again highlighting the importance of the intersections of various components of identities.

Older Age

In recent years, we have seen older groups – first 85 and older in 2019, then 75–85, and 85+ in 2020 – having suicide rates greater than those in middle age. And while older adults (75+ years) account for a small percentage of all suicides, they currently have the highest suicide rate, which seems to be a worldwide phenomenon (Conwell & Thompson, 2008; WHO, 2014). Within this age group, non-Hispanic White men have particularly high suicide rates (CDC, 2022b).

There are unique risk factors and aspects to geriatric suicide. Older adults tend to experience physical illness, cognitive decline, loneliness, low social support, physical and logistical barriers to care, and financial stress, which can exacerbate suicide risk (Conwell & Thompson, 2008). Further, older adults tend to have more lethal attempts (Conwell, 2014) due to being more planful about their suicide, and less likely to demonstrate warning signs or be identified as at risk (Conwell et al., 1998). The greater lethality of suicidal behavior in later life may also be attributed to physical frailty that may decrease odds of survival or social isolation that may limit opportunities for interruption or rescue. Finally, older adults tend to use more lethal means than younger people; larger proportions of suicides are by firearm among older people than other age groups, and firearm suicides have been increasing among the elderly, particularly elderly White males (Price & Khubchandani, 2021). As the U.S. population ages (Vespa, 2018), older groups are the fastest growing segment of the population, making later-life suicide a major public health issue.

Race and Ethnicity

Suicide rates differ across racial and ethnic groups. However, our understanding of such differences is limited by underreporting in some communities, limitations in data collection methods, as well as limited research and information on individuals who identify with two (or more) racial groups (Kegler et al., 2022; Oh et al., 2022; Stone, Jones, & Mack, 2021; Subica & Wu, 2018). Additionally, many, if not all, of the racial and ethnic groups summarized in suicide literature are comprised of many subgroups that differ in religion, culture, traditions, and other variables that may drive within-group differences that are obscured by combining subgroups into larger categories.

American Indian and Alaska Native

In 2020, those who identified as AI/AN alone (i.e., not in conjunction with another race) accounted for 1.1% of the U.S. population (Jones et al., 2021). Unique risk factors that impact this group of people include historical trauma, colonialization, poverty, and geographic isolation and other traumas resulting from forced resettlement onto reservations (Frakt, 2021). Despite these similarities, people who identify as AI/AN are diverse descendants of North, South, or Central America and vary in their cultural heritage, tribes, and traditions. Thus, there may be very real differences between subgroups of AI/AN that are obscured by consolidating them into a single group. However, disaggregating data for AI/AN subgroups have challenges (NCAI Policy Research Center, 2016) and may fail to detect differences given small sample sizes. Further challenges to understanding suicide among AI/AN include the lack of tribal affiliation documented in state data, tribes may have their own independent suicide monitoring systems, tribes may use different or be lacking definitions for suicide, and there may be hesitancy to share suicide data with state or federal organizations (Stone et al., 2022).

Among all racial/ethnic groups, AI/AN people have the highest reported suicide rates. It has been suggested that younger men who specifically identify as American Indian, particularly those living in the Northern Plains region, are at high suicide risk relative to other groups (SAMHSA, 2022). Among AI/AN populations, suicide rates peak during adolescence and young adulthood, and then decline through age 85+ (SPRC, 2022). This differs from the aforementioned age pattern among the overall U.S. population where there is a peak in middle age, a dip until 74, and then increases in later life. In terms of sex, similar to the overall U.S. population, suicide rates among AI/AN men are more than three times greater than the rates for AI/AN women, though both groups have rates greater than the overall U.S. population rate (SPRC, 2022).

Asian or Pacific Islander

About 6% of the 2020 U.S. population was comprised of people who identified as Asian, Native Hawaiian, or Other Pacific Islander alone (not in combination with another race) (Monte & Shin, 2022). Unique suicide risk factors among Asian or Pacific Islander populations in the United States may include racism and recent racially motivated violence, mental health stigma, or conflict between collectivistic and individualistic identities (Leong et al., 2007). However, this is a group comprised of diverse people that span a wide geographical, linguistic, and cultural range. Thus, there may be differences between Asian or Pacific Islander subpopulations that are obscured by combining them in suicide-related data. For example, adults who identify as Native Hawaiian or Other Pacific Islander have a greater rate of suicide attempts in the past year than either the Asian population or the overall U.S. population (Center for Behavioral Health Statistics and Quality, 2021; SPRC, 2022). However, there is limited research that specifically targets Asian or Pacific Islander mental health and suicide (Takeuchi et al., 2012), and less that disaggregates these groups, limiting what is known.

Generally, the Asian or Pacific Islander population has suicide rates lower than the overall U.S. rate and follows a unique lifespan trajectory similar to the broader U.S. population. In Asian or Pacific Islander populations, suicide rates follow a U-shaped pattern, with the second-highest rates in the 15–24 age group and then peaking again at 85 and older. Like the overall U.S. population, among this group, men have a suicide rate greater than that of women, though only about two times greater (SPRC, 2022).

Black or African American

In 2020, the Black or African American (not in combination with another race) population accounted for 12.4% of the U.S. population (Jones et al., 2021). Like other demographic groups, the Black or African American population is comprised of people from numerous regions, cultures, histories, and heritages (Tamir, 2021), and combining them into a larger aggregated population may hide more micro-level trends or differences that could be targeted to reduce suicide among certain subpopulations.

Similar to other racially minoritized groups, Black/African American individuals have unique risk factors including historical trauma, colonialization, racism, race-based violence, discrimination, oppression, and systemic barriers to physical, psychological, social, and financial wellness. Despite these risk factors, the age-adjusted suicide rate for Black populations from 2011 to 2020 was less than half the overall U.S. suicide rate (SPRC, 2022). Similar to the overall U.S. population, Black males have a suicide rate that is greater than three times the suicide rate for Black females. For Black men, experiences of racism may contribute to suicide risk directly and indirectly via depression symptoms (Goodwill et al., 2021). With regard to age, the Black or African American population diverges from the pattern evident in the general U.S. population in that we see suicide rates peak in adolescence and young adulthood, and then steadily decline through age 85+ (SPRC, 2022). Suicide among young Black or African American children has garnered particular attention (Coleman, 2019).While this group traditionally has lower suicidality rates, these have increased in recent years, compared to decreases among non-Hispanic White peers (Bath & Njoroge, 2021). Black or African American children are an at-risk group that warrants further attention in terms of understanding how suicide risk develops and manifests for these youths, as well as developing racially, culturally, developmentally sensitive prevention and intervention efforts (Robinson et al., 2022).

Hispanic

Data for the Hispanic population are not only impacted by the aforementioned subgroup diversity but also the fact that individuals who identify as Hispanic *and* another race are often combined into a single Hispanic category. In other words, individuals would be categorized as Hispanic regardless of race (Office of Management and Budget, 1997; SAMHSA, 2022).

Hispanic individuals in the United States face unique risks including acculturative stress (Silva & Van Orden, 2018), decreased likelihood of receiving mental health treatment (Office of Minority Health, 2021), discrimination (Perez-Rodriguez et al., 2014), and increasing anti-immigrant ideologies (Goldstein & Wilson, 2022). Among Hispanic individuals, acculturative stress has been associated with suicide ideation, behaviors, and deaths, potentially as a result of the loss of protective factors such as traditional cultural values, religiosity, and strong social networks (Silva & Van Orden, 2018). However, historically, suicide mortality has not been as high as would be anticipated given the general degree of stressors and socioeconomic disadvantage experienced by this group (Silva & Van Orden, 2018), and has historically been lower than other groups.

In 2020, the age-adjusted suicide rate among Hispanic individuals was just over half of what the suicide rate was for the overall United States, and interestingly, suicide rates do not fluctuate significantly across the lifespan. For example, from 2011 to 2020, suicide rates ranged from 6.5 to 9.7 for all age groups from 15 years old and above (SPRC, 2022). Even though U.S. Hispanics have historically had relatively low suicide rates, suicide risk among Hispanics in the United States has steadily increased over the last two decades (Khubchandani & Price, 2022; Martínez-Alés et al., 2022). Further, suicide was the second leading cause of death among the Hispanic population between 15 and 34 years of age in 2019 (Office of Minority Health, 2021). And although Hispanic males have greater suicide rates than Hispanic females (Ehlman, 2022; Khubchandani & Price, 2022), there has been particular concern about young Hispanic females (Silva & Van Orden, 2018), who have recently demonstrated greater suicide attempts than White peers (Ivey-Stephenson et al., 2020; Office of Minority Health, 2021) and have had concerning increases in suicide deaths (Silva & Van Orden, 2018). Culturally tailored prevention efforts, particularly those that bolster culturally relevant protective factors (Oquendo et al., 2005), may be needed to address suicide risk among those identifying as Hispanic.

White

The monoracial White (i.e., not in combination with another race or ethnicity) population made up 61.6% of all people living in the United States in 2020 (Jones et al., 2021). Like all other groups, the U.S. White population can include a broad range of people, including those who are descendants of people from Europe, the Middle East, or North Africa (U.S. Census Bureau, 2022), which includes numerous cultures, religions, languages, and heritages. Indeed, it has been reported that Middle Eastern and North African (MENA) Americans may not be viewed, nor perceive themselves, as White. It has been suggested that this group may warrant a new U.S. Census race category such that potential disparities and inequalities faced by MENA Americans can be elucidated (Maghbouleh,

Schachter, & Flores, 2022). Such differences should be kept in mind when considering suicide among those identifying as White.

The age-adjusted suicide rate for White populations has consistently been higher than that for the overall United States (SPRC, 2022), and this group had the second highest age-adjusted suicide rate of all racial and ethnic groups (CDC, 2022b). Optimistically, we have seen recent drops in suicide rates among this group, which may be driving the reductions seen in the overall U.S. suicide rate (Ehlman et al., 2022). Suicide trends among White populations generally follow the overall U.S. population, in terms of rates over the life course and in sex disparities. For example, for Whites, suicide rates increase from 15 to 54 years of age, then decline from ages 55 to 74, and then increase again in late life, mirroring larger U.S. trends (SPRC, 2022). Also, similar to the U.S. population, White males tend to die by suicide at three to four times the rate of White females (e.g., Curtin, 2022). In fact, in 2020, White males accounted for almost 70% of *suicide deaths* (AFSP, 2022).

The aforementioned differences in rates, trends over the lifespan, and trends over time between the various racial and ethnic groups within the United States highlight the potential impacts of health disparities, historical trauma, marginalization, and other social and systemic factors (e.g., social isolation, access to means, access to opioids) that contribute to suicide. The impact of multiracial and intersecting identities and multiple marginalization on suicide ideation, behavior, and death, which have begun to gain attention, remain an area in need of research (Rosario-Williams et al., 2022; Wiglesworth et al., 2022). Even within racial groups, there is significant heterogeneity that research and prevention efforts must begin to address. Despite the optimism provided by the recent decreases in the overall U.S. suicide rate, monitoring national suicide rates can mask the very real disparities in suicide deaths among diverse groups. Indeed, it has been suggested that the national decrease in suicide rates has largely been driven by decreasing suicide trends among White people, and that suicide rates are rising or stable among all non-White racial and ethnic groups (Ehlman et al., 2022; Martínez- Alés, 2020). From 2019 to 2020, the overall suicide rate declined significantly by 3.0%. However, during this same period, non-Hispanic White people experienced a 4.5% decline in suicide rate whereas no other racial/ethnic groups experienced significant changes (Ehlman et al., 2022). In fact, suicide rates increased by 4.0% among non-Hispanic Black people and 6.2% among non-Hispanic AI/AN people (CDC, 2022b). These differences also suggest that following trends of the overall U.S. suicide rate is necessary, but not sufficient, if we are to address the unique needs of subpopulations within the United States.

Beyond the challenges posed by a national-level focus on suicide rates, small sample sizes and limited research or data on subgroups inhibit our understanding of the suicide risks among non-White groups, multiracial groups, and other groups that may be vulnerable to disparities. It would be beneficial to now target efforts to replicate the reductions in White and U.S. suicide rates across all groups, and learn from them to enhance further prevention efforts (McKoy, 2022).

Sex

In the United States, males and females have consistently demonstrated differences in suicide ideation, behaviors, and deaths. Better understanding of these differences and their underlying causes can help target prevention efforts and interventions specific to male or female audiences.

Females

For years, from 1999 to 2017, female suicide rates had increased, and at a pace greater than that for males (Hedegaard et al., 2018). Promisingly, between 2019 and 2020, the suicide rate among females declined by 8.0%. However, while the rates decreased for the overall U.S. female population and the non-Hispanic White female population (down by 9.9%), the suicide rate for non-Hispanic multiracial females *increased* by almost 30% (Ehlman et al., 2022). Thus, there is likely a disparity in suicide among women that falls along racial and ethnic lines that must be addressed. With regard to age, the 2020 female suicide rate was highest for those aged 45–54 though this group and others saw decreases between 2019 and 2020 (Ehlman et al., 2022). Recently, means of suicide have changed among females, with a shift away from self-poisoning and greater rates of suicide by firearm and suffocation (Hedegaard, Curtin, & Warner, 2021).

Females engage in self-directed suicide behaviors more frequently than men (Bommersbach et al., 2022; Canetto & Sakinofsky, 1998) and have a greater lifetime prevalence of SI (Nock et al., 2013). However, they die by suicide less often than males, a discrepancy that emerges during puberty. Female adolescents are twice as likely to experience suicide ideation and behaviors than males (Labelle et al., 2013). Recently, female adolescents have been increasingly seen in the ED for suicide attempts, increasing

50.6% during February to March 2021 for adolescent girls (aged 12–17) when compared with the same timeframe in 2019. This is in stark contrast to a 3.7% increase for similarly aged males during the same period (Yard et al., 2021). Although male adolescents are more likely to die by suicide (Miranda-Mendizabal et al., 2019), there is some suggestion that this gap has been closing (Ruch et al., 2019).

The potential reasons behind greater suicide ideation and behavior among females include a wide range of explanations. For one, this may, in part, be related to the fact that suicide risk is increased by traumas that are more commonly experienced by women: sexual abuse (Copersino et al., 2008), sexual trauma (Gradus et al., 2012), and IPV (Brown & Seals, 2019). Aside from trauma, females are also generally afforded less power and privilege than males, and improving gender equality can result in significant reductions in female suicide (Milner et al., 2020). Lifespan-related factors may also influence differences between males and females regarding suicide ideation and behavior: oral contraceptive use, premenstrual dysphoric disorder, increased risk during menses and luteal phases of their cycle, perimenopause, and menopausal hormone therapy, among others (Behera et al., 2019; Stacy, Kremer, & Schulkin, 2022). Pregnancy and postpartum periods are both times with their own unique presentations and predictors of suicide risk (Mangla et al., 2019; Stacy, Kremer, & Schulkin, 2022). In fact, suicide is a leading cause of maternal mortality (Campbell et al., 2021). Given the lifespan, menstrual cycle, peripartum, and perimenopausal factors that influence suicidality as well as the fact that sex differences in suicidality emerge during puberty, hormones have been implicated as a potential driver for suicide risk. Specifically, it has been suggested that dysregulation in the immune system and altered sex hormones may drive sex differences. For example, in females, suicide attempts have been associated with decreased levels of estrogen (Sublette, 2020) and increased levels of testosterone (Zhang et al., 2015). Further, testosterone levels are correlated with the number of lifetime suicide attempts among females with bipolar disorder (Sher et al., 2014). Thus, social and biological factors must be considered in understanding and addressing the reasons behind sex differences in suicide ideation, behavior, and deaths.

Males

Males are more likely to die by suicide than females, and in 2020, the suicide rate among U.S. males was almost four times greater than that of females (22.0 vs. 5.5 per 100,000; CDC, 2023; see Figure 4.1). The highest

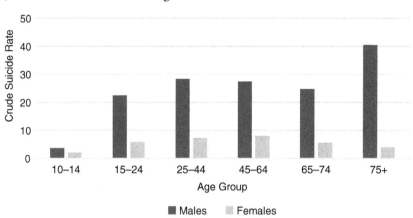

Figure 4.1　2020 crude suicide rates categorized by sex and age (NIMH, 2022).

suicide rate overall was among males aged ≥85 years (52.0 per 100,000) (Ehlman et al., 2022). Similar to what we see in females, there has recently been a decline in suicide among males, but largely driven by White males. From 2019 to 2020, the suicide rate among males declined by 1.9% overall. However, while there was a 3.1% decrease among non-Hispanic White males, there was a 5.7% *increase* among Hispanic males (Ehlman et al., 2022). There were also differences in suicide rate changes between age groups, with decreases of 5–12% for males aged 45–54, 55–64, and 65–74 years, whereas rates increased by 5.0% in males aged 25–34 years. Again, this shows the importance of reviewing suicide trends among subgroups within any population and potentially creating interventions targeted to the unique factors that increase suicide risk among them.

Why do males make up such a large proportion of suicide deaths? There are many proposed explanations, including social, psychological, and biological differences. In males, suicide deaths and suicide attempts are associated with increased androgen levels (Sublette 2020; Zhang et al., 2015). Other studies have shown that those who made violent suicide attempts had lower testosterone levels compared with those who made non-violent attempts (Tripodianakis et al., 2007). Beyond hormonal causes, males are less likely to seek professional help when they are depressed (Addis & Mahalik, 2003; Sierra Hernandez et al., 2014) or suicidal (Cleary, 2017; Oliffe et al., 2020), especially as they age (Mackenzie et al., 2012). Males are more likely to own firearms (Wolfson, Azrael, & Miller, 2020) and use firearms as the most common means of suicide (though suffocation has increased in recent years) (Hedegaard,

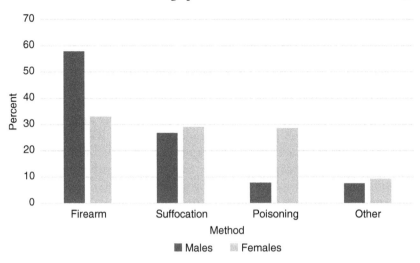

Figure 4.2   Suicide method by sex in the United States (2020) (NIMH, 2022).

Curtin, & Warner, 2021). Indeed, males use more lethal means in their suicide attempts than do females (Denning et al., 2000; see Figure 4.2). Some, but not all (Denning et al., 2000), have demonstrated that males have stronger suicidal intent than females (Hariss, Hawton, & Zahl, 2005) and more favorable attitudes around suicide (Eskin et al., 2016), which could result in more lethal or subsequent attempts. Interestingly, the transition from ideation to action appears to be briefer among males (Neeleman et al., 2004; Van Heeringen, 2001), which offers less opportunity for the person or others to recognize the need for or to seek out help. These factors may all coalesce, likely with other factors, to result in the greater greater risk of suicide death among males.

Sexual Orientation and Gender Identity

Like the other demographic variables discussed earlier, the LGBT community is diverse and is comprised of individuals with varied experiences, identities, and challenges. However, research has largely combined these groups, and many studies omit trans individuals or are specifically focused on the subgroup of transsexuals within the larger trans population (e.g., Haas et al., 2010). Further, research is hampered by lacking or limited documentation of sexual orientation or gender identity on death records. Still, we do know that individuals who identify as LGBT are disproportionately at risk for suicide behavior, suicide death, and other mental health and substance use disorders (Coker et al., 2010; Haas et al., 2010; King et al., 2008). Sexual minority youth are particularly at risk and are several times more likely to attempt suicide compared to heterosexual peers (Russell & Joyner, 2001; Stuart-Maver et al., 2021). Startlingly, almost 25% of high school students identifying as LGBT reported attempting suicide in the prior 12 months (Ivey-Stephenson et al., 2020). This is in line with findings that in a sample of suicide deaths, those who had been identified as LGBT were younger than those identified as non-LGBT (Patten et al., 2022). Suicide attempts among this group of people tend to decrease with age, with most attempts occurring during adolescence and young adulthood (de Graaf et al., 2006; Paul et al., 2002; Russell & Toomey, 2010).

Many studies have shown that mental health diagnoses, which are more prevalent in LGBT populations, are associated with suicidal ideation and behavior among LGBT individuals (Haas et al., 2010). Thus, some of the elevated suicide risks among this population may be a result of increased prevalence of mental health disorders. However, even after adjusting for mental health diagnoses, suicide attempt rates remain significantly higher among LGBT individuals compared with the general population (Bolton & Sareen, 2011; Haas et al., 2010). Thus, there are factors beyond the relatively high rates of psychopathology that are driving high rates of suicide among this group. Some have suggested that perhaps some of the increased rates of suicide among LGBT populations may be related to HIV/AIDS diagnoses (Cooperman & Simoni, 2005); however, some have found that this relationship is mediated by other factors such as substance use, psychiatric diagnoses, and previous suicide attempts (Komiti et al., 2001). Further, it has also been suggested that the suicide risk among those who are HIV-positive may be decreasing as treatments improve (Haas et al., 2010), though it should be noted that some types of antiretroviral therapies have been associated with increased suicide risk (Mollan et al., 2017).

Experiences of prejudice, discrimination, harassment, and victimization may also be driving suicide rates among the LGBT community, particularly among adolescents (Irwin et al., 2014; Mustanski & Liu, 2013). It has been reported that over 80% of LGBT youth reported being assaulted or threatened in the 2021–2022 school year (GLSEN, 2022). LGBT-specific victimization, general victimization, bullying, and negative family treatment have been significantly associated with suicidal ideation and attempts (de Lange et al., 2022). This supports the minority stress theory, which suggests that minorities experience frequent, chronic, unique stressors related to their identity, in this case their sexual orientation and/or gender identity, that contribute to health disparities (Meyer & Frost, 2013). It has further been suggested that minority stress can increase suicidogenic cognitions such as entrapment, defeat, and perceived burdensomeness among LGBT communities (Levi-Belz et al., 2022; Li et al., 2016).

There have been recent advancements in the U.S. sociopolitical environment for LGBT individuals (e.g., Pride Month, marriage equality) and some improvements in community attitudes around same-sex relationships and other forms of sexual and gender diversity (Lewis et al., 2022; Poushter & Kent, 2020). One would hope that as the social environment improves, so would the well-being and health of those identifying as LGBT. However, Meyer et al. (2021) compared generational cohorts and found no indication that these improvements have translated to reduced minority stress (e.g., discrimination, victimization), psychological distress, or suicide. Although younger cohorts tended to come out earlier, their psychological distress and suicide outcomes were worse than older cohorts. Thus, it is possible that although the political environment and overall social attitudes have improved, it has not been sufficient to eradicate the heteronormative history and culture that promotes heterosexism and homophobia that contribute to victimization. Indeed, victimization of and discrimination against those who identify as LGBT persist in the United States (Mallory & Sears, 2020; Myers et al., 2020).

As mentioned above, there are group differences between those who identify as lesbian, gay, bisexual, or transgender, but there is limited research that disaggregates these groups. What does exist suggests that each subgroup has its own risk levels (Robinson & Espelage, 2013). Individuals who identify as transgender are at greatest suicide risk, followed by those who identify as bisexual (Blosnich & Bossarte, 2012; Robin et al., 2002), and then as lesbian or gay (Di Giacomo et al., 2018). Transgender individuals, particularly transgender youth, have very high rates of suicidal ideation and behavior (Austin et al., 2022; Patten et al., 2022; Tebbe & Moradi, 2016). It has also been demonstrated that transgender individuals who died by suicide were more likely to have mental health problems, prior attempts, and a history of child abuse than LGB individuals who died by suicide (Patten et al., 2022). Similarly, in an online survey of LGBT adults in Israel, transgender people reported the highest levels of depression, entrapment, hopelessness, perceived burdensomeness, and stigma-related life events relative to respondents who identified as LGB (Levi-Belz et al., 2022). The same study reported that these variables (depression, entrapment, etc.) were second highest among those who identified as bisexual. Those who identify as bisexual may uniquely bear the brunt of discrimination and harassment from two communities, both outside and within the LGBT community (Zivony & Lobel, 2014), which may exacerbate risk relative to those who identify as lesbian or gay. Further investigation into the differences in suicide risk factors, behaviors, and protective factors that exist between the subgroups of the LGBT community is essential if we are to address disparities among these groups.

Geography and Location

There is a place-based component to suicide, particularly along rural–urban lines, with suicide rates inversely related to population density. In the United States, suicide rates have consistently been greater in rural areas than urban areas for at least two decades (CDC, 2022c; see Table 4.2). This is true across sex, race/ethnicity, age, and means of suicide (Ivey-Stephenson et al., 2017). Further, rural residents have 1.5 times the rate of ED visits for self-directed harm than urban residents (Wang et al., 2022). Rural areas have also had greater suicide rate increases over time, widening the urban–rural gap (e.g., Kegler et al., 2017). For example, from 2000 to 2020, suicide rates increased by 46% in non-metro areas but only by 27.3% in metro areas (CDC, 2022c).

This place-driven component of suicide has been attributed to multiple factors. For example, rural areas tend to have larger physical distances between individuals, which is a challenge in addressing community integration and belongingness needs. The physical distance further compounds suicide risk by increasing barriers to healthcare in areas that traditionally have fewer infrastructure/transportation resources, limited mental health providers, and financial barriers to care (Casant & Helbich, 2022; Steelesmith et al., 2019). Some rural areas are mountainous (e.g., North Dakota, West Virginia) and, in the United States, suicide risk is related to increased altitude (Ha & Tu, 2018; Haws et al., 2009; Brenner et al., 2011), which may be a stronger predictor of suicide than population density or gun ownership (Kim et al., 2011). Other potential contributors to rural suicide include greater rates of heavy alcohol use (Center for Behavioral Health Statistics and Quality, 2020), stigma (Hirsch, 2006), and socioeconomic challenges (Hirsch, 2006). In farming areas, fluctuations around crops can also exacerbate stressors and financial concerns, and drive suicide rates (Turvey et al., 2002).

Table 4.2 *Suicide rate by urbanicity, 2020 (Ehlman et al., 2022)*

Urbanicity	Suicide rate (per 100,000)
Large central metropolitan	10.5
Large fringe metro	12.0
Medium metro	14.9
Small metro	16.9
Micropolitan (non-metro)	18.2
Noncore (non-metro)	20.6

In the United States, individuals in rural areas tend to have greater access to lethal means, namely firearms and opioids, both of which can facilitate suicide (Ilgen et al., 2016; Nestadt et al., 2017; Spark et al., 2021). The density of gun shops has been associated with suicide rates in rural areas (Steelesmith et al., 2019). About half of rural adults own a gun, a rate much greater than urban and suburban residents (Parker et al., 2017), and many gunowners report storing them in an unsecured manner (Ramchand, 2022). As a result, firearm-related suicides are more prevalent in rural than urban areas (Ivey-Stephenson et al., 2017). Indeed, it has been suggested that the gap between suicide rates in urban and rural areas is driven by firearm-related suicide deaths among males (Nestadt et al., 2017). Opioids are particularly relevant to rural suicide, as these areas have been particularly, though variably, impacted by the opioid epidemic (Monnat, 2020; Rigg et al., 2018). Opioid use increases suicide risk (Agyemang et al., 2022; Bensley et al., 2022; Ilgen et al., 2016), and in rural areas, there are particular concerns about the combined use of opioids and benzodiazepines in suicide attempts (Bensley et al., 2022). The intersection of increased opioid availability and access to firearms may further exacerbate suicide risk in certain rural locations (Kalesan et al., 2020). Thus, these lethal means and their combination can be prevalent in rural areas and should be considered in prevention efforts. These efforts should also leverage unique protective factors that may exist in these areas: close-knit communities, multigenerational families, resilience, or Christian beliefs (Hirsch, 2006; Mohatt et al., 2021).

It should be noted that there are limitations to the literature on urban–rural differences in suicide. The constructs of rurality and urbanicity are multifaceted and poorly defined, with oversimplified typologies that lack a nuanced understanding of the social, political, cultural, and economic

Table 4.3 *States with the greatest suicide rates in 2020 (CDC, 2022d)*

State	Suicide rate (per 100,000)
Wyoming	30.5
Alaska	27.5
Montana	26.1
New Mexico	24.2
Idaho	23.2

factors present in any given environment (Bennett et al., 2019; Mohatt et al., 2021). Using this single rural–urban continuum to investigate suicide trends and risk factors is insufficient. For example, The American Communities Project highlighted that among young people aged 10–24, areas they defined as "Hispanic Centers" and "African American South" have lower rates of suicide than the national average, despite many of them being rural (Chinni, 2021). Thus, suicide rates cannot be understood solely based on rurality alone, and other factors must be considered in combination.

Another place-based component of suicide is the state in which one lives. State lines are relatively arbitrary and comprised of both urban and rural areas such that reviewing state-level data can mask regional differences. At the same time, states are governed by laws and other policies that can influence suicide (e.g., gun laws, minimum wage, mental health access), so understanding state trends is also important. From 2019 to 2020, seven states saw significant declines in their overall suicide rate (California, Connecticut, Florida, New Jersey, Ohio, Oregon, and Pennsylvania); however, rates remained stable in all other states and DC. Table 4.3 lists the states with the greatest 2020 suicide rates.

The discussions above are limited in their ability to capture all identities and their intersections (e.g., females who identify as biracial, Christian, lesbian, and live in a rural area). While a basic understanding of suicide of various groups is important, suicide is a far more complex picture when risk and rates are considered as a function of age, sex, race, occupation, and other variables. Further, there are other aspects of identity that may influence our understanding of suicide that go beyond the core demographic variables discussed above. For example, Veterans, those with disabilities, and individuals in certain occupations (e.g., mining, quarrying) have increased rates of suicide (Khazem, 2018; Peterson et al., 2020; U.S.

Department of Veterans Affairs, 2022). Better understanding of the many variables that may drive suicide risk and the intersections of these identities are crucial to maximize effectiveness of prevention and interventions, and identify potential regions or locations (e.g., workplaces, religious communities, primary care settings, schools, and other community organizations) where such efforts can be implemented to reach and benefit individuals with diverse identities.

CHAPTER 5

Prevention, Identification, and Intervention

The field of suicide prevention, risk identification, and intervention has become increasingly specialized given that the issue is complicated, healthcare reform in the United States is focused on cost-effectiveness and evidence-based care in the least restrictive settings, and the field is rife with liability issues (Jobes, Au, & Siegelman, 2015). As a result of these changes and repeated calls for action (The White House, 2022; U.S. Department of Veterans Affairs, 2018; U.S. Office of the Surgeon General and National Action Alliance for Suicide Prevention, 2012), there has been a wave of innovation and research on suicide prevention and treatment.

Suicide prevention efforts include primary prevention (e.g., anti-stigma campaigns), secondary prevention (e.g., gatekeeper training), tertiary prevention (e.g., clinical interventions), and postvention (e.g., survivor support groups). Suicide prevention interventions can be applied for different groups: universal (i.e., general population), selective (e.g., high-risk groups, such as Veterans or LGBT youth), and indicated (i.e., high-risk groups where risk is acutely elevated, such as people in inpatient settings), or integrated and applied at multiple levels within a social–ecological model (SEM; Cramer & Kapusta, 2017; Turecki et al., 2019).

The CDC provides a four-level framework to guide prevention strategies at the individual, relational, community, and societal levels (see Chapter 2, Figure 2.3). This model is particularly helpful in that it informs multilevel intervention and prevention efforts. In line with this, a U.S. national suicide prevention strategy was developed, with four foci (U.S. Office of the Surgeon General and National Action Alliance for Suicide Prevention, 2012):

1. Healthy and empowered individuals, families, and communities;
2. clinical and community preventive services;
3. treatment and support services; and
4. surveillance, research, and evaluation.

There have been numerous gains in implementing this National Strategy, and in 2021 the Surgeon General issued a call to action to reinvigorate efforts for *full* implementation (U.S. Office of the Surgeon General and National Action Alliance for Suicide Prevention, 2021). This document emphasized six actions necessary for the National Strategy to be fully implemented:

1. Activate broad-based public health response to suicide;
2. address upstream factors that impact suicide;
3. ensure lethal means safety;
4. support adoption of evidence-based care for suicide risk;
5. enhance crisis care and care transitions; and
6. improve the quality, timeliness, and use of suicide-related data.

This chapter highlights evidence-based and promising suicide prevention practices at each ecological level, beginning with the individual level and ending with societal-level efforts.

Individual Level

Screening and Assessment

An essential component of suicide prevention is screening and assessment of suicide risk, which has historically been challenging (Hawton, 1987). One challenge in the assessment of suicide risk is the fact that suicide is a low base rate event. Because suicide is relatively rare, it would only be able to be predicted using methods able to discriminate between lower- and higher-risk groups, and current methods have relatively limited predictive value (McHugh & Large, 2020). Thus, in clinical practice, even when identifying those most at risk, we are likely to generate a significant number of false positives (i.e., incorrectly identify people as at risk for suicide when they do not ultimately go on to die by suicide). This high false positive rate may be tolerable given the consequences of overlooking someone at risk for suicide; however, it may also be problematic in that it can cause unwarranted concern, result in restriction or loss of autonomy for those who are incorrectly identified as at risk, or divert limited resources to individuals who do not need them.

Another challenge in risk assessment is that there are certain *groups* who are at elevated risk; however, that does not necessarily translate into an *individual's* behavior. The presence or absence of risk factors is malleable over the course of one's life, and the impact or perceptions of risk factors is not universal. Further, risk factors differ in terms of the risk they confer in the immediate and long-term future, and may be poorly documented such that they cannot even inform a risk assessment (McHugh & Large, 2020; Su et al., 2020). A final barrier is the varying language used in research and clinical work (Bryan & Rudd, 2006), and even in this very book, given the variable terms used in the primary sources we cited. Over the years, the nomenclature used to describe suicide behavior has varied and included suicide attempts, suicidal self-directed violence, parasuicidal behavior, and self-harm, among others. These labels can be stigmatizing, and inconsistent language results in decreased clarity, difficulty drawing inferences from the literature, and has contributed to the inaccurate perception that clinicians should be able to "predict" suicide rather than identify and respond to individuals who are at increased suicide risk (Bryan & Rudd, 2006; Gold & Frierson, 2020).

These and other challenges are reflected in the literature on suicide screening and risk assessment. There have already been many reviews of suicide risk assessment tools and techniques (Carter & Spittal, 2018; Chan et al., 2016; Powsner et al., 2023; Runeson et al., 2017; Turecki et al., 2019; Velupillai et al., 2019). Our goal here is not to duplicate those efforts but to highlight a few key issues in the field. For example, not all scales have demonstrated an association with death by suicide (Brown, 2001), nor are they all statistically strong in terms of sensitivity, specificity, or positive predictive power (e.g., Chan et al., 2016; Cramer & Kapusta, 2017; Large et al., 2016). Even methods that combine multiple risk factors or classify individuals into high- or low-risk categories may not increase the association between suicide and individual risk factors (Carter & Spittal, 2018; Large et al., 2016, 2022; Wyder et al., 2021). Further, some assessment tools have complex scoring systems (Weissinger et al., 2022), a significant hurdle given that clinicians who may conduct screenings (e.g., primary care providers, emergency department physicians, ob/gyns) report a lack of training in suicide assessment (Carter & Spittal, 2018; Diamond et al., 2012; Stacy et al., 2022).

For some settings where complex assessment is not possible or warranted, some have evaluated the use of a single item (#9) on the Patient Health Questionnaire-9 (PHQ-9; Kroenke et al., 2001; see Box 5.1), as a universal screening instrument to identify suicide risk. While this question is positively associated with suicide death (Louzon et al., 2016; Simon et al., 2013), a majority of suicide deaths occurred among individuals who responded "not at all" to item 9 on their most recent PHQ-9 (Louzon et al., 2016). Further, one study indicated that the

---

Box 5.1 PHQ-9 item 9 and responses (Kroenke et al., 2001)

ITEM 9 QUESTION
Over the past two weeks, how often have you been bothered by thoughts that you would be better off dead or of hurting yourself in some way?

RESPONSE OPTIONS
- Not at all
- Several days
- More than half the days
- Nearly every day

PHQ-9 item resulted in false negatives for 11% of the sample who had recent SI (Uebelacker et al., 2011). Thus, while the PHQ-9 item 9 may be beneficial in primary care settings and as an initial screening tool (Kim, Lee, & Lee, 2021), relying on it exclusively may fail to identify patients at risk.

The Columbia-Suicide Severity Rating Scale (C-SSRS; Posner et al., 2008) is a commonly used tool to screen for suicide risk that has predictive value in adolescents and adults, and is endorsed by the U.S. Food and Drug Administration (FDA) for pharmaceutical trials (Brown & Jager-Hyman, 2014). However, there is a smaller research literature to support its use as a screening tool (Runeson et al., 2017; Sall et al., 2019), and it may not be feasible in every clinical encounter (Su et al., 2020). A short version, C-SSRS Screen, was created for initial screening purposes, and the C-SSRS Screen's Ideation Severity and Behavior Scales have been associated with death by suicide at one week, one month, and one year time points for individuals visiting a psychiatric emergency room (Bjureberg et al., 2021). However, the screener may be insensitive to risk immediately after discharge from the ED (Simpson et al., 2021), and thus may have limited utility during some high-risk periods.

Currently, there is no single recommended instrument or method to assess suicide risk in clinical practice (Chan et al., 2016; Sall et al., 2019; U.S. Department of Veterans Affairs and Department of Defense, 2019), nor is there a reliable tool by which to classify patient risk level (Large et al., 2018). This lack of guidance on risk assessment has likely contributed to the lack of formal training for mental health and other healthcare providers in suicide risk assessment (Jacobson et al., 2012; Schmitz et al., 2012; Stacy et al., 2022). Further, numerous patients may not endorse SI

(Richards et al., 2019) or reports may be discrepant with what is reported in medical records (Katz et al., 2020), so clinicians should not rely on a single tool for screening or assessment.

Indeed, suicide risk assessment requires a thorough evaluation incorporating data from numerous sources (e.g., patient, family, medical record) using different modalities (e.g., interview, self-report survey measures). Gold and Frierson (2020) suggest that risk assessment is a semi-structured process by which a clinician gathers information from multiple sources and weighs the various presenting acute risk factors (e.g., current ideation, insomnia), chronic risk factors (e.g., past suicide attempts), and protective factors (e.g., strong social support network). Similarly, Simon (2012) suggests that suicide risk assessment entails identifying unique individual risk factors, acute risk factors, protective factors, medical history and labs, collateral information from other clinical providers, significant other interviews, collaboration with current mental health provider (if any), and reviewing medical records. More recently, the VA/DoD Clinical Practice Guideline for the Assessment and Management of Suicide Risk (U.S. Department of Veterans Affairs and Department of Defense, 2019) emphasizes the need for a non-judgmental assessment of suicidal thoughts, intent, and behavior, and a comprehensive assessment of protective factors, warning signs, and risk factors. The Guideline also emphasizes the need to observe and attend to patient behavior in the interview.

There is significant overlap across the literature in the recommended domains to be covered by a suicide risk assessment, and the repeated suggestion that this must include very direct and non-judgmental questions about suicidal thoughts and behaviors. The domains that are essential to a comprehensive suicide risk evaluation have been detailed in multiple sources and are summarized in Table 5.1 (Gold & Frierson, 2020; Rudd, 2014; Silverman et al., 2015).

One meta-analysis (Franklin et al., 2017) of 365 studies concluded that the ability of risk-factor models to predict suicide has not significantly improved over 50 years of research, and recommended a shift in focus from risk factors to machine-learning-based risk algorithms. Indeed, machine learning is a promising tool for improving suicide prevention and even prediction. Multiple studies have demonstrated that machine learning techniques may improve suicide prediction accuracy (Barak-Corren et al., 2017; Choi et al., 2018; Gradus et al., 2020; Kessler et al., 2017; Simon et al., 2018; Walsh, Ribeiro, & Franklin, 2017, 2018). While machine learning approaches to suicide prediction have the potential to improve the field, there are barriers, limitations, and ethical issues that need to be considered before integration into clinical practice (Bernert

Table 5.1 *Recommended components of a suicide risk assessment (Gold & Frierson, 2020; Rudd, 2014; Silverman et al., 2015)*

Demographics	Age Sex Race Ethnicity Sexual orientation Gender identity Religion
Personal history	History of sexual, physical, emotional abuse, and trauma Medical history Family history of suicide
Precipitants or stressors	Perceived stressors Financial stressors Legal stressors Acute or chronic medical problems Relationship loss or problems
Mental health	History of mental health and substance use diagnoses Current mental health and substance use symptoms Recent discharge from inpatient care Hopelessness duration and severity Feeling trapped Lacking purpose Impulsivity and self-control
Suicide cognition	Past suicide ideation and intent Current suicide ideation and intent (frequency, intensity, duration) Suicide plan Motivation for suicide (e.g., revenge, command hallucinations) Suicidogenic cognitions (e.g., burdensomeness and belongingness)
Suicide behavior	Past suicide attempts • Frequency • Dates • Triggers/context • Perceived lethality and outcomes • Opportunity for interruption, rescue, help • Reaction to previous attempts and survival Past self-injury Availability of means (firearms, medications, etc.) Access to means Preparatory behavior or rehearsal
Protective factors	Presence, accessibility of social support Problem-solving skills Coping skills Engagement in treatment and therapeutic alliance Hopefulness Children or grandchildren in the home Cultural or religious beliefs against suicide Life satisfaction Intact reality testing Fear of social disapproval Fear of pain, suicide, or death

et al., 2020; Linthicum, Schafer, & Ribeiro, 2019; McHugh & Large, 2020). Machine learning efforts have also been met with some skepticism. For example, there are criticisms that algorithms cannot account for the idiosyncratic and nuanced ways risk factors are perceived and impact an individual and their risk level (Michel, 2021). Others suggest that the prediction improvements are only modestly better than existing methods and should be met with tempered enthusiasm (McHugh & Large, 2020).

In clinical practice, clinically derived or algorithm-derived risk-factor-based screening can be used as an initial step leading to a robust person-centered risk assessment and evaluation (Bjureberg et al., 2021; Michel, 2021). This then can identify and ensure that individuals at increased risk are provided the appropriate level of intervention and support, which is the focus of the remainder of this chapter.

Treatment and Intervention

In suicide prevention, treatments can target suicide ideation and behavior indirectly or directly. Because of the strong association between mental illness and suicide risk, there is support that effective psychological or pharmacological mental health treatment, particularly for depression, may indirectly reduce suicide risk (Rihmer, 2001; Turecki et al., 2019; Wasserman et al., 2012). However, there is also evidence that specifically targeting suicidality and suicide behaviors, regardless of diagnosis, is beneficial for reducing suicide risk (Bryan, 2019; Sullivan et al., 2021; Turecki et al., 2019). In fact, suicidal ideation and behavior may best be addressed by treatments that target them directly (Meerwijk et al., 2016; Torok et al., 2020). Here, we primarily, though not exclusively, focus on studies of interventions directly targeting suicide ideation and behaviors, first discussing pharmacologic and medical treatments with evidence of anti-suicide effects, and then transition to focus on psychosocial treatments and community interventions.

Biologic/Medical Interventions

Pharmacological and medical interventions for suicide prevention have been investigated, with some promising interventions that reduce suicide attempts and deaths (D'Anci et al., 2019; Zalsman et al., 2016; U.S. Department of Veterans Affairs and Department of Defense, 2019). The most commonly highlighted interventions in this domain are lithium, clozapine, ketamine, and electroconvulsive therapy (ECT).

Lithium has historically been used as a treatment for bipolar disorder and has been the hallmark mood stabilizer in psychiatry for over half a century (Malhi et al., 2013; Shorter, 2009). A systematic review (D'Anci et al., 2019) reported that there was moderate-strength evidence to support the use of lithium for reducing suicide. However, while lithium was associated with significantly lower rates of suicide than placebo, suicide rates did not differ between lithium and other treatments (D'Anci et al., 2019). Further, it has also been suggested that lithium may not confer additional protection as an augmentation of an existing medication regimen (Katz et al., 2022). Despite these potential limitations, lithium remains the only medication associated with lowered suicide rates in bipolar disorder (Miller & Black, 2020), and has been recommended as a means to decrease suicide risk among patients with mood disorders (U.S. Department of Veterans Affairs and Department of Defense, 2019).

Clozapine is an atypical antipsychotic used for treatment-resistant schizophrenia (Warnez & Alessi-Severini, 2014). This medication has also demonstrated anti-suicide effects for individuals with schizophrenia and schizoaffective disorder (Masdrakis & Baldwin, 2023; Meltzer et al., 2003; Wasserman et al., 2012), even after controlling for the amount of clinical contact required by clozapine protocols (Meltzer et al., 2003). Indeed, clozapine is the only medication with a specific U.S. FDA indication for reducing the risk of recurrent suicidal behavior in patients with schizophrenia or schizoaffective disorder (FDA, 2022). Clozapine is also recommended as a treatment to reduce suicide deaths among adults with schizophrenia or schizoaffective disorder in the VA/DoD Clinical Practice Guidelines (U.S. Department of Veterans Affairs and Department of Defense, 2019).

A more recently identified pharmacological intervention for suicidality is ketamine, an NMDA (N-methyl-D-aspartate) antagonist used as a rapid-acting antidepressant (Kirby, 2015; Krystal et al., 2019). A review of ketamine's impact on SI (Witt et al., 2020) suggests that a single infusion of ketamine may provide individuals with affective disorder short-term relief from SI, reducing acute suicidality for up to 3 days. D'Anci and colleagues (2019) reported moderate-strength evidence that supports the use of short-term intravenous ketamine as a means of reducing SI. However, these authors highlight that much of the data on ketamine are relatively short term, often with only a week of follow-up. A more recent study using two infusions of ketamine found results persisted out to six weeks, though this varied by diagnosis (Abbar et al., 2022). Interestingly, the effect of ketamine in this study was mediated by mental pain, and these authors suggest that the anti-suicide effects of ketamine may be the result of its ability to mitigate mental pain (Abbar et al., 2022). Thus, a ketamine infusion may be a beneficial adjunctive treatment for short-term reduction in SI (U.S. Department of Veterans Affairs and Department of Defense, 2019), though diagnostic considerations may be warranted, as well as consideration of concern about abuse and treatment restrictions (De Giorgi, 2022; U.S. Department of Veterans Affairs and Department of Defense, 2019).

ECT is another biological treatment that has long been suggested as effective in reducing suicidality among people with mental health diagnoses (Prudic & Sackeim, 1999). Kellner et al. (2005) reported that most patients with depression who had expressed high suicidal intent and then completed an acute course of ECT reported no intent by the end of treatment. A study of Medicare-insured patients who were 65+ years old and receiving inpatient mental healthcare highlighted the potential short-term effects of ECT, although protective effects waned and were no longer significant at 12-month follow-up (Rhee et al., 2021). It is for this reason that it has been suggested that ECT should be considered earlier in treatment, particularly when suicide risk is present (Kellner et al., 2005). Though not all studies have demonstrated anti-suicide effects (Peltzman et al., 2020), several professional organizations across the globe highlight suicide risk as an indication for consideration of treatment with ECT (American Psychiatric Association, 2008; Baldaçara et al., 2020; Banken, 2002).

Despite this support and its demonstrated effectiveness, ECT has historically been underutilized and often offered as a last resort (Grover et al., 2019; Kellner et al., 2005; Patel et al., 2006) due to misconceptions, myths, and stigma (Dowman et al., 2005). It is also noteworthy that patients from racial-ethnic minority groups are less likely to be referred for ECT when compared with White peers (Black Parker et al., 2021). It has been suggested that clinicians' diagnosis and treatment recommendations are impacted by unconscious biases, resulting in unequal access to ECT. As such, the creation and implementation of treatment algorithms for objective and evidence-based decision-making for access to ECT may be beneficial in improving healthcare equity (Black Parker et al., 2021) and suicide prevention.

Psychosocial Interventions

Psychosocial interventions have also had promising results in terms of suicide prevention, with a particular focus on safety or crisis response planning, cognitive behavioral therapy (CBT), dialectical behavior therapy

(DBT), and problem-solving therapy (PST). Postvention efforts have also had some success in suicide prevention following exposure to suicide. We should note that the range of potential psychosocial and psychotherapeutic interventions for suicide prevention is not limited to these. For example, Teachable Moment Brief Intervention (O'Connor et al., 2020), Attempted Suicide Short Intervention Program (Gysin-Maillart et al., 2016), and Systems Training for Emotional Predictability and Problem Solving (Alesiani et al., 2014; Boccalon et al., 2017) are among the promising interventions that warrant further investigation.

Cognitive Behavioral Therapy

CBT (Beck & Beck, 2011) is a typically brief, collaborative, problem-focused, and goal-oriented treatment that is empirically supported treatment for depression, chronic pain, and insomnia. A cognitive-behavioral approach helps patients notice and change maladaptive cognitive and behavioral processes, which then influence downstream emotional reactivity and experiences. Many CBT studies targeted depression with an indirect attempt at reducing suicidality, and it has been suggested that directly targeting suicidality may be more effective than indirectly targeting factors that drive suicidality, like depression (Torok et al., 2020). Direct interventions that focus on the treatment target (e.g., CBT-insomnia, CBT-chronic pain) are more effective than general CBT (Torok et al., 2020). Given suggestions that suicide ideation and behavior may be distinct phenomena that require targeted treatment (Meerwijk et al., 2016; Torok et al., 2020), a CBT modality tailored specifically to suicide has been developed. CBT for suicide prevention (CBT-SP) directly focuses on suicidality, identifying the thoughts, beliefs, and behaviors that occur prior to SI or self-directed violence, and the application of CBT techniques to challenge or limit the impact of those cognitions (Bryan & Rudd, 2018; Stanley et al., 2009).

There is evidence that CBT for suicide prevention is effective (Brown et al., 2005; Bryan, 2019; Gøtzsche & Gøtzsche, 2017; Leavey & Hawkins, 2017; Méndez-Bustos et al., 2019; Tarrier et al., 2008; Wu et al., 2022). Brown et al. (2005) conducted an RCT of 120 adults who had attempted suicide and compared cognitive therapy and treatment as usual (TAU) plus tracking and referral services. They reported that over the course of eighteen months, individuals who had received cognitive therapy were more likely to remain attempt-free, had lower reattempt rates, and were half as likely to reattempt suicide than individuals in the TAU group.

Interestingly, the groups did not differ on SI at any point, though the cognitive therapy group reported less depression and hopelessness at several time points. An RCT with a group of active-duty military service members who had current SI and/or a recent attempt reported that a brief CBT intervention was effective at reducing subsequent suicide attempts (Rudd et al., 2015), and that brief CBT contributed to low rates of suicide behavior regardless of risk level (Bryan et al., 2018). Interestingly, within the CBT group, individuals who gradually improved were 2.78 times more likely to attempt suicide during the twenty-four-month follow-up period than rapid improvers (Lee, Bryan, & Rudd, 2020).

Systematic reviews have also identified CBT as an effective suicide intervention. For example, D'Anci et al. (2019) reported that CBT reduces suicide attempts, SI, and hopelessness compared with TAU. Gøtzsche and Gøtzsche (2017) found that, among studies with patients who had attempted suicide in the past six months, CBT reduced the risk of reattempt in half when compared to those who received usual care. Hawton and colleagues (2016) conducted a systematic review and reported improved outcomes (self-directed violence, SI, hopelessness) for those who received CBT-based psychotherapy as opposed to usual care. A systematic review by Leavey and Hawkins (2017) similarly reported benefits of CBT in that there was a statistically significant, small to medium effect for in-person (but not electronically delivered) CBT for SI and suicidal behavior. However, it should be noted that although these reviews highlighted beneficial outcomes of CBT in terms of SI and suicidal behavior, there is some question of whether CBT is effective at preventing suicide death (D'Anci et al., 2019; Riblet et al., 2017), and as such, further research is warranted.

Problem-Solving Therapy

PST (D'Zurilla & Nezu, 2010; Nezu & Nezu, 2001) is an iteration of CBT that focuses on improving one's ability to cope and adopt an adaptive problem-solving style. It has also been identified as a potential suicide prevention intervention. An early systematic review (Hawton et al., 1998) found a non-significant trend indicating that those who received PST had reductions in repetition of deliberate self-harm, though it suggested that the lack of significance was due to the varied outcomes across studies. Indeed, while a number of studies have suggested that PST-type interventions may improve hopelessness, repeated self-injury, and problem-solving skills, the sample, interventions, and outcomes of the studies varied. An early RCT (Salkovskis, Atha, & Storer, 1990) assigned twenty patients at high risk of repeated suicide attempts to a problem-solving intervention or TAU. Those who received the problem-solving intervention had significantly greater improvements in depression, hopelessness, and SI at the end of treatment and for up to one year afterward. The intervention group also demonstrated a lower rate of suicide attempts at six-month follow-up. McLeavey et al. (1994) provided an interpersonal problem-solving skills training intervention to individuals hospitalized for self-poisoning and compared that with a problem-oriented, crisis intervention control treatment. Both treatments were effective in reducing hopelessness and the number of presenting problems reported, but the problem-solving intervention was superior in terms of interpersonal cognitive problem-solving, self-rated problem-solving ability, and a reduction of repeated self-poisoning at twelve months. Hatcher et al. (2011) randomized individuals with recent self-poisoning or self-injury to PST plus usual care or usual care alone. Those receiving PST had significantly greater three- and twelve-month improvements in hopelessness, problem-solving, anxiety, depression, and suicidal thinking, especially if they received four or more sessions. Interestingly, at one-year follow-up, PST had little effect on repeated self-harm across all participants but *was* effective at reducing future episodes of self-harm for people who had initially presented with *repeated* self-harm (i.e., for those whom the index event was not their first self-harm event). This subgroup was 39% less likely to be seen again for self-harm a year later. Further, for those who did present to the hospital, they engaged in hospital care earlier than the usual care group.

Stewart et al. (2009) compared PST, CBT, and TAU for individuals who were hospitalized for a recent suicide attempt. Both CBT and PST resulted in significant improvements and outperformed TAU in several areas. PST was associated with reduced hopelessness and SI, as well as increased problem-solving and treatment satisfaction (the same pattern was reported for CBT). When compared with TAU, PST had greater improvements in satisfaction and SI, but there were interestingly no significant differences in problem-solving outcomes. These authors further reported that PST and CBT groups did not differ in their self-reported problem-solving ratings. The authors conclude that both CBT and PST are possibly effective and acceptable brief treatments for reducing repeated suicide behaviors.

Beyond the promising outcomes of PST on problem-solving, hopelessness, SI, and/or suicide behavior among various diverse groups, it has been reported that even brief video interventions based on PST can reduce SI and depression among a nonclinical sample of college students who had endorsed SI (Fitzpatrick & Schmidt, 2005; Fitzpatrick, Witte, & Schmidt, 2005). Group-based PST has also been shown to reduce depression, hopelessness, and SI, with corresponding increases in self-perceived interpersonal problem-solving (Bannan, 2010; Cooper & Bates, 2019). PST's effectiveness in reducing suicide risk, ideation, and behavior among diverse groups (Beaudreau et al., 2022; Choi et al., 2016; Gustavson et al., 2016; Hopko et al., 2013; Xavier et al., 2019) has contributed to it being recommended for certain individuals with the aim of reducing self-harm and SI (SPRC, 2017; U.S. Department of Veterans Affairs and Department of Defense, 2019).

Dialectical Behavior Therapy

DBT integrates components of CBT and skills training, and has modules that focus on mindfulness, distress tolerance, emotion regulation, and interpersonal effectiveness. As it was initially designed, DBT involves twelve months of weekly individual and group sessions, with additional telephone support and a therapist consultation team (Linehan, 1993; Linehan et al., 1991). Given that DBT is relatively long and intensive, it can be viewed as resource-heavy, costly, and challenging to implement (Chugani & Landes, 2016; Flynn, Kells, & Joyce, 2021; Landes et al., 2021). Originally developed as a treatment for people diagnosed with Borderline Personality Disorder (BPD), who often have chronic suicide behaviors (Linehan et al., 1991), DBT has since been extended to groups without BPD diagnoses as a potential suicide prevention intervention (Perepletchikova et al., 2011).

Numerous, but not all (McMain et al., 2009), studies have highlighted the potential of DBT to reduce suicide behaviors and self-harm. Turner (2000) conducted a naturalistic evaluation of DBT and client-centered therapy for individuals with BPD and reported that DBT had superior outcomes in terms of suicide behavior and self-harm, impulsivity, anger, and depression. Similarly, Linehan et al. (2006) conducted an RCT with women with BPD and recent suicide behavior and self-injury, and DBT was superior to community treatment in numerous domains: less attrition, fewer suicide attempts, lower medical risk across all suicide and self-injury behaviors, fewer psychiatric hospitalizations, and fewer psychiatric ED visits.

Several systematic reviews have suggested cautious optimism around DBT as a suicide prevention intervention, though they generally highlight the need for higher quality research before reaching conclusions.

One meta-analysis demonstrated that the effect sizes for CBT and DBT were robust and comparable in terms of reducing suicide behavior (Tarrier et al., 2008). Hawton et al. (2016) found that, when compared with TAU, DBT resulted in significantly reduced frequency of self-harm (regardless of suicidal intent) at follow-up but did not reduce the proportion of people repeating self-harm. They also reported that when compared to some, but not all, therapies DBT was associated with a significant reduction in repeated self-harm at follow-up. A systematic review by D'Anci and colleagues (2019) concluded that both CBT and DBT offered modest reductions in SI relative to TAU, and provided some evidence that DBT can reduce SI relative to some, but not all, other treatments tested. They also reported that although it may reduce SI, DBT did not have a significantly different impact on suicide attempts or deaths, though the studies reviewed were small. However, a Cochrane review (Witt et al., 2021) specifically on interventions for self-harm (with or without suicidal intent) failed to find evidence of an effect for DBT, compared to either TAU or another psychotherapy, on SI or suicide deaths. Taken together, these findings have contributed to cautious optimism that DBT is a means to reduce non-suicidal and suicidal self-directed violence among people with BPD and/or recent self-harm (Sall et al., 2019), but further research is needed.

Given the potential implementation challenges of DBT, some have investigated abbreviated versions of DBT or independent components of DBT as possible alternatives to the relatively unwieldy standard DBT. Some adaptations of DBT may be effective at reducing SI and improving other suicide-related outcomes (Berk et al., 2020; Katz et al., 2004; McMain et al., 2017). McMain and colleagues (2017) provided brief (twenty weeks) DBT skills training for individuals with BPD and reported significantly reduced suicide behaviors and self-injury compared to a waitlist group. A small study by Berk and colleagues (2019) found that a six-month DBT intervention was associated with significant reductions in suicide attempts, non-suicidal self-injury behaviors, SI, emotion dysregulation, depression, impulsivity, psychiatric symptoms, and substance use. It was also associated with improved family expressiveness, increased reasons for living, as well as high treatment satisfaction and retention rates. Katz et al. (2004) conducted a feasibility study to implement a brief adaptation of DBT on a child/adolescent inpatient unit and found that it significantly reduced behavioral incidents during hospitalization relative to TAU. Perepletchikova et al. (2011) provided children a relatively low dose of DBT (twice weekly for six weeks) and reported a decrease in SI and depression, and a corresponding increase in coping skills. Decker and colleagues (2019) implemented a DBT skills group as an adjunctive treatment for Veterans. This uncontrolled trial demonstrated that SI was reduced immediately post-treatment and this effect persisted at three-month follow-up.

The potential efficacy of briefer versions of DBT and skills groups to reduce SI is promising, though it should be noted that many of these are smaller studies that warrant replication, and not all studies demonstrated the superiority of DBT (Goodman et al., 2016). Further, the quality of evidence for DBT for suicide prevention is low (D'Anci et al., 2019; U.S. Department of Veterans Affairs and Department of Defense, 2019). As such, further research is needed evaluating DBT as a suicide-specific treatment, particularly in terms of briefer iterations of DBT or DBT for those without BPD diagnoses, as well as the feasibility of telehealth-based DBT.

Crisis Response Planning and Safety Planning Intervention

Safety plans are often suggested as an intervention for individuals with recent SI or a past suicide attempt (U.S. Department of Veterans Affairs and Department of Defense, 2019), or are deemed to be at increased risk for suicide (Stanley & Brown, 2012). Safety plans are adaptable to multiple settings, even those without ongoing contact with clients (Ferguson et al., 2021; Labouliere et al., 2020; Rudd et al., 2022; Stanley et al., 2018). Beyond this, safety plans are transdiagnostic, transtheoretical, and can be incorporated into other evidence-based psychosocial interventions (Barnes et al., 2017, 2022; Jobes, 2006; Rudd, 2012; Tyndal, Zhang, & Jobes, 2022). A meta-analysis of varied safety-planning type interventions (Nuij et al., 2021) suggests that they are effective at preventing suicidal behavior but not SI.

Two interventions have dominated the safety plan literature: Safety Planning Intervention (SPI; Stanley & Brown, 2012; Stanley et al., 2008) and Crisis Response Planning (CRP; Rudd, Joiner, & Rajab, 2001). Both collaboratively identify warning signs of a suicidal crisis, internal coping skills clients can use to manage distress and suicidal thoughts, and, if those fail, a list of social contacts who can distract from or assist in resolving the crisis, and a list of professional contacts (e.g., clinicians, crisis lines) to contact if their distress cannot be resolved. CRP and SPI share similar steps and objectives, and both generate a collaboratively built document that clients can use to manage future crises (McGhee, 2020). Both are effective in reducing the likelihood of suicide attempts during follow-up (Bryan et al., 2017; Stanley et al., 2018) and address concerns around the use of no suicide contracts (Stanley & Brown, 2012), which are neither evidence based nor legally defensible (Matarazzo, Homaifar, & Wortzel, 2014; McGhee, 2020). It has been suggested that interventions like CRP and SPI may work via providing distraction, increasing connection, promoting autonomy, building competence, reducing engagement in impulsive urges, hindering engagement in suicidal behavior, and reducing cognitive load by providing alternatives and solutions (Rogers et al., 2022).

Despite overlap between SPI and CRP, CRP is unique in that it incorporates reasons for living. Bryan and colleagues (2017) compared CRP and safety contracts among soldiers with SI during the past week and/ or a lifetime history of suicide attempts; CRP was associated with a significantly lower number and proportion of suicide attempts, as well as a lower number of inpatient days, when compared to safety contracts. They also demonstrated that CRP was associated with a more rapid decline in SI and negative emotional states than safety contracts. They suggest that including reasons for living in CRP may increase positive emotional states, contribute to faster reductions in suicide risk, and reduce the likelihood of inpatient hospitalization (Bryan et al., 2018, 2019). Others similarly suggest that discussing reasons for living during CRP increases positive emotional states, such as optimism (Rozek et al., 2019). However, when comparing CRP with and without incorporating reasons for living, the additional inclusion of reasons for living did not augment protection against attempts at six-month follow-up (Bryan et al., 2017).

SPI includes a semi-structured interview that collaboratively builds a safety plan document. SPI uniquely incorporates lethal means safety, which promotes safe environments via safe storage practices (of firearms, medications, etc.), naloxone provision, and other preventive measures. These conversations may also include the distribution of safety devices (e.g., gun lock, medication lockbox), which is more effective at increasing safe storage practices compared to counseling alone or financial incentives to buy one's own device (Rowhani, Simonetti, & Rivara, 2016). The transition from SI to suicide behavior can be rapid (Deisenhammer et al., 2009) and means substitution generally does not occur (i.e., when a firearm is unavailable people tend not to use another method; Anestis & Houtsma, 2018). Thus, secure storage for lethal means is likely beneficial in preventing suicide by delaying the progression from ideation to action. This is particularly true for suicide among children, for whom 80% of firearm suicides result from having access to a family member's firearm (Johnson et al., 2010). Indeed, one case–control study found that storing firearms locked, unloaded, and separate from locked ammunition was protective against suicide attempts among children and adolescents (Grossman et al., 2005).

Like CRP, SPI is effective at reducing suicide ideation and behavior. One small study (Zonana et al., 2018) compared clinical outcomes among patients for six months before and after the creation of a safety plan, and reported that hospitalizations were significantly reduced and use of crisis calls significantly increased after implementation of safety plans, suggesting the use of less-intensive resources prior to escalating to inpatient care. This study was limited by a relatively small sample but reported trends toward significance suggesting that suicide attempts, ED visits, number of inpatient days, and outpatient mental healthcare utilization all may improve following the creation of a safety plan. Many studies provide SPI in conjunction with additional follow-up. Vijayakumar et al. (2017) provided regular contact and safety planning cards to refugees and found significant reductions in suicide attempts, as well as suicide attempts and deaths combined (though not suicide deaths alone). Stanley et al. (2018) provided SPI and follow-up to Veterans in the ED experiencing SI. SPI was associated with about 50% fewer suicidal behaviors over six-month follow-up and twice the likelihood of engaging in outpatient mental health treatment. One systematic review (Ferguson et al., 2021) reported that SPI is associated with improvements in SI, suicide behavior, depression, hopelessness, and treatment attendance, as well as fewer hospitalizations. However, they point out that there is significant heterogeneity in the studies examined, with some offering SPI alone, others offering it with other treatments, and some offering Internet-based SPI. Ferguson and colleagues (2021) also note that many studies were conducted in adults or U.S. Veteran populations, which limit the ability to generalize findings, a concern relayed elsewhere (Rogers et al., 2022).

Despite these limitations of the literature, SPI has gained traction in the field for a number of reasons. SPI is extremely flexible and easily adapted (Ferguson et al., 2021) and various disciplines can be trained to complete SPI with relatively low amounts of training (Stanley & Brown, 2012) (though higher quality safety plans are associated with better outcomes; Gamarra et al., 2015; Green et al., 2018). Given its ease of use and its positive clinical results, SPI has been implemented in numerous settings (Labouliere et al., 2020; Rudd et al., 2022; Stanley et al., 2018), recognized as a best practice (Stanley & Brown, 2012; The White House, 2021; U.S. Department of Veterans Affairs and Department of Defense, 2019), and iterated upon in numerous ways (Bloch-Elkouby & Barzilay, 2022; Chesin et al., 2015; Czyz, King, & Biermann, 2019; Goodman et al., 2021; Micol,

Orouty, & Czyz, 2022). SPI can be administered in conjunction with other treatments or independently, electronically or on paper, in person or via Internet (Ferguson et al., 2021). Some have augmented SPI with text messages (e.g., Czyz et al., 2020), smartphone applications ("apps"; Buus et al., 2019; Melvin et al., 2019; Nuij et al., 2018; Skovgaard Larsen, Frandsen, & Erlangsen, 2016), and ecological momentary interventions (Jiménez-Muñoz et al., 2022). Some adaptations have demonstrated positive outcomes such as improvements in suicide ideation and behavior, as well as suicide-related coping (Czyz, King, & Biermann, 2019; Melvin et al., 2019); however, many have not been thoroughly researched.

Postvention

Clinical interventions have also been focused on the survivors of those who have died by suicide. These interventions are broadly called post-vention, a term introduced by Edwin Shneidman. Although postvention initially had two goals – to support survivors of an attempt, and/or alleviate the stress of experiencing a suicide loss (Ross et al., 1971) – the current postvention literature primarily focuses on the latter. About 135 people are directly affected by a single suicide (Cerel et al., 2019), and suicide has significant consequences for survivors (Barman & Kablinger, 2021; Cerel, 2008; Jordan & McIntosh, 2010; McDaid et al., 2010; Ruskin et al., 2004), including increased suicide risk and mental health concerns (National Action Alliance for Suicide Prevention, 2015). As such, postvention efforts aim to help those impacted by suicide-related grief, reduce suicide risk among survivors, and prevent contagion. Postvention is, in and of itself, a suicide prevention effort (Aguirre & Slater, 2010; U.S. Office of the Surgeon General; National Action Alliance for Suicide Prevention, 2012).

Early in bereavement, suicide survivors may benefit from information, practical assistance, and non-judgmental support (McGill et al., 2023). Postvention efforts have included on-the-scene post-suicide support teams (Campbell, 2011), school interventions (Cha et al., 2018; Espelage et al., 2022; Williams et al., 2022), support for healthcare workers (Figueroa & Dalack, 2013; Kinman & Torry, 2021; Leaune et al., 2020), or military families (Ruocco et al., 2022) who experience suicide, grief-focused therapy (Supiano et al., 2017; Zisook et al., 2018), online support (Kramer et al., 2015), short-term retreats (Figueroa & Dalack, 2013; Scocco et al., 2019), communication and media guidelines on reporting suicides (e.g., Andriessen & Krysinska, 2012; Cox et al., 2016; Ramchand et al., 2015), among others (Hybholt et al., 2022; McDaid et al., 2008; Peters et al., 2015). Many postvention efforts include a range of interventions that can be tailored to survivors' needs, the degree of impact the suicide had on a person, and/or when they seek postvention (Dyregrov, 2011; Kinman & Torry, 2021; Leaune et al., 2020; Ruocco et al., 2022; Williams et al., 2022). Guidelines from the United States, the United Kingdom, and Australia similarly suggest tailoring interventions based on how greatly individuals are impacted (Australian Institute for Suicide Research and Prevention & Postvention Australia, 2017; National Action Alliance, 2015; Public Health England, 2016).

Postvention efforts have been shown to be acceptable (Scocco et al., 2019; Zisook et al., 2018), reduce mental health concerns (Cha et al., 2018; Kramer et al., 2015; Scocco et al., 2019), promote effective griev-ing (Supiano et al., 2017), and may reduce suicidality (Visser et al., 2014; Zisook et al., 2018). However, the empirical support for postven-tion is limited, of low quality, and complicated by the varied nature of postvention interventions, settings, and audiences (Andriessen et al., 2019; Baldaçara et al., 2020; McDaid et al., 2008; U.S. Department of Veterans Affairs and Department of Defense, 2019). Thus, it cannot be concluded that postvention is effective at reducing suicide deaths (Andriessen et al., 2019; Baldaçara et al., 2020; McDaid et al., 2008; U.S. Department of Veterans Affairs and Department of Defense). It has also been suggested there is a possibility that postvention efforts could cause harm, and further investigation is necessary (Andriessen et al., 2018; Hybholt et al., 2022; U.S. Department of Veterans Affairs and Department of Defense, 2019).

Technology and Clinical Interventions for Suicide Prevention

Technology-based interventions (e.g., telehealth, apps) have become increasingly important (Di Carlo et al., 2021; Li et al., 2022; Torous et al., 2021) and can overcome barriers to care (e.g., transportation, stigma, social distancing) for a wide range of individuals, including those at high suicide risk (Jiménez-Muñoz et al., 2022; Torous et al., 2021). Indeed, some have highlighted the unique benefits that modalities such as telehealth may pro-vide when working with individuals at risk for suicide (Godleski et al., 2008; McGinn et al., 2019; Pruitt et al., 2014). For example, digital safety plans can include photos of loved ones, relaxation videos, links to websites and crisis lines, or maps to emergency services (Jiménez-Muñoz et al., 2022), which can reduce the cognitive load required to problem-solve during a crisis. However, there are diverse forms of telehealth and technology-based interventions, and there is minimal high-quality research regarding the effectiveness of telehealth or technology-based interventions for reducing SI or suicide behavior (Rojas et al., 2020; Sullivan et al., 2022).

Teletherapy has consistently demonstrated similar outcomes to in-person therapy (Batastini et al., 2021; Carlbring et al., 2018; Giovanetti et al., 2022; Lin, Heckman, & Anderson, 2022; Novella et al., 2022), and telehealth and other technology-based interventions may be effective for managing clinical emergencies and/or reducing SI (Batterham et al., 2022; De Jaegere et al., 2019; Finlayson et al., 2023; McGinn et al., 2019; Rojas et al., 2020). Several reviews of telehealth interventions for suicide highlight beneficial outcomes (e.g., reduced SI, reduced suicide behavior, or longer time to next attempt), but caution against firm conclusions due to the heterogeneity and small number of studies (Leavey & Hawkins, 2017; Sullivan et al., 2022).

Guided and unguided online interventions have been highlighted as potentially scalable, stigma-reducing, suicide prevention interventions. However, many internet treatment studies look at the impact of depression treatment on suicide-related outcomes (Mewton & Andrews, 2015; Watts et al., 2012), and few have specifically targeted SI. An internet-based, guided DBT intervention for those with SI and heavy episodic drinking significantly reduced SI, alcohol use severity, alcohol quantity, and emotion dysregulation over four months (Wilks et al., 2018). An RCT demonstrated that an unguided, internet-based CBT for individuals with SI was associated with lower rates of deterioration than a control intervention (an internet-based wellness intervention of similar length (Batterham et al., 2022)). Even a brief (i.e., 30 minutes per week for 4 weeks) preventive web-based CBT intervention was associated with lower rates of SI among medical interns when compared to a control intervention of mental health-related emails (Guille et al., 2015). One systematic review and meta-analysis of internet-based CBT-based interventions targeting SI concluded that such interventions are associated with significant reductions in SI compared to controls, but that more information was needed about suicide behavior (Buscher et al., 2020). Further, D'anci and colleagues (2019) conclude that there is very low strength evidence that internet-based CBT may be better than controls, but not other active treatments. Internet-based treatments may be helpful in reducing SI and, given their scalability and lack of evidence suggesting they would be harmful, may present an opportunity for enhancing suicide prevention efforts.

Mental health apps have been researched with studies of varying levels of quality. One meta-analysis of online-based and mobile phone–based apps for self-management of SI and self-harm reported that they were associated with decreased SI but not self-harm or suicide attempts (Witt et al., 2017). This is in line with Malakouti et al. (2020) whose systematic review concluded a small number of studies suggested that apps were associated with reduced SI and increased coping skills. Jiménez-Muñoz and colleagues (2022) similarly expressed cautious optimism that about half of the suicide prevention apps using ecological momentary interventions (EMI) they reviewed may reduce suicidal thoughts and behaviors; however, they also stated that many apps had yet to be demonstrated to be efficacious and that the literature is limited by small samples. Less optimistically, Melia et al. (2020) concluded that none of the apps evaluated significantly decreased SI when compared to controls, but still suggested they may be a beneficial tool to augment suicide prevention treatment given that they may improve other suicide risk factors: depression, distress, and self-efficacy. However, in light of findings that using suicide-specific apps as adjuncts to treatment may be associated with worse outcomes (O'Toole et al., 2019), further research and consideration are needed.

Despite the potential promise of technology-based interventions for suicide prevention and advocacy for the use of such interventions, particularly when access is limited (Brenna et al., 2021; Pruitt et al., 2022; Torok et al., 2020; Torous et al., 2020), there are still perceptions that suicide prevention treatment is too high risk for telehealth (Gilmore & Ward-Ciesielski, 2019). Further, many studies exclude individuals at risk for suicide (McGinn et al., 2019), and some guidelines have remained agnostic (U.S. Department of Veterans Affairs and Department of Defense, 2019) or against (Alqahtani et al., 2021) the use of telehealth and internet-based interventions for suicide prevention. Research is needed to determine how to best incorporate technology into suicide prevention such that individuals with the greatest needs and barriers can access life-saving care.

More rigorous research is needed to evaluate the effects of these digital health interventions on suicide behavior and identify mediating and moderating variables to elucidate the mechanisms underlying the impact of these interventions (Buscher et al., 2020). Apps and other digital applications should be evaluated similarly to other interventions and clinicians would be wise to thoroughly review the apps (both the research on them and the app itself) they recommend. Many suicide prevention health apps have not been empirically supported (Jiménez-Muñoz et al., 2022), and some include incorrect information (Martinengo et al., 2019) or do not align with evidence-based care (Larsen, Nicholas, & Christensen, 2016). Some apps and other technology-based interventions may not be able to accommodate the relatively greater need for support among individuals with high suicide risk; clinicians should be wary of incorporating low-intensity interventions that may exacerbate distress or hopelessness. Accountability mechanisms within the health app industry and the platforms that offer them may also be warranted (Martinengo et al., 2019).

There have been many promising advances in the clinical realm of suicide prevention, both in terms of medical and psychosocial interventions. However, there are also concerns and limitations that persist. For example, given the low base rate of suicide, there is a lack of RCTs that have sufficient power to determine whether suicide *deaths* (as opposed to ideation or attempts) can be prevented by psychosocial intervention (Brown & Jager-Hyman, 2014). A further complication is that when interventions have been demonstrated to reduce ideation or attempts, we cannot assume that this translates into reducing suicide *deaths* (Brown & Jager-Hyman, 2014), particularly given there are likely qualitative differences between individuals who experience SI and the approximately one-third of those who transition to suicide behaviors (Cha et al., 2010; Klonsky & May, 2014, 2015; Nock et al., 2008; Smith et al., 2016). While some research has been conducted in high-risk settings, more is needed to understand how treatments and technology can be implemented in high-risk settings, such as prisons, EDs, inpatient units, and crisis hotlines. Further concerns have been expressed regarding the fact that the general effect sizes for interventions like CBT and DBT have been small and do not differ from other less mainstream treatments' effect sizes, and that efficacy has not improved as more research has been conducted (Fox et al., 2020). High-quality research on suicide-specific interventions, with an emphasis on RCTs, larger sample sizes, and inclusion of diverse populations, will decrease heterogeneity and improve our ability to generalize findings, make firm recommendations, and tailor interventions to specific populations and settings.

A challenge that will persist despite ongoing intervention research is the fact that effective pharmacological and psychological suicide prevention interventions can only help those who engage with clinical care. Unfortunately, many individuals who experience SI or engage in suicide behavior are not in clinical care (Jobes & Chalker, 2019). Broadening the focus of suicide prevention to include the larger population is likely to be impactful in reducing suicide morbidity and mortality.

Community Interventions

Public health approaches to suicide prevention include a focus on population-level and community-based interventions. U.S. efforts (U.S. Office of the Surgeon General and the National Action Alliance for Suicide Prevention, 2012, 2021) similarly emphasize community-based strategies, such as gatekeeper training, education programs, media campaigns, and lethal means safety. However, some have concluded that there is insufficient evidence about community-based interventions to recommend any particular one as a stand-alone intervention (U.S. Department of Veterans Affairs and Department of Defense, 2019). Indeed, Zalsman et al. (2016) highlighted that there was too little evidence to determine the effectiveness of interventions such as primary care screening, general public education, or media guidelines. Despite these limitations, many of these interventions have been implemented widely.

Gatekeeper training, which teaches people (e.g., students, teachers, clergy, coaches, family) to recognize suicide warning signs and help individuals at risk access services, has been recommended and implemented in numerous settings (Burnette et al., 2015; Isaac et al., 2009; Terpstra et al., 2018). Gatekeeper training can increase knowledge and confidence around suicide prevention (Holmes et al., 2021; Mo, Ko, & Xin, 2018; Terpstra et al., 2018; Zalsman et al., 2016), but this training effect decays over time and does not necessarily translate into intervention behavior (Holmes et al., 2021; Kawashima et al., 2022). A review by Mann and colleagues (2005) suggested that gatekeeper training's effectiveness may depend on the setting, with a suggestion that educating gatekeepers may reduce suicide behavior in settings where there are clear roles and accessible treatment. However, there have been no RCTs that demonstrate gatekeeper training is associated with a reduction in population-level suicide rates (Sareen et al., 2013; Zalsman et al., 2016), and one systematic review was unable to conduct a meta-analysis due to significant heterogeneity of the studies reviewed (Yonemoto et al., 2019). As such, many groups have concluded that the evidence to support gatekeeper training is weak and insufficient to indicate for or against gatekeeper training as a solo intervention to reduce population-level suicide rates (Burnette et al., 2015; Isaac et al., 2009; Mo, Ko, & Xin, 2018; U.S. Department of Veterans Affairs and Department of Defense, 2019; Yonemoto et al., 2019). Further, some (Sareen et al., 2013), but not all (Gould et al., 2005), have expressed concern that gatekeeper training may increase SI among those who participate.

Restricting access to lethal means, such as guns or opioids (Mann et al., 2005; Zalsman et al., 2016; U.S. Department of Veterans Affairs and

Department of Defense, 2019), is effective for indicated, clinical populations, and, similarly, legislation and environmental changes that restrict access to lethal means can be effective at reducing population-level suicide rates. Environmental changes targeting high-risk locations (i.e., hot spots) as opposed to people at risk can be beneficial (Beautrais, 2001; Pirkis et al., 2015). For example, altering suicide hot spots, such as by creating high barriers on bridges, have been shown to reduce suicide (Perron et al., 2013; Pirkis et al., 2015). There is also evidence that there are not corresponding increases of jumps at other local bridges, suggesting intervention effectiveness and a lack of location substitution (Perron et al., 2013). The inverse has also been demonstrated, where the removal of such barriers on bridges has been associated with immediate increases in suicides by jumping at the location (Beautrais, 2001).

Overall, rigorous research is lacking into community-based interventions, inhibiting the ability to make evidence-based recommendations for or against any single intervention (U.S. Department of Veterans Affairs and Department of Defense, 2019). What research exists often provides interventions in tandem or part of a larger suicide prevention program, making it difficult to parse out the independent effects of interventions. Understanding the impacts of stand-alone interventions will help identify mechanisms of change and identify for what groups these interventions are most beneficial, so efforts can be tailored to local communities. Although there is limited evidence to support community interventions, these efforts should not be abandoned. Instead, effort should be directed toward conducting high-quality research of these initiatives.

Societal-Level Interventions

Just as creating safe environments at the individual and community levels is effective at reducing suicide risk, law- and policy-backed means restriction for the larger society is also effective. In general, policies about the accessibility of materials that can be used for self-poisoning have been effective. Limiting the length, quantity, and renewal of prescriptions or over-the-counter medications can reduce related suicides or hospitalizations (Daniel, 2006; Fink et al., 2020; Hawton et al., 2004; Hughes et al., 2003). State and federal efforts in the United States, such as Medicare formulary restrictions and controlled physician prescribing, have led to reductions in opioid misuse and overdoses (Fink et al., 2020). In the United Kingdom, restricting paracetamol (acetaminophen) package size is associated with fewer paracetamol-related deaths and hospital admissions (Hawton et al.,

2004; Hughes et al., 2003). In Sri Lanka – where in the mid-1990s a significant proportion of suicides were due to pesticide self-poisonings – bans on several lethal pesticides resulted in a significant reduction in suicide (44% between 1995 and 2005; Knipe et al., 2017). One systematic review (Lim et al., 2021) reported that means restriction of various types of poison (e.g., pesticides, medications, domestic gas, vehicle exhaust) decreased suicide rates by poison without an associated increase in other methods, again suggesting an absence of means substitution. Thus, limiting access to particularly lethal suicide methods can be important in driving down suicide rates at the population level.

Firearms legislation is particularly relevant to this discussion. Suicide attempts involving firearms are particularly lethal (Conner et al., 2019; Elnour & Harrison, 2008) and are responsible for a significant and rising proportion of suicide deaths in the United States (Kegler et al., 2022). Thus, laws that limit access to firearms, though politically charged in the United States, are likely beneficial in inhibiting the progression from ideation to action. Research from multiple countries has concluded that greater access to firearms is associated with greater firearm suicide rates, and that legislation limiting gun ownership reduces firearm suicide rates (Anestis & Anestis, 2015; Beautrais et al., 2006; Gius, 2015; Kapusta et al., 2007; Kivisto & Phalen, 2018; Lambert & Silva, 1998; Mann & Michel, 2016; Ozanne-Smith et al., 2004). Although Kleck (2022) argued that firearm availability only impacted the means by which suicide occurred and not the total number of suicides, this was challenged by a replication study (Lane, 2022) that found a significant and positive association between firearm availability and total suicides. Similarly, Cerdá et al. (2022) used a model to determine the impact of disqualifying individuals with alcohol- or drug-related misdemeanors from purchasing firearms. They reported that such a restriction, over the course of five years, would reduce the suicide rate by 3% (alcohol related) and 4.6% (drug related). Similarly, Anestis and colleagues (2017) demonstrated that the absence of firearm regulation policies (e.g., universal background checks, mandatory waiting periods) is associated with faster increases in statewide suicide rates. Thus, there is support for societal-level interventions to enhance the safety of environments; however, the level of evidence is still weak and further research, particularly RCTs to elucidate the population-level impacts of polices and regulations, is needed.

The degree of liberalism in a region is also associated with lower suicide rates. Further, left-leaning state governments are associated with decreased suicide (Flavin & Radcliff, 2009), and suicide rates decrease when a country shifts to a more liberal government (Matsubayashi &

Udea, 2012). One potential reason for this is that public efforts, such as economic support, that are more aligned with liberal governments result in structural changes that can also protect against suicide. Increasing certain social welfare programs has been shown to prevent suicide deaths in the United States (Minoiu & Andres, 2008; Rambotti, 2020) and elsewhere (Tuttle, 2018; Yuryev et al., 2012), and has been highlighted as a potential reason for why suicide rates have risen in the United States but fallen in Europe (Case & Deaton, 2020; Sterling & Platt, 2022). For example, Rambotti (2020) demonstrated that increasing Supplemental Nutrition Assistance Program (SNAP) support by 4.5% during a 15-year period would have prevented almost 32,000 suicides. Similarly, increasing the minimum wage above and beyond the inflation rate may reduce suicide. Estimates suggest that for every \$1 increase in minimum wage, there would be a 1.9%–5.9% reduction in suicide rates. The impact of a minimum wage increase would likely be greatest for those with a high school education or less, and some studies found a greater impact among women (Gertner et al., 2019; Kaufman et al., 2020). While greater per capita public assistance spending is associated with lower suicide rates, it should be noted that increased expenditures specifically for public mental health may not predict lower suicide rates (Ross et al., 2012; Stack, 2021). This highlights the structural and sociopolitical contributions to suicide, and how macro-level policies, which are not necessarily intended as a suicide prevention intervention, may be just that.

The sociopolitical context can influence suicide rates via legislation, policies, and financial supports that reduce suicide risk by eliminating the structural antecedents of suicide. Creating a stronger government-driven social safety net (Case & Deaton, 2020) may be a key piece of the suicide prevention puzzle. Future research is needed to assess which state and federal policies (e.g., welfare, minimum wage legislation) may work the best at suicide prevention (Yuryev et al., 2012). While this line of research is being pursued, it is also likely that multi-pronged approaches spanning multiple social–ecological levels to suicide prevention are needed.

Indeed, multimodal, multilevel prevention programs are promising. For example, a multilevel intervention consisting of eleven initiatives (e.g., community education and training, critical incident stress management, suicide surveillance) to decrease stigma, increase help-seeking, and strengthen support and coping was implemented in the U.S. Air Force (Knox et al., 2003). This initiative was associated with a sustained reduction in suicide rates, with a 33% relative risk reduction after the intervention. This suggests that multilevel interventions to promote help-seeking and training can reduce suicide risk at a population level. Similarly, Nuremberg, Germany, implemented a four-level, two-year depression and suicide prevention program. The program offered physician training, media campaigns, community partnerships, self-help activities, and support for high-risk groups. The program was associated with reduced suicide attempts when compared to a control region (Hegerl et al., 2006), an effect that was cost-effective and sustained after the intervention ended (Hegerl et al., 2010). This program has been implemented elsewhere, with promising results (Hegerl et al., 2013). In Japan, one study compared a multi-layered program (comprised of education and awareness programs, gatekeeper training, screening programs for at-risk individuals, and grief support for survivors) in rural areas with high suicide rates to prevention-as-usual in similar rural areas. The intervention regions demonstrated reductions in relative risk of completed suicides and suicide attempts requiring hospitalization. However, there is some suggestion that model fidelity and effectiveness may vary by community (Ono et al., 2013), and some similar intervention programs, like the Multi-level Intervention for Suicide Prevention in New Zealand, failed to find reductions in rates of suicide behavior (Collings et al., 2018). Thus, questions remain around the effectiveness of multilevel interventions and their appropriateness in all settings. Despite these questions, there are some recommendations for what multilevel suicide prevention programs should incorporate (see Box 5.2; Cramer & Kapusta, 2017; van der Feltz-Cornelis et al., 2011).

Box 5.2 Recommended qualities of multilevel interventions (Cramer & Kapusta, 2017; van der Feltz-Cornelis et al., 2011)

RECOMMENDED QUALITIES

1. Training for general practitioners on depression and suicide
2. Community facilitator training
3. Access to mental healthcare
4. Restricting access to lethal means
5. Application of risk and protective factors with strongest empirical support relevant to the target population
6. Implementation of prevention strategies at each ecological level
7. Program evaluation strategy including stakeholder opinions and patient outcomes
8. Informed by theory regarding mechanisms of change
9. Primary and secondary prevention techniques, at a minimum when possible

Any intervention – regardless of type (e.g., medication vs. psychotherapy) or level (e.g., individual vs. community) – will likely be impactful to the extent it decreases diverse forms of pain, increases hope, improves connection, and/or reduces suicide capacity (Klonsky & May, 2015; Klonsky et al., 2021), and would ideally target as many of these as possible. It is potentially for this reason that multi-pronged, multilevel interventions are beneficial, given that they can simultaneously directly and indirectly address the multitude of contributors to suicide risk and the transition from suicide ideation to action. Further evaluation of these integrated public health models is needed to identify components that are most effective, how, where, and for which populations.

CHAPTER 6

Building Resilient Individuals, Communities, and Societies to Prevent Suicide

Decades of suicide prevention efforts have had a limited impact on suicide rates, and suicide remains a critical public health problem in the United States. Throughout the course of this book, questions have emerged and remained, at least partially, unanswered. Despite this, we can be optimistic about best practices and the lessons learned in the preceding chapters. Indeed, this is the positive note on which we begin to conclude this book: summarizing lessons learned, remaining questions, and providing optimism about next steps toward building resilience among individuals, communities, and society.

We have learned a significant amount that can help us understand risk, particularly about rates and demographics of suicide, as well as risk and protective factors. We understand a multitude of cognitive, affective, behavioral, and biological aspects that promote and perpetuate suicidal thoughts and behaviors, and many of these are incorporated into contemporary suicide theories, interventions, and practice guidelines. Further, we have elucidated the sociopolitical and various environmental factors that can drive population-level suicide rates and have begun to incorporate them into suicide theories and interventions. This shift from attributing suicide to individual causes, to incorporating environmental contributions into suicide models is promising. It signals that we have – partially – overcome our collective cognitive bias, the fundamental attribution error (Ross, 1977), the tendency to overemphasize individual, dispositional, or personality-based explanations for behaviors, while under-acknowledging situational causes. Thus, we have made progress in decreasing suicide stigma and established the need for adding a population-level focus on suicide rates. However, research on higher-level interventions includes varied samples and design, leaving us with no firm conclusions about what higher-level interventions are effective, especially as stand-alone interventions.

Several key questions remain, perhaps the greatest of which is *how can we identify who will attempt to take their own life or die by suicide?* While the field has identified risk factors for suicide, this does not successfully enable clinicians to identify those who will die by suicide with a high degree of certainty. Lists of risk factors, risk categorizations, and predictive modeling have made some progress in identifying those at increased risk, but has not improved accuracy or positive predictive power significantly. Machine learning has the potential to improve this; however, current machine learning efforts cannot accommodate the minute-by-minute (or even more rapidly) fluctuating risk within an individual, nor can they capture the idiosyncratic and nuanced features and circumstances that may propel a person from ideation to action.

Once identified, clinicians must be able to mitigate suicide risk. This raises questions about *what interventions are most effective at reducing suicide?* Despite the encouraging findings presented in Chapter 5, questions remain as to exactly which clinical and community interventions, or their components and combinations, are most effective or *what interventions are effective for whom?* Although there is evidence supporting suicide-targeted treatments for certain groups (e.g., CBT or PST for those with recent self-directed violence, clozapine for those with schizophrenia, DBT for BPD), there are numerous subpopulations (and their intersections) for whom ideal treatments have not been identified. There is a pressing need for interventions that are effective for various subsections of the population with high levels of risk.

Much effort has been expended to identify and address risk factors for suicide. These approaches are often deficit oriented, focused on changing maladaptive thoughts, emotions, behaviors, and environments to decrease distress. This can be helpful in the short term or in periods of crisis but may be limited in the long term if skills or supportive environments are not maintained. There may be an opportunity to expand the focus beyond deficits, pathology, and distress. This raises the question of *what is missing in existing suicide prevention efforts?* The answer may be found in going beyond addressing risk factors, even beyond efforts to bolster protective factors, and focusing on building resilience. Without this, interventions may overlook positive states, such as optimism and gratitude, that have been associated with reduced hopelessness, SI, and suicide behavior (Huffman et al., 2016). Positive emotions may improve problem-solving among individuals experiencing SI (Joiner et al., 2001), and having a positive future orientation may be more important in reducing suicide behaviors than reducing hopelessness (Hirsch et al., 2006). Some highlight that improving future orientation may also reduce hopelessness (Mac Giollabhui et al., 2018). Thus, interventions directly addressing positive cognitive and affective states may provide benefits beyond those provided by traditional deficit-oriented approaches (Hirsch et al., 2018). Although there has been some research on what protective factors are, there is even less information on how interventions can promote positive emotional experiences or foster resilience to potentially prevent suicide.

Resilience

Resilience can be defined as "the process and outcome of successfully adapting to difficult or challenging life experiences, especially through mental, emotional, and behavioral flexibility and adjustment to external and internal demands…" (American Psychological Association, n.d.). Resilience buffers against psychological and physical consequences of adversity (Catalano et al., 2011; Rudd & Yates, 2020; Yi et al., 2008) and is associated with successful adaptation, recovery, and psychological growth (Babić et al., 2020; Ong et al., 2006; Tu et al., 2020; Yeager & Dweck, 2012).

Resilient people tend to worry less, have more cognitive flexibility, and are more likely to use an optimistic or positive attributional style to explain negative events (Gillham et al., 2001; Johnson et al., 2017; Ram et al., 2019). Greater resilience has also been associated with greater purpose or meaning in life (Winger, Adams, & Mosher, 2016), positive beliefs about the self, self-awareness of character strengths, and higher self-efficacy (Kidd & Shahar, 2008; Martínez-Martí & Ruch, 2017; Schwarzer & Warner, 2013). Thus, resilience influences both how an event is appraised and the appraisal of one's own capacity to deal with that event, all of which have clear implications in terms of problem-solving, future orientation, and suicide.

There has been debate about whether resilience should be viewed as a personality trait or a process resulting from both personality and environment/experience (Garcia-Dia et al., 2013; Sisto et al., 2019). However, research has shown that the capabilities and skills that are associated with resilience can be taught (Newman, 2005), suggesting that aspects of resilience go beyond the presence or absence of a trait. Thus, resilience is likely the result of person–environment interaction and can be fostered through learning and successful experiences interacting with and navigating the environment (Egeland, Carlson, & Sroufe, 1993; Herrenkohl, 2013; Seery, 2011). Promoting opportunities for such positive interactions and learning at the individual, community, and societal levels may contribute to increased resilience.

Resilience interventions must help people build self-awareness, reflect on existing strategies used to manage challenges and their effectiveness, and assess what changes are needed (Baker et al., 2021; Cowden & Meyer-Weitz, 2016; Gogo et al., 2019; Kreibich et al., 2020). Interventions to build resilience must also accommodate the fact that resilience fluctuates over time and scenario, and should not only build capacity for resilience but also improve self-appraisals of one's own ability to cope with adversity (Baker et al., 2021). Research also tells us that successful attempts at managing adversity increase self-confidence to handle future challenges (Baker et al., 2021). Thus, resilience-oriented interventions can promote self-efficacy and support individuals' capacity to navigate current and future challenges, and could potentially be adapted to reduce suicide risk (Sher, 2019). Resilience interventions adapted for suicide prevention may consider targeting self-regulation of negative emotions, distress tolerance, cognitive reappraisal, and strategies aimed at reducing unhelpful coping behaviors and building more helpful coping behaviors (Helmreich et al., 2017; Sher, 2019). Several established resilience interventions (Baker et al., 2021; Padesky & Mooney, 2012) focus on these domains with a heavy influence from Positive Psychology (Seligman, 2002).

Positive Psychology and Positive Suicidology

Positive psychology (Seligman, 2002) is the study of conditions and processes that contribute to the thriving, flourishing, and the optimal functioning of people, groups, and institutions (Gable & Haidt, 2005). Based on three pillars (positive emotions, positive traits, and positive institutions), positive psychology expanded psychology beyond deficits and studies what is good, including well-being, hope, optimism, flow, and happiness (Chafouleas & Bray, 2004; Gable & Haidt, 2005; Seligman, 2002). These characteristics are viewed as applicable to all humans, including those who have mental health concerns or experience suicidality (Seligman & Csikszentmihalyi, 2000), although their cross-cultural applicability has been questioned (Cole & Wingate, 2018).

Positive psychologists have developed a wide range of interventions that aim to increase pleasure, engagement, and meaning in life (Seligman, Steen, Park, & Peterson, 2005). Although many have been employed in nonclinical settings (e.g., classrooms, workplaces), they are likely beneficial to clinical populations as well, given that mental illness and well-being are not mutually exclusive (Iasiello & Van Agteren, 2020). The alleviation of psychiatric symptoms does not necessarily result in increased well-being, and an individual can simultaneously experience happiness and mental illness, well-being and distress (Bergsma, Ten Have, Veenhoven, & de Graaf, 2011; Bergsma, Veenhoven, ten Have, & de Graaf, 2011). Focusing on human strengths and virtues has been suggested as an important component to effectively prevent and treat psychopathology (Seligman & Csikszentmihalyi, 2000), including suicide. In general, applying positive psychological principles to the promotion of physical and mental well-being has been successful, with growing evidence that positive psychological characteristics are associated with better social and health outcomes (Aspinwall & Tedeschi, 2010; Boehm & Kubzansky, 2012; Hefferon & Boniwell, 2011; Kubzansky et al., 2018).

It may be beneficial to expand the scope of suicide prevention to include bolstering meaning, purpose, and well-being independent of, or in spite of, suicide risk. Indeed, positive psychology theories have been applied to suicide prevention (Davidson et al., 2009; Fredrickson & Joiner, 2018; Hill & Pettit, 2013; Hirsch, Chang, & Kelliher Rabon, 2018). Suicidal ideation and behavior may be a possible target for positive psychological intervention by shifting the focus from the causes of the suicidal behavior toward a better understanding of resilience factors and processes that may decrease suicide risk, such as positive experiences and problem-solving (Wingate et al., 2006). Positive characteristics like optimism, hope, and coping ability, among others, may also play a role in reducing suicidality (Ong & Thompson, 2019; Quintana-Orts & Rey, 2018; Sher, 2019; Wingate et al., 2006) by interrupting the associated pathway between stressors and suicidal responses (Wingate et al., 2006). For example, positive psychological factors of reasons for living, meaning in life, social support, and gratitude are negatively related to SI, depression, and loneliness (Costanza et al., 2019; Heisel, Neufeld, & Flett, 2016; Kleiman, Riskind, & Schaefer, 2014), and may reduce suicide risk directly or indirectly (Kleiman, Riskind, & Schaefer, 2014; Krysinska et al., 2015; Wingate et al., 2006).

Theory, research, and clinical evidence suggest that there is a role for such positive psychological variables in suicide prevention. Early predecessors of positive-focused treatment approaches to suicide include Linehan and colleagues' focus on reasons for living (Linehan et al., 1983). More recently the subfield of positive suicidology has emerged, with a focus on applying strengths or adaptive characteristics to prevent suicide (Hefferon & Boniwell, 2011; Hirsch, Chang, & Kelliher Rabon, 2018). Some interventions focus on cultivating or amplifying a specific positive cognition or emotion, such as expressing optimism, generating gratitude, and reestablishing life purpose (Huffman et al., 2014), which are associated with lower suicidality (Heisel et al., 2016; Kleiman et al., 2014; Krysinska et al., 2015; Wingate et al., 2006). Other positive interventions for suicidality focus on improving future orientation, promoting forgiveness, enhancing social communication and self-disclosure, and promoting healthy behaviors, and mindfulness (Hirsch, Chang, & Kelliher Rabon, 2018).

Positive interventions for suicidality have had some success. For example, Huffman and colleagues (2014) demonstrated that varied positive psychological exercises (e.g., gratitude practice, use of personal strengths) were associated with reductions in hopelessness and increased optimism among individuals hospitalized for suicidality. An intervention focused on creating meaningful goals among older adults with suicidal thoughts led to greater hope, future outlook, goal realization, and decreased depression and distress (Lapierre et al., 2007). An RCT compared combined sertraline and positive psychotherapy to sertraline alone and reported that the combined treatment had superior hopelessness and SI outcomes (Shaygan et al., 2022). However, others found that brief positive interventions were superior to control treatments in improving depression, anxiety, and optimism, but not SI or hopelessness (Celano et al., 2020; Ducasse et al., 2019). Still other studies failed to demonstrate the superiority of positive psychology interventions, with Celano et al. (2017) demonstrating the potential superiority of a cognition-focused control intervention.

Despite these conflicting results, positive interventions may still be beneficial to implement given that they generally require minimal provider training, are straightforward and acceptable to patients, can be incorporated into numerous settings, and are accessible to a variety of individuals, including who do not have formal mental health diagnoses (Brouzos et al., 2021; Celano et al., 2020; Huffman et al., 2017). Positive interventions have been suggested as an adjunctive intervention early in treatment (Shaygan et al., 2021) or in crisis and acute settings to improve positive psychological states at discharge (Ducasse et al., 2019; Huffman et al., 2014), which is known to be a high-risk period (Olfson et al., 2014). Further, positive psychology exercises can potentially enhance existing evidence-based interventions for suicide prevention that promote emotion regulation, social well-being, and adaptive cognitive-emotional functioning (e.g., CBT, PST, and DBT).

Similar to traditional clinical treatments, positive psychology interventions at one level (e.g., individual) may not be sufficient to drive resilience or optimism in others (e.g., workplace) (Farmer & Stevenson, 2017). Thus, positive interventions likely must occur at multiple ecological levels, a natural fit for positive psychology interventions given that they have been broadly implemented in nonclinical and organizational settings. Positive psychology also has an inherent focus on promoting factors that allow individuals *and communities* to thrive (Hefferon & Boniwell, 2011). Thus, our final remaining question is: *how do we build societies, cultures, organizations, teams, units, etc., that prioritize and support such resilience?* The third pillar of positive psychology, positive institutions, may provide useful tools for developing resilience-focused, positively oriented systems.

Positive psychology's initial discussions of positive organizations reference constructs like democracy, free inquiry, and strong families, which touch on larger societal needs. Since then, the research literature on positive *organizational* psychology has expanded into workplaces, healthcare systems, neighborhoods, schools, and other contexts (Luthans & Youssef-Morgan, 2021; Resnick & Leddy, 2015; Tao, Yang, & Chai, 2020) and can inform our work on positive higher-level interventions for suicide prevention. Positive interventions that transform workplaces, organizations, and other settings suggest that effective strategies are promoting positive deviance (e.g., altruistic behavior), virtuous actions without expecting reciprocity (e.g., compassion, forgiveness), affirmative biases (e.g., focusing on what is going well), incorporating everyone's strengths, social capital (e.g., trust, communication), rewarding environments, and a culture of change and improvement (Lewis, 2011).

Luthans and colleagues (Luthans & Avolio, 2014; Luthans & Youssef-Morgan, 2017, 2021; Youssef-Morgan & Luthans, 2015) highlight the role of psychological capital (PsyCap), which is comprised of the psychological constructs of hope, self-efficacy, resilience, and optimism. Those who develop PsyCap tend to confidently engage with and persevere through obstacles, pursue goals, be optimistic about the odds of success, and shift course if necessary. Those with higher levels of PsyCap are able to be resilient in the face of adversity to attain success. Not surprisingly, PsyCap is inversely correlated with SI (Ray, 2020) and mediates the relationship between job stress and SI (Gao et al., 2020; Shen et al., 2014). Importantly, PsyCap can be taught, practiced, and developed. While PsyCap can be fostered in individuals, it is included here in this discussion of positive organizations because it can also be passed along via social contagion (Luthans & Broad, 2022) to others to promote health, positive organizations, communities, and cultures. PsyCap interventions are brief and easy to implement (Luthans & Youssef-Morgan, 2017) and have been adapted to address suicide prevention (Luthans & Broad, 2022). PsyCap elements can be reinforced across all ecological levels to promote more positive environments that support individual and community well-being. Some have argued that building strengths, rather than rectifying weaknesses, in individuals and communities is the most efficient way to improve well-being (Clifton & Harter, 2003). This can result in upward spirals and escalating positive phenomena in organizations (Cameron, Dutton, & Quinn, 2003) and may be a foundational first step for communities, organizations, and governments to take in their efforts toward positive suicide interventions.

Beyond embracing positive psychological principles, positive suicidology (Hirsch, Chang, & Kelliher Rabon, 2018) encourages community-based approaches that incorporate local needs and values. For example, community-based participatory empowerment strategies for suicide prevention can involve community members as co-owners/designers of the effort, democratize prevention decision-making and implementation, and maximize community benefit by incorporating local culture, knowledge, and history. Tailoring prevention efforts to the cultural values, understandings, and goals of the community will help to sustain these programs and foster community growth and wellness. Indeed, these approaches have successfully been adapted to support socioeconomically disadvantaged and at-risk communities (Bruck, 2017; Cox et al., 2014; Grattidge et al., 2021; Kral & Idlout, 2016; Mohatt, 2014). There may also be potential synergy with a more recent area of study, critical suicidology, which integrates diverse stakeholders to revamp the study of suicide and create more culturally sensitive and less oppressive prevention strategies that capitalize on community strengths, as opposed to the deficit-focused biomedical model of suicide (White et al., 2015).

One potential way to offer culturally sensitive, values-driven suicide prevention efforts is through local coalitions. Coalitions are a common health promotion mechanism for addressing community-wide problems, including suicide (Kaslow et al., 2012; Reifels et al., 2021). Coalitions can be comprised of individuals from public and private local organizations, including those with lived experience of suicidality or suicide loss, and can play a part in identifying the values, needs, and goals, within a given community. They can also develop and use local infrastructure to promote suicide prevention at state and community levels (Quinlan et al., 2021). Suicide prevention coalitions have a potential to implement risk mitigation (e.g., risk screening, lethal means safety) and positive psychology (e.g., PsyCap) interventions in a culturally meaningful way and drive suicide prevention at local, community, and state levels. Regardless of the specific intervention, it is essential that federal, state, and local governments partner with public and private organizations to establish suicide prevention efforts, dedicate resources and staff, collect and use suicide data, and build capacity for their implementation (Quinlan et al., 2020).

There are many unresolved questions and suicide remains a public health problem in the United States. Our society is challenged by a history of colonialism, oppression, and inequity, and an increasingly disconnected society, with a growing reliance on virtual platforms for social interaction. While being aware of these challenges and having risk and deficit-focused models are essential to understanding suicide, they likely must be combined with strengths- and values-based models to have a greater impact. Just like clinical models and treatment are critical to prevent suicide among indicated populations, we must continue to augment them with public health approaches and social policies (e.g., economic supports, housing stability) that target the whole population if we are to impact national suicide rates. As we embrace positive psychology into suicide prevention, we can also embrace its tenets of optimism, hope, and resilience: optimism that prevention efforts can have an impact, that societies will improve, and suicide rates will decline; hope that there are more answers to be found; and resilience in the face of a perpetually negative news cycle and stubborn suicide rates.

CHAPTER 7

Hope

Suicide has long been part of social discourse, with numerous depictions in art, literature, philosophy, and so forth, across cultures and time periods. It is evident that suicide has touched every corner of this world, with no demographic, social group, or geography unscathed. With the ever-expanding reach of social media and increased globalization, it seems the number of people impacted by every suicide is only increasing. From celebrities, politicians, and fashion designers to colleagues, friends, or family, suicide is seemingly everywhere. Either through confirmation bias or an actual increase in suicide behavior in the people around us, we were concerned with the number of media and personal stories of suicide we were encountering. In an effort to grapple with difficult emotions and incomplete understandings of what could drive friends, family, or clients to suicide, we came together to write this book and answer, in part, the question of "Why?"

Our book had two aims: to provide a biopsychosocial perspective on suicide and prevention, and to serve as a public health intervention by increasing awareness about and destigmatizing suicide. As we reflect on what we have written, we see that we have also answered another question for ourselves: *why should we have hope?* Indeed, perhaps a third purpose of this book is one that goes beyond awareness and decreased stigma, to include: *help our audience shift their perspective to a place of hope and optimism, and even agency, such that they feel they can be part of suicide prevention.*

As much as suicide has been a part of our social history, hope has also been a construct prevalent in culture, literature, religion, and so forth, everywhere. Hope is a common human experience, and it has been highlighted as a necessary survival trait without which humans would perish (Goodall & Abrahams, 2021). Hope has indeed been shown to be related to recovery from illness, injury, as well as mental health and substance use conditions (Bonney & Stickley, 2008; Davidson et al.,

2008; Stickley & Wright, 2011). Hope is very clearly tied to our species' well-being and resilience. Hope can improve the current state of suicide prevention both by reducing suicidality and by increasing the hope we have about suicide prevention such that we take action. We intend for this final chapter to unify readers toward the common goal of engaging in suicide prevention efforts (at any level), offer concrete next steps, and provide a realistic perspective on the barriers we will encounter in working toward that end.

In the preceding chapters, we have expanded our understanding of the causes, treatments, and next steps in the realm of suicide prevention. We have incorporated strengths, hope, and other positive aspects into the discussion of what many would agree is the least positive topic possible. We landed, firmly planted, in a place of hope for change, lives saved. Along the way, we have challenged the *myths* that have historically maintained stigma and silence around suicide:

- **Suicide ideation, behavior, and death are a problem *within* an individual**: While there are individual risk factors for suicide, a vast array of interpersonal, community, and societal-level factors drive suicide.
- **People who have suicidal thoughts and behaviors are weak or unstable**: Numerous external factors drive suicide, including genetic factors that are outside of an individual's control. We also do not know the perceptions others have in the face of challenges or chronic stress.
- **People who die by suicide are selfish**: The assumption here is that individuals who die by suicide do not think or care about how their death will impact others. However, interpersonal-based models of suicide highlight the role of distorted cognitions about perceived burdensomeness and thwarted belonging. Individuals who die by suicide often *do* consider how their death will impact others; they just assume others will be better off if they are dead.
- **Nothing can be done if a person wants to die by suicide**: Connecting people to treatment can reduce suicide risk, treatments like CBT for suicide prevention are effective, and creating safe environments (e.g., removing firearms, medication lockboxes) can prevent suicide. We also know that most people who attempt suicide *don't* go on to die by suicide. Suicide can be prevented.
- **I personally can't do anything to prevent it if someone wants to die by suicide**: You can notice when people are not acting like themselves and ask if they need help. While individuals experiencing

SI have a need for clinical support, we can *all* help via emotional support and encouragement. Practical support – like securing the environment (e.g., removing firearms), not leaving them alone, encouraging them to talk, identifying resources, or helping them plan for the future – can prevent suicide. In emergencies, you can call 9-1-1 or crisis lines (e.g., "9-8-8") on behalf of the person.

- **Asking about suicide will put the idea in their head**: Social support *reduces* suicide risk. Beyond immediate practical and logistical support, providing an opportunity to talk about suicidal thoughts or problems can help alleviate their pain and find solutions.
- **People with a history of a suicide attempt can't help someone who is suicidal**: Individuals with lived experience of suicide ideation or behavior can improve prevention efforts. Community empowerment strategies and coalitions can be informed by the experiences and needs that people with lived experience can elucidate. Further, individuals with suicidal thoughts may have never encountered others with similar experiences. Peer support and sharing such stories, carefully and ethically (Fitzpatrick, 2016), can mitigate feelings of loneliness and isolation. Another benefit: sharing recovery stories is beneficial to the recovery of the storyteller (Koenig Kellas et al., 2015; Niederhoffer & Pennebaker, 2009).

It is on these notes of positivity, optimism, hope, and resilience that we hope to conclude this book. Borne out of strife, we partnered together to answer the frustrating, nagging, unending question of "Why did he/she/they die by suicide?" Starting from a place of pain, and early chapters that paint a grim picture of despair and lives cut short, we have learned about numerous heartening interventions, prevention efforts, and paths forward. We encourage you to identify what *you* can do in your community to prevent suicide (American Psychiatric Association, 2018; SAMHSA, 2023).

- **Pay attention to warning signs**:
  - Talking or writing about death, dying, or suicide
  - Expressing hopelessness, helplessness, or worthlessness
  - Saying they have no purpose or reason to live
  - Increased alcohol/drug use
  - Withdrawal from others and social activities
  - Reckless behavior or more risky activities
  - Drastic mood changes
  - Talking about feeling trapped or being a burden

- **Ask friends/family how they are doing**: Sometimes our discomfort with suicide keeps us from saying anything. Don't be afraid to ask directly if someone is thinking about hurting himself. It's okay to *not* be okay.
- **Ask friends/family if they need help**: The best you can do is offer to support someone and ask, "What can I do?" "What do you need from me?" "How can I support you?" A simple "I'm thinking of you" can be a supportive statement.
- **Connect to help:** Not sure where to start? Your physician or local National Alliance on Mental Illness chapter can likely connect you with local resources, or you can look at Substance Abuse and Mental Health Services Administration's Behavioral Health Treatment Services Locator (https://findtreatment.samhsa.gov/). If you need emergency support, call 9-1-1 for emergencies or 9-8-8 for the 988 Suicide and Crisis Lifeline.
- **Don't give up:** You can be an important advocate for yourself or a loved one. Beyond helping individuals with whom you are in contact, get involved at the local and state levels.

Our personal experiences with suicide drove us together toward action. Using the primary platform available to us (academia), we turned our discomfort, frustration, and fear of futility into agency. We hope that, now equipped with more information and concrete next steps, our readers will have the self-efficacy and sense of urgency to get involved in prevention efforts however possible. The important thing, for all involved, is to take a first step.

References

Abbar, M., Demattei, C., El-Hage, W., Llorca, P.M., Samalin, L., Demaricourt, P., ... & Jollant, F. (2022). Ketamine for the acute treatment of severe suicidal ideation: Double blind, randomised placebo controlled trial. *BMJ, 376*, e067194.

Abramson, L.Y., Alloy, L.B., Hogan, M.E., Whitehouse, W.G., Gibb, B.E., Hankin, B.L., & Cornette, M.M. (2002). The hopelessness theory of suicidality. In T. Joiner & M.D. Rudd (Eds.), *Suicide science* (pp. 17–32). Springer.

Addis, M.E., & Mahalik, J.R. (2003). Men, masculinity, and the contexts of help seeking. *American Psychologist, 58*(1), 5.

Adler, A. (1964). *Superiority and social interest: A collection of later writings* (H.L. Ansbacher & R.R. Ansbacher, Eds.). Northwestern University Press.

Adynski, H., Zimmer, C., Thorp Jr, J., & Santos Jr, H.P. (2019). Predictors of psychological distress in low-income mothers over the first postpartum year. *Research in Nursing & Health, 42*(3), 205–216.

Adu, A., Brown, S.V., Asaolu, I., & Sanderson, W. (2019). Understanding suicide in pregnant and postpartum women, using the National Violent Death Reporting System Data: Are there differences in rural and urban status? *Open Journal of Obstetrics and Gynecology, 9*, 547–565.

AFSP. (2022). *Suicide statistics*. Retrieved March 16, 2023, from https://afsp.org/suicide-statistics/.

Aguirre, R.T., & Slater, H. (2010). Suicide postvention as suicide prevention: Improvement and expansion in the United States. *Death Studies, 34*(6), 529–540.

Agyemang, D.O., Madden, E.F., English, K., Venner, K.L., Rod, H., Singh, T.P., & Qeadan, F. (2022). A trend analysis of the prevalence of opioid misuse, social support, and suicide attempt among American Indian/Alaska native high school students in New Mexico: 2009–2019 Youth Risk Resiliency Survey (YRRS). *BMC Public Health, 22*(1), 1–15.

Ahmedani, B.K., Simon, G.E., Stewart, C., Beck, A., Waitzfelder, B.E., Rossom, R., ... & Solberg, L.I. (2014). Health care contacts in the year before suicide death. *Journal of General Internal Medicine, 29*, 870–877.

Aiello, G., Horowitz, M., Hepgul, N., Pariante, C.M., & Mondelli, V. (2012). Stress abnormalities in individuals at risk for psychosis: A review of studies in subjects with familial risk or with "at risk" mental state. *Psychoneuroendocrinology, 37*(10), 1600–1613.

Alesiani, R., Boccalon, S., Giarolli, L., Blum, N., & Fossati, A. (2014). Systems Training for Emotional Predictability and Problem Solving (STEPPS): Program efficacy and personality features as predictors of drop-out – An Italian study. *Comprehensive Psychiatry, 55*(4), 920–927.

Alfonso, C.A., & Schulze, T.G. (2021). Early-life adversity, suicide risk and epigenetics of trauma. In C.A. Alfonso, P.S. Chandra, & T.G. Schulze (Eds.), *Suicide by self-immolation* (pp. 157–167). Springer.

Alhabib, S., Nur, U., & Jones, R. (2010). Domestic violence against women: Systematic review of prevalence studies. *Journal of Family Violence, 25*(4), 369–382.

Alhusen, J.L., Frohman, N., & Purcell, G. (2015). Intimate partner violence and suicidal ideation in pregnant women. *Archives of Women's Mental Health, 18*, 573–578.

Altinanahtar, A., & Halicioglu, F. (2009). A dynamic econometric model of suicides in Turkey. *The Journal of Socio-Economics, 38*(6), 903–907.

Alqahtani, M.M.J., Alkhamees, H.A., Alkhalaf, A.M., Alarjan, S.S., Alzahrani, H.S., AlSaad, G.F., ... & Alqahtani, K.M.M. (2021). Toward establishing telepsychology guideline. Turning the challenges of COVID-19 into opportunity. *Ethics, Medicine, and Public Health, 16*, 100612.

American Psychiatric Association. (2008). *The practice of electroconvulsive therapy: Recommendations for treatment, training, and privileging: A task force report of the American Psychiatric Association*. American Psychiatric Publishing.

American Psychiatric Association. (2013). *Diagnostic and statistical manual of mental disorders*, Fifth Edition. American Psychiatric Publishing.

American Psychiatric Association. (2018). *Suicide prevention*. Retrieved March 16, 2023, from www.psychiatry.org/patients-families/suicide-prevention.

American Psychological Association. (n.d.). *Resilience*. Retrieved March 16, 2023, from https://dictionary.apa.org/resilience.

American Psychiatric Association. (2022). *Diagnostic and statistical manual of mental disorders* (5th ed., text rev.). https://doi.org/10.1176/appi.books.9780890425787.

Anacker, C., Zunszain, P.A., Carvalho, L.A. & Pariante, C.M. (2011). The glucocorticoid receptor: Pivot of depression and of antidepressant treatment? *Psychoneuroendocrinology, 36*(3), 415–425.

Andres, A.R., & Hempstead, K. (2011). Gun control and suicide: The impact of state firearm regulations in the United States, 1995–2004. *Health Policy, 101*, 95–103.

Andriessen, K., & Krysinska, K. (2012). Essential questions on suicide bereavement and postvention. *International Journal of Environmental Research and Public Health, 9*(1), 24–32.

Andriessen, K., Krysinska, K., Draper, B., Dudley, M., & Mitchell, P.B. (2018). Harmful or helpful? A systematic review of how those bereaved through suicide experience research participation. *Crisis, 39*(5), 364–376.

Andriessen, K., Krysinska, K., Hill, N.T., Reifels, L., Robinson, J., Reavley, N., & Pirkis, J. (2019). Effectiveness of interventions for people bereaved through suicide: A systematic review of controlled studies of grief, psychosocial and suicide-related outcomes. *BMC Psychiatry, 19*, 1–15.

Anestis, M.D., & Anestis, J.C. (2015). Suicide rates and state laws regulating access and exposure to handguns. *American Journal of Public Health, 105*(10), 2049–2058.

Anestis, M.D., & Houtsma, C. (2018). The association between gun ownership and statewide overall suicide rates. *Suicide and Life-Threatening Behavior, 48*(2), 204–217.

Anestis, M.D., Selby, E.A., & Butterworth, S.E. (2017). Rising longitudinal trajectories in suicide rates: The role of firearm suicide rates and firearm legislation. *Preventive Medicine, 100*, 159–166.

Anglemyer, A., Horvath, T., & Rutherford, G. (2014). The accessibility of firearms and risk for suicide and homicide victimization among household members: A systematic review and meta-analysis. *Annals of Internal Medicine, 160*(2), 101–110.

Ansbacher, H.L. (1969). Suicide as communication: Adler's concept and current applications. *Journal of Individual Psychology, 25*(2), 174.

Aquinas, T. (2020). Whether one is allowed to kill oneself. In T. Timmerman & M. Cholbi (Eds.), *Exploring the philosophy of death and dying: Classical and contemporary perspectives* (pp. 211–212) Routledge.

Arango, V., Ernsberger, P., Marzuk, P.M., Chen, J.S., Tierney, H., Stanley, M., ... & Mann, J.J. (1990). Autoradiographic demonstration of increased serotonin 5-HT2 and β-adrenergic receptor binding sites in the brain of suicide victims. *Archives of General Psychiatry, 47*(11), 1038–1047.

Arnsten, A.F., & Goldman-Rakic, P.S. (1998). Noise stress impairs prefrontal cortical cognitive function in monkeys: Evidence for a hyperdopaminergic mechanism. *Archives of General Psychiatry, 55*(4), 362–368.

Aspinwall, L.G., & Tedeschi, R.G. (2010). The value of positive psychology for health psychology: Progress and pitfalls in examining the relation of positive phenomena to health. *Annals of Behavioral Medicine, 39*(1), 4–15.

Austin, A., Craig, S.L., D'Souza, S., & McInroy, L.B. (2022). Suicidality among transgender youth: Elucidating the role of interpersonal risk factors. *Journal of Interpersonal Violence, 37*(5–6), NP2696–NP2718.

Australian Institute for Suicide Research and Prevention & Postvention Australia. (2017). *Postvention Australia guidelines: A resource for organisations and individuals providing services to people bereaved by suicide.* www.griffith.edu.au/__data/assets/pdf_file/0038/359696/Postvention_WEB.pdf.

Babić, R., Babić, M., Rastović, P., Ćurlin, M., Šimić, J., Mandić, K., & Pavlović, K. (2020). Resilience in health and illness. *Psychiatria Danubina, 32*(suppl. 2), 226–232.

Baker, F.R.L., Baker, K.L., & Burrell, J. (2021). Introducing the skills-based model of personal resilience: Drawing on content and process factors to build resilience in the workplace. *Journal of Occupational and Organizational Psychology, 94*(2), 458–481.

Baldaçara, L., Grudtner, R.R., da S Leite, V., Porto, D.M., Robis, K.P., Fidalgo, T.M., ... & da Silva, A.G. (2020). Brazilian Psychiatric Association guidelines for the management of suicidal behavior, Part 2: Screening, intervention, and prevention. *Brazilian Journal of Psychiatry, 43*, 538–549.

Baller, R.D., & Richardson, K.K. (2009). The "dark side" of the strength of weak ties: The diffusion of suicidal thoughts. *Journal of Health and Social Behavior, 50*(3), 261–276.

Banerjee, R., Ghosh, A.K., Ghosh, B., Bhattacharyya, S. & Mondal, A.C. (2013). Decreased mRNA and protein expression of BDNF, NGF, and their receptors in the hippocampus from suicide: An analysis in human postmortem brain. *Clinical Medicine Insights: Pathology, 6*, 1–11.

Banken, R. (2022). *Agence d'Évaluation des Technologies et des Modes d'Intervention en Santé: The Use of Electroconvulsive Therapy in Québec*. AETMIS.

Bannan, N. (2010). Group-based problem-solving therapy in self-poisoning females: A pilot study. *Counselling and Psychotherapy Research, 10*(3), 201–213.

Barak-Corren, Y., Castro, V.M., Javitt, S., Hoffnagle, A.G., Dai, Y., Perlis, R.H., ... & Reis, B.Y. (2017). Predicting suicidal behavior from longitudinal electronic health records. *American Journal of Psychiatry, 174*(2), 154–162.

Barman, R., & Kablinger, A. (2021). Prevalence of trauma-and stress-related symptoms in psychiatrists and trainees following patient suicide in the United States. *Social Psychiatry and Psychiatric Epidemiology, 56*(7), 1283–1288.

Barnes, S.M., Borges, L.M., Sorensen, D., Smith, G.P., Bahraini, N.H., & Walser, R.D. (2022). Safety planning within acceptance and commitment therapy. *Cognitive and Behavioral Practice, 30*(1), 55–63.

Barnes, S.M., Monteith, L.L., Gerard, G.R., Hoffberg, A.S., Homaifar, B.Y., & Brenner, L.A. (2017). Problem-solving therapy for suicide prevention in veterans with moderate-to-severe traumatic brain injury. *Rehabilitation Psychology, 62*(4), 600–608.

Barr, B., Taylor-Robinson, D., Scott-Samuel, A., McKee, M., & Stuckler, D. (2012). Suicides associated with the 2008–10 economic recession in England: Time trend analysis. *BMJ, 345*, e5142.

Barry, R. (1995). The development of the Roman Catholic Teachings on suicide. *Notre Dame Journal Ethics & Public Policy, 9*, 449.

Batastini, A.B., Paprzycki, P., Jones, A.C., & MacLean, N. (2021). Are video-conferenced mental and behavioral health services just as good as in-person? A meta-analysis of a fast-growing practice. *Clinical Psychology Review, 83*, 101944.

Bath, E., & Njoroge, W.F. (2021). Coloring outside the lines: Making Black and Brown lives matter in the prevention of youth suicide. *Journal of the American Academy of Child and Adolescent Psychiatry, 60*(1), 17–21.

Batterham, P.J., Calear, A.L., & Christensen, H. (2013). Correlates of suicide stigma and suicide literacy in the community. *Suicide and Life-Threatening Behavior, 43*(4), 406–417.

Batterham, P.J., Christensen, H., Calear, A.L., Werner-Seidler, A., & Kazan, D. (2022). Rates and predictors of deterioration in a trial of internet-delivered cognitive behavioral therapy for reducing suicidal thoughts. *Archives of Suicide Research, 26*(2), 937–947.

Battin, M.P. (2015). *The ethics of suicide: Historical sources.* Oxford University Press.

Baumeister, R.F. (1990). Suicide as escape from self. *Psychological Review, 97*(1), 90.

Bearman, P.S., & Moody, J. (2004). Suicide and friendships among American adolescents. *American Journal of Public Health, 94*(1), 89–95.

Beauchaine, T.P., Hinshaw, S.P., & Bridge, J.A. (2019). Nonsuicidal self-injury and suicidal behaviors in girls: The case for targeted prevention in preadolescence. *Clinical Psychological Science, 7*, 643–667.

Beauchamp, T.L. (1989). Suicide in the age of reason. In A.B. Brody (Ed.), *Suicide and euthanasia. Philosophy and medicine, vol 35.* (pp. 183–220) Springer.

Beaudreau, S., Karel, M., Funderburk, J., Nezu, A., Nezu, C., Aspnes, A., & Wetherell, J. (2022). Problem-solving training for Veterans in home based primary care: An evaluation of intervention effectiveness. *International Psychogeriatrics, 34*(2), 165–176.

Beautrais, A.L. (2001). Effectiveness of barriers at suicide jumping sites: A case study. *Australian & New Zealand Journal of Psychiatry, 35*(5), 557–562.

Beautrais, A.L., Fergusson, D.M., & Horwood, L.J. (2006). Firearms legislation and reductions in firearm-related suicide deaths in New Zealand. *Australian & New Zealand Journal of Psychiatry, 40*(3), 253–259.

Beck, J.S., & Beck, A.T. (2011). *Cognitive behavior therapy.* Guilford Publication.

Beck, A.T., Kovacs, M., & Weissman, A. (1975). Hopelessness and suicidal behavior: An overview. *JAMA, 234*(11), 1146–1149.

Beckie, T.M., Duffy, A., & Groer, M.W. (2016). The relationship between allostatic load and psychosocial characteristics among women veterans. *Women's Health Issues, 26*(5), 555–563.

Beghi, M., & Rosenbaum, J. F. (2010). Risk factors for fatal and nonfatal repetition of suicide attempt: A critical appraisal. *Current Opinion in Psychiatry, 23*(4), 349–355.

Beghi, M., Rosenbaum, J.F., Cerri, C., & Cornaggia, C.M. (2013). Risk factors for fatal and nonfatal repetition of suicide attempts: A literature review. *Neuropsychiatric Disease and Treatment, 9*, 1725–1736.

Behera, C., Sikary, A.K., Mridha, A.R., Pandey, R.M., Satapathy, S., Lalwani, S., & Gupta, S. (2019). Association of menstruation cycle with completed suicide: A hospital-based case-control study. *Archives of Women's Mental Health, 22*, 771–777.

Bennett, K.J., Borders, T.F., Holmes, G.M., Kozhimannil, K.B., & Ziller, E. (2019). What is rural? Challenges and implications of definitions that inadequately encompass rural people and places. *Health Affairs, 38*(12), 1985–1992.

Bensley, K.M.K., Kerr, W.C., Barnett, S.B., & Mulia, N. (2022). Postmortem screening of opioids, benzodiazepines, and alcohol among rural and urban suicide decedents. *The Journal of Rural Health, 38*(1), 77–86.

Ben-Zeev, D., Corrigan, P.W., Britt, T.W., & Langford, L. (2012). Stigma of mental illness and service use in the military. *Journal of Mental Health, 21*(3), 264–273.

Berardelli, I., Serafini, G., Cortese, N., Fiaschè, F., O'Connor, R.C., & Pompili, M. (2020). The involvement of hypothalamus–pituitary–adrenal (HPA) axis in suicide risk. *Brain Sciences, 10*(9), 653.

Berger, M., Juster, R.P., Westphal, S., Amminger, G.P., Bogerts, B., Schiltz, K., … & Sarnyai, Z. (2018). Allostatic load is associated with psychotic symptoms and decreases with antipsychotic treatment in patients with schizophrenia and first-episode psychosis. *Psychoneuroendocrinology, 90*, 35–42.

Bergsma, A., Ten Have, M., Veenhoven, R., & Graaf, R.D. (2011). Most people with mental disorders are happy: A 3-year follow-up in the Dutch general population. *The Journal of Positive Psychology, 6*(4), 253–259.

Bergsma, A., Veenhoven, R., Ten Have, M., & de Graaf, R. (2011). Do they know how happy they are? On the value of self-rated happiness of people with a mental disorder. *Journal of Happiness Studies, 12*, 793–806.

Bering, J. (2018). *Suicidal: Why we kill ourselves.* University of Chicago Press.

Berk, M.S., Starace, N.K., Black, V.P., & Avina, C. (2020). Implementation of dialectical behavior therapy with suicidal and self-harming adolescents in a community clinic. *Archives of Suicide Research, 24*(1), 64–81.

Bertolote, J.M., Fleischmann, A., De Leo, D., & Wasserman, D. (2004). Psychiatric diagnoses and suicide: Revisiting the evidence. *Crisis, 25*, 147–155.

Bernert, R.A., Hilberg, A.M., Melia, R., Kim, J.P., Shah, N.H., & Abnousi, F. (2020). Artificial intelligence and suicide prevention: A systematic review of machine learning investigations. *International Journal of Environmental Research and Public Health, 17*(16), 5929.

Beurel, E., & Jope, R.S. (2014). Inflammation and lithium: Clues to mechanisms contributing to suicide-linked traits. *Translational Psychiatry, 4*(12), e488–e488.

Bey, G.S., Waring, M.E., Jesdale, B.M., & Person, S.D. (2018). Gendered race modification of the association between chronic stress and depression among Black and White US adults. *American Journal of Orthopsychiatry, 88*(2), 151.

Bhatt, M., Perera, S., Zielinski, L., Eisen, R.B., Yeung, S., El-Sheikh, W., … & Samaan, Z. (2018). Profile of suicide attempts and risk factors among psychiatric patients: A case-control study. *PLoS One, 13*(2), e0192998.

Bhatta, M.P., Jefferis, E., Kavadas, A., Alemagno, S.A., & Shaffer-King, P. (2014). Suicidal behaviors among adolescents in juvenile detention: Role of adverse life experiences. *PLoS One, 9*(2), e89408.

Birkenæs, V., Elvsåshagen, T., Westlye, L.T., Høegh, M.C., Haram, M., Werner, M.C., … & Aas, M. (2021). Telomeres are shorter and associated with number of suicide attempts in affective disorders. *Journal of Affective Disorders, 295*, 1032–1039.

Bjureberg, J., Dahlin, M., Carlborg, A., Edberg, H., Haglund, A., & Runeson, B. (2021). Columbia-Suicide Severity Rating Scale Screen Version: Initial screening for suicide risk in a psychiatric emergency department. *Psychological Medicine, 52*, 1–9.

Black Parker, C., McCall, W.V., Spearman-McCarthy, E.V., Rosenquist, P., & Cortese, N. (2021). Clinicians' racial bias contributing to disparities in electroconvulsive therapy for patients from racial-ethnic minority groups. *Psychiatric Services, 72*(6), 684–690.

Bloch-Elkouby, S., & Barzilay, S. (2022). Alliance-focused safety planning and suicide risk management. *Psychotherapy, 59*(2), 157.

Blosnich, J., & Bossarte, R. (2012). Drivers of disparity: Differences in socially based risk factors of self-injurious and suicidal behaviors among sexual minority college students. *Journal of American College Health, 60*(2), 141–149.

Blosnich, J.R., Garfin, D.R., Maguen, S., Vogt, D., Dichter, M.E., Hoffmire, C.A., Bernhard, P.A., & Schneiderman, A. (2021). Differences in childhood adversity, suicidal ideation, and suicide attempt among veterans and nonveterans. *American Psychologist, 76*, 284–299.

Boccalon, S., Alesiani, R., Giarolli, L., & Fossati, A. (2017). Systems training for emotional predictability and problem solving program and emotion dysregulation: A pilot study. *The Journal of Nervous and Mental Disease, 205*(3), 213–216.

Boehm, J.K., & Kubzansky, L.D. (2012). The heart's content: The association between positive psychological well-being and cardiovascular health. *Psychological Bulletin, 138*(4), 655.

Boldrini, M., Underwood, M.D., Hen, R., Rosoklija, G.B., Dwork, A.J., John Mann, J., & Arango, V. (2009). Antidepressants increase neural progenitor cells in the human hippocampus. *Neuropsychopharmacology, 34*(11), 2376–2389.

Bolton, S. L., & Sareen, J. (2011). Sexual orientation and its relation to mental disorders and suicide attempts: Findings from a nationally representative sample. *The Canadian Journal of Psychiatry, 56*(1), 35–43.

Bommersbach, T.J., Rosenheck, R.A., Petrakis, I.L., & Rhee, T.G. (2022). Why are women more likely to attempt suicide than men? Analysis of lifetime suicide attempts among US adults in a nationally representative sample. *Journal of Affective Disorders, 311*, 157–164.

Bonelli, R., Dew, R.E., Koenig, H.G., Rosmarin, D.H., & Vasegh, S. (2012). Religious and spiritual factors in depression: Review and integration of the research. *Depression Research and Treatment.* https://doi.org/10.1155/2012/962860.

Bonney, S., & Stickley, T. (2008). Recovery and mental health: A review of the British literature. *Journal of Psychiatric and Mental Health Nursing, 15*(2), 140–153.

Bowlby, J. (1973). *Attachment and loss, Volume II: Separation, anxiety and anger.* The Hogarth Press and the Institute of Psycho-analysis.

Braga, M.F.M., Aroniadou-Anderjaska, V., Manion, S.T., Hough, C.J. & Li, H., 2004. Stress impairs α1A adrenoceptor-mediated noradrenergic facilitation of GABAergic transmission in the basolateral amygdala. *Neuropsychopharmacology, 29*(1), 45–58.

Brenna, C.T., Links, P.S., Tran, M.M., Sinyor, M., Heisel, M.J., & Hatcher, S. (2021). Innovations in suicide assessment and prevention during pandemics. *Public Health Research & Practice, 31*, 3132111.

Brenner, B., Cheng, D., Clark, S., & Camargo, C.A. (2011). Positive association between altitude and suicide in 2584 U.S. counties. *High Altitude Medicine & Biology 12*, 31–5.

Brent, D.A., Moritz, G., Bridge, J., Perper, J., & Canobbio, R. (1996). The impact of adolescent suicide on siblings and parents: A longitudinal follow-up. *Suicide and Life-Threatening Behavior, 26*(3), 253–259.

Bridge, J.A., Goldstein, T.R., & Brent, D.A. (2006). Adolescent suicide and suicidal behavior. *Journal of Child Psychology and Psychiatry, 47*(3–4), 372–394.

Briere, J., Madni, L.A., & Godbout, N. (2016). Recent suicidality in the general population: Multivariate association with childhood maltreatment and adult victimization. *Journal of Interpersonal Violence, 31*(18), 3063–3079.

Brouzos, A., Vassilopoulos, S.P., Baourda, V.C., Tassi, C., Stavrou, V., Moschou, K., & Brouzou, K.O. (2021). "Staying Home–Feeling Positive": Effectiveness of an on-line positive psychology group intervention during the COVID-19 pandemic. *Current Psychology, 42*, 1–13.

Brown, G.K. (2001). *A review of suicide assessment measures for intervention research with adults and older adults.* Available at: https://sprc.org/sites/default/files/migrate/library/BrownReviewAssessmentMeasuresAdultsOlderAdults.pdf.

Brown, S.M., Henning, S., & Wellman, C.L. (2005). Mild, short-term stress alters dendritic morphology in rat medial prefrontal cortex. *Cerebral Cortex, 15*(11), 1714–1722.

Brown, G.K., & Jager-Hyman, S. (2014). Evidence-based psychotherapies for suicide prevention: Future directions. *American Journal of Preventive Medicine, 47*(3), S186–S194.

Brown, S., & Seals, J. (2019). Intimate partner problems and suicide: Are we missing the violence? *Journal of Injury and Violence Research, 11*, 53.

Bruck, D.K. (2017). *Engaging Teenagers in Suicide Research through Youth Participatory Action Research* [Doctoral dissertation, University of Cincinnati]. OhioLINK Electronic Theses and Dissertations Center. http://rave.ohiolink.edu/etdc/view?acc_num=ucin1504799248601175.

Brunner, J., Stalla, G.K., Stalla, J., Uhr, M., Grabner, A., Wetter, T.C., & Bronisch, T. (2001). Decreased corticotropin-releasing hormone (CRH) concentrations in the cerebrospinal fluid of eucortisolemic suicide attempters. *Journal of Psychiatric Research, 35*(1), 1–9.

Bryan, C.J. (2019). Cognitive behavioral therapy for suicide prevention (CBT-SP): Implications for meeting standard of care expectations with suicidal patients. *Behavioral Sciences & the Law, 37*(3), 247–258.

Bryan, C.J., Bryan, A.O., Rozek, D.C., & Leifker, F.R. (2019). Meaning in life drives reductions in suicide risk among acutely suicidal soldiers receiving a crisis response plan. *Journal of Social and Clinical Psychology, 38*(9), 774–787.

Bryan, C.J., Mintz, J., Clemans, T.A., Burch, T.S., Leeson, B., Williams, S., & Rudd, M.D. (2018). Effect of crisis response planning on patient mood and clinician decision making: A clinical trial with suicidal US soldiers. *Psychiatric Services, 69*(1), 108–111.

Bryan, C.J., Mintz, J., Clemans, T.A., Leeson, B., Burch, T.S., Williams, S.R., … & Rudd, M.D. (2017). Effect of crisis response planning vs. contracts for safety on suicide risk in U.S. Army Soldiers: A randomized clinical trial. *Journal of Affective Disorders, 212*, 64–72.

Bryan, C.J., Peterson, A.L., & Rudd, M.D. (2018). Differential effects of brief CBT versus treatment as usual on posttreatment suicide attempts among groups of suicidal patients. *Psychiatric Services, 69*(6), 703–709.

Bryan, C.J., & Rozek, D.C. (2018). Suicide prevention in the military: A mechanistic perspective. *Current Opinion in Psychology*, *22*, 27–32.

Bryan, C.J., & Rudd, M.D. (2006). Advances in the assessment of suicide risk. *Journal of Clinical Psychology*, *62*(2), 185–200.

Bryan, C.J., & Rudd, M.D. (2018). *Brief cognitive-behavioral therapy for suicide prevention*. Guilford Publications.

Bryan, C.J., Rudd, M.D., Wertenberger, E., Etienne, N., Ray-Sannerud, B.N., Morrow, C.E., … & Young-McCaughon, S. (2014). Improving the detection and prediction of suicidal behavior among military personnel by measuring suicidal beliefs: An evaluation of the Suicide Cognitions Scale. *Journal of Affective Disorders*, *159*, 15–22.

Bryan, C.J., Wastler, H., Allan, N., Khazem, L.R., & Rudd, M.D. (2022). Just-in-time adaptive interventions (JITAIs) for suicide prevention: Tempering expectations. *Psychiatry*, *85*(4), 341–346.

Burnette, C., Ramchand, R., & Ayer, L. (2015). Gatekeeper training for suicide prevention: A theoretical model and review of the empirical literature. *Rand Health Quarterly*, *5*(1), 1–38.

Burshtein, S., Dohrenwend, B.P., Levav, I., Werbeloff, N., Davidson, M., & Weiser, M. (2016). Religiosity as a protective factor against suicidal behaviour. *Acta Psychiatrica Scandinavica*, *133*(6), 481–488.

Burton, N. (2022). The Stoics' view of suicide: The circumstances under which the Stoics considered suicide acceptable. *Psychology Today*. www.psychologytoday.com/us/blog/hide-and-seek/202204/the-stoics-view-suicide#:~:text=Musonius%20too%20was%20open%20to,would%20be%20helpful%20to%20more.

Büscher, R., Torok, M., Terhorst, Y., & Sander, L. (2020). Internet-based cognitive behavioral therapy to reduce suicidal ideation: a systematic review and meta-analysis. *JAMA Network Open*, *3*(4), e203933–e203933.

Buus, N., Juel, A., Haskelberg, H., Frandsen, H., Larsen, J.L.S., River, J., … & Erlangsen, A. (2019). User involvement in developing the MYPLAN mobile phone safety plan app for people in suicidal crisis: Case study. *JMIR Mental Health*, *6*(4), e11965.

Calati, R., Ferrari, C., Brittner, M., Oasi, O., Olié, E., Carvalho, A.F., & Courtet, P. (2019). Suicidal thoughts and behaviors and social isolation: A narrative review of the literature. *Journal of Affective Disorders*, *245*, 653–667.

Cameron, K.S., Dutton, J.E., & Quinn, R.E. (2003). *Positive organizational scholarship*. Berrett-Koehler.

Campbell, F.R. (2011). Baton Rouge crisis intervention center's LOSS team active postvention model approach. In J.R. Jordan & J.L. McIntosh (Eds.), *Grief after suicide* (pp. 357–362). Routledge.

Campbell, J., Matoff-Stepp, S., Velez, M.L., Cox, H.H., & Laughon, K. (2021). Pregnancy-associated deaths from homicide, suicide, and drug overdose: Review of research and the intersection with intimate partner violence. *Journal of Women's Health*, *30*(2), 236–244.

Canetto, S.S., & Sakinofsky, I. (1998). The gender paradox in suicide. *Suicide and Life-Threatening Behavior*, *28*(1), 1–23.

Cannistraro, P.A., & Rauch, S.L. (2003). Neural circuitry of anxiety: Evidence from structural and functional neuroimaging studies. *Psychopharmacology Bulletin, 37*(4), 8–25.

Carbone, J.T. (2021). Allostatic load and mental health: A latent class analysis of physiological dysregulation. *Stress, 24*(4), 394–403.

Caribé, A.C., Nunez, R., Montal, D., Ribeiro, L., Sarmento, S., Quarantini, L.C., & Miranda-Scippa, Â. (2012). Religiosity as a protective factor in suicidal behavior: A case-control study. *The Journal of Nervous and Mental Disease, 200*(10), 863–867.

Carlbring, P., Andersson, G., Cuijpers, P., Riper, H., & Hedman-Lagerlöf, E. (2018). Internet-based vs. face-to-face cognitive behavior therapy for psychiatric and somatic disorders: An updated systematic review and meta-analysis. *Cognitive Behaviour Therapy, 47*(1), 1–18.

Carlson, E.D., & Chamberlain, R.M. (2005). Allostatic load and health disparities: A theoretical orientation. *Research in Nursing & Health, 28*, 306–315.

Carpenter, C. (2004). Heavy alcohol use and youth suicide: Evidence from tougher drunk driving laws. *Journal of Policy Analysis and Management, 23*(4), 831–842.

Carpenter, L.L., Shattuck, T.T., Tyrka, A.R., Geracioti, T.D., & Price, L.H. (2011). Effect of childhood physical abuse on cortisol stress response. *Psychopharmacology, 214*, 367–375.

Carpiniello, B., Girau, R., & Orrù, M. (2007). Mass-media, violence and mental illness. Evidence from some Italian newspapers. *Epidemiology and Psychiatric Sciences, 16*(3), 251–255.

Carpiniello, B., & Pinna, F. (2017). The reciprocal relationship between suicidality and stigma. *Frontiers in Psychiatry, 8*, 35.

Carrà, G., Bartoli, F., Crocamo, C., Brady, K.T., & Clerici, M. (2014). Attempted suicide in people with co-occurring bipolar and substance use disorders: Systematic review and meta-analysis. *Journal of Affective Disorders, 167*, 125–135.

Carroll, D., Kearney, LK., & Miller, M.A. (2020). Addressing suicide in the veteran population: Engaging a public health approach. *Frontiers in Psychiatry, 11*, 569069.

Carroll, J.E., Seeman, T.E., Olmstead, R., Melendez, G., Sadakane, R., Bootzin, R., … & Irwin, M.R. (2015). Improved sleep quality in older adults with insomnia reduces biomarkers of disease risk: Pilot results from a randomized controlled comparative efficacy trial. *Psychoneuroendocrinology, 55*, 184–192.

Carter, G., & Spittal, M.J. (2018). Suicide risk assessment. *Crisis, 39*, 229–234

Casant, J., & Helbich, M. (2022). Inequalities of suicide mortality across urban and rural areas: A literature review. *International Journal of Environmental Research and Public Health, 19*(5), 2669.

Case, A., & Deaton, A. (2020). *Deaths of despair and the future of capitalism.* Princeton University Press.

Catalano, D., Chan, F., Wilson, L., Chiu, C.Y., & Muller, V.R. (2011). The buffering effect of resilience on depression among individuals with spinal cord injury: A structural equation model. *Rehabilitation Psychology, 56*(3), 200.

CDC. Web-based Injury Statistics Query and Reporting System. 10 Leading Causes of Death, 2020. https://wisqars.cdc.gov/data/lcd/home.

CDC. (2020). *CDC WONDER: Underlying cause of death, 1999–2019*. Atlanta, GA: US Department of Health and Human Services. https://wonder.cdc.gov/Deaths-by-Underlying-Cause.html.

CDC. (2015). *Suicide trends among persons aged 10–24 years, United States, 1994–2012*. Morbidity and Mortality Weekly Report. www.cdc.gov/mmwr/pdf/wk/mm6408.pdf.

CDC. (2022). *Facts about suicide.* www.cdc.gov/suicide/facts/index.html#:~:text=Suicide%20is%20death%20caused%20by,a%20result%20of%20their%20actions.&text=Many%20factors%20can%20increase%20the%20risk%20for%20suicide%20or%20protect%20against%20it.

CDC. (2022b). *Disparities in suicide.* www.cdc.gov/suicide/facts/disparities-in-suicide.html.

CDC. (2022c). *Suicide in rural America.* www.cdc.gov/ruralhealth/Suicide.html#:~:text=Suicide%20is%20a%20leading%20cause,to%2027.3%25%20in%20metro%20areas.

CDC. (2022d). *Suicide mortality by state.* www.cdc.gov/nchs/pressroom/sosmap/suicide-mortality/suicide.htm.

CDC. (2023). *Suicide data and statistics.* www.cdc.gov/suicide/suicide-data-statistics.html.

Celano, C.M., Beale, E.E., Mastromauro, C.A., Stewart, J.G., Millstein, R.A., Auerbach, R.P., … & Huffman, J.C. (2017). Psychological interventions to reduce suicidality in high-risk patients with major depression: A randomized controlled trial. *Psychological Medicine, 47*(5), 810–821.

Celano, C.M., Gomez-Bernal, F., Mastromauro, C.A., Beale, E.E., DuBois, C.M., Auerbach, R.P., & Huffman, J.C. (2020). A positive psychology intervention for patients with bipolar depression: A randomized pilot trial. *Journal of Mental Health, 29*(1), 60–68.

Center for Behavioral Health Statistics and Quality. (2020). *Results from the 2019 National survey on drug use and health: Detailed tables*. Substance Abuse and Mental Health Services Administration. www.samhsa.gov/data/.

Center for Behavioral Health Statistics and Quality. (2021). *2020 National Survey on Drug Use and Health: Detailed tables*. Substance Abuse and Mental Health Services Administration, Rockville, MD. www.samhsa.gov/data/report/2020-nsduh-detailed-tables

Center for Mental Health Services; Office of the Surgeon General (2001). *National strategy for suicide prevention: Goals and objectives for action.* U.S. Public Health Service.

Cerdá, M., Hamilton, A.D., Tracy, M., Branas, C., Fink, D., & Keyes, K.M. (2022). Would restricting firearm purchases due to alcohol-and drug-related misdemeanor offenses reduce firearm homicide and suicide? An agent-based simulation. *Injury Epidemiology, 9*(1), 17.

Cerel, J. (2008). The impact of suicide on the family. *Crisis, 29*(1), 38.

Cerel, J., Brown, M.M., Maple, M., Singleton, M., Van de Venne, J., Moore, M., & Flaherty, C. (2019). How many people are exposed to suicide? Not six. *Suicide and Life-Threatening Behavior, 49*(2), 529–534.

Cha, J.M., Kim, J.E., Kim, M.A., Shim, B., Cha, M.J., Lee, J.J., … & Chung, U.S. (2018). Five months follow-up study of school-based crisis intervention for Korean high school students who experienced a peer suicide. *Journal of Korean Medical Science, 33*(28), e192.

Cha, C.B., Najmi, S., Park, J.M., Finn, C.T., & Nock, M.K. (2010). Attentional bias toward suicide-related stimuli predicts suicidal behavior. *Journal of Abnormal Psychology, 119*(3), 616.

Chafouleas, S.M., & Bray, M.A. (2004). Introducing positive psychology: Finding a place within school psychology. *Psychology in the Schools, 41*(1), 1–5.

Chan, M.K., Bhatti, H., Meader, N., Stockton, S., Evans, J., O'Connor, R.C., … & Kendall, T. (2016). Predicting suicide following self-harm: Systematic review of risk factors and risk scales. *The British Journal of Psychiatry, 209*(4), 277–283.

Chaney, A., Carballedo, A., Amico, F., Fagan, A., Skokauskas, N., Meaney, J., & Frodl, T. (2014). Effect of childhood maltreatment on brain structure in adult patients with major depressive disorder and healthy participants. *Journal of Psychiatry and Neuroscience, 39*(1), 50–59.

Chang, S.S., Gunnell, D., Sterne, J.A., Lu, T.H., & Cheng, A.T. (2009). Was the economic crisis 1997–1998 responsible for rising suicide rates in East/Southeast Asia? A time–trend analysis for Japan, Hong Kong, South Korea, Taiwan, Singapore and Thailand. *Social Science & Medicine, 68*(7), 1322–1331.

Chang, S.S., Stuckler, D., Yip, P., & Gunnell, D. (2013). Impact of 2008 global economic crisis on suicide: Time trend study in 54 countries. *BMJ, 347*, 1–15.

Chatzittofis, A., Nordström, P., Hellström, C., Arver, S., Åsberg, M., & Jokinen, J. (2013). CSF 5-HIAA, cortisol and DHEAS levels in suicide attempters. *European Neuropsychopharmacology, 23*, 1280–1287.

Chaudron, L.H., & Caine, E.D. (2004). Suicide among women: A critical review. *Journal of the American Medical Women's Association (1972), 59*(2), 125–134.

Chen, Y., Koh, H.K., Kawachi, I., Botticelli, M., & VanderWeele, T.J. (2020). Religious service attendance and deaths related to drugs, alcohol, and suicide among US health care professionals. *JAMA Psychiatry, 77*(7), 737–744.

Chesin, M.S., Jeglic, E.L., & Stanley, B. (2010). Pathways to high-lethality suicide attempts in individuals with borderline personality disorder. *Archives of Suicide Research, 14*(4), 342–362.

Chesin, M.S., Sonmez, C.C., Benjamin-Phillips, C.A., Beeler, B., Brodsky, B.S., & Stanley, B. (2015). Preliminary effectiveness of adjunct mindfulness-based cognitive therapy to prevent suicidal behavior in outpatients who are at elevated suicide risk. *Mindfulness, 6*, 1345–1355.

Chinni, D. (2021). *Unpacking the geography of America's youth suicide epidemic.* American Communities Project. Available at: www.americancommunities.org/chapter/unpacking-the-geography-of-americas-youth-suicide-epidemic/.

Chioqueta, A.P., & Stiles, T.C. (2007). The relationship between psychological buffers, hopelessness, and suicidal ideation: Identification of protective factors. *Crisis*, *28*(2), 67–73.

Chitwood, A. (1986). The death of Empedocles. *The American Journal of Philology*, *107*(2), 175–191.

Choi, N.G., DiNitto, D.M., Marti, C.N., & Segal, S.P. (2017). Adverse childhood experiences and suicide attempts among those with mental and substance use disorders. *Child Abuse & Neglect*, *69*, 252–262.

Choi, S.B., Lee, W., Yoon, J.H., Won, J.U., & Kim, D.W. (2018). Ten-year prediction of suicide death using Cox regression and machine learning in a nationwide retrospective cohort study in South Korea. *Journal of Affective Disorders*, *231*, 8–14.

Choi, N.G., Marti, C.N., & Conwell, Y. (2016). Effect of problem-solving therapy on depressed low-income homebound older adults' death/suicidal ideation and hopelessness. *Suicide and Life-Threatening Behavior*, *46*(3), 323–336.

Chu, J.P., Goldblum, P., Floyd, R., & Bongar, B. (2010). The cultural theory and model of suicide. *Applied and Preventive Psychology*, *14*(1–4), 25–40.

Chugani, C.D., & Landes, S.J. (2016). Dialectical behavior therapy in college counseling centers: Current trends and barriers to implementation. *Journal of College Student Psychotherapy*, *30*(3), 176–186.

Cicchetti, D., & Rogosch F.A. (2001). The impact of child maltreatment and psychopathology on neuroendocrine functioning. *Development and Psychopathology*, *13*(4):783–804.

Cicchetti, D., Rogosch, F.A., Toth, S.L., & Sturge-Apple, M.L. (2011). Normalizing the development of cortisol regulation in maltreated infants through preventive interventions. *Development and Psychopathology*, *23*(3), 789–800.

Classen, T.J., & Dunn, R.A. (2010). The politics of hope and despair: The effect of presidential election outcomes on suicide rates. *Social Science Quarterly*, *91*(3), 593–612.

Cleary, A. (2017). Help-seeking patterns and attitudes to treatment amongst men who attempted suicide. *Journal of Mental Health*, *26*(3), 220–224.

Clifton, D.O., & Harter, J.K. (2003). Investing in strengths. In K.S. Cameron, J.E. Dutton, & R.E. Quinn (Eds.), *Positive organizational scholarship: Foundations of a new discipline* (pp. 111–121). Berrett-Koehler Publishers.

Coker, T.R., Austin, S.B., & Schuster, M.A. (2010). The health and health care of lesbian, gay, and bisexual adolescents. *Annual Review of Public Health*, *31*, 457–477.

Coffey, C.E. (2006). Pursuing perfect depression care. *Psychiatric Services*, *57*(10), 1524–1526.

Coffey, C.E. (2007). Building a system of perfect depression care in behavioral health. *Joint Commission Journal on Quality and Patient Safety*, *33*(4):193–199.

Coffey, C.E., Coffey M.J., & Ahmedani, B.K. (2013). An update on perfect depression care. *Psychiatric Services*, *64*(4), 396.

Coffey, M., Coffey, C., & Ahmedani, B.K. (2015). Suicide in a health maintenance organization population. *JAMA Psychiatry*, *72*(3), 294–296.

Cohen, S., & Wills, T.A. (1985). Stress, social support, and the buffering hypothesis. *Psychological Bulletin, 98*(2), 310.

Cole, A.B., & Wingate, L.R. (2018). Considering race and ethnicity using positive psychological approaches to suicide. In J. Hirsch, E. Chang, & J. Kelliher Rabon, (Eds.), *A positive psychological approach to suicide. Advances in mental health and addiction.* Springer, Cham. https://doi.org/10.1007/978-3-030-03225-8_6.

Coleman, B.W. (2019). *Ring the alarm: The crisis of black youth suicide in America.* Emergency Taskforce on Black Youth Suicide and Mental Health; https://watsoncoleman.house.gov/uploadedfiles/full_taskforce_report.pdf.

Colla, M., Kronenberg, G., Deuschle, M., Meichel, K., Hagen, T., Bohrer, M., & Heuser, I. (2007). Hippocampal volume reduction and HPA-system activity in major depression. *Journal of Psychiatric Research, 41*(7), 553–560.

Collings, S., Jenkin, G., Stanley, J., McKenzie, S., & Hatcher, S. (2018). Preventing suicidal behaviours with a multilevel intervention: A cluster randomised controlled trial. *BMC Public Health, 18*(1), 1–13.

Conner, A., Azrael, D., & Miller, M. (2019). Suicide case-fatality rates in the United States, 2007 to 2014: A nationwide population-based study. *Annals of Internal Medicine, 171*(12), 885–895.

Conner, K.R., Meldrum, S., Wieczorek, W.F., Duberstein, P.R., & Welte, J.W. (2004). The association of irritability and impulsivity with suicidal ideation among 15- to 20-year-old males. *Suicide and Life-Threatening Behavior, 34*(4), 363–373.

Conwell, Y. (2014). Suicide later in life: Challenges and priorities for prevention. *American Journal of Preventive Medicine, 47*(3), S244–S250.

Conwell, Y., Duberstein, P.R., Cox, C., Herrmann, J., Forbes, N., & Caine, E.D. (1998). Age differences in behaviors leading to completed suicide. *The American Journal of Geriatric Psychiatry, 6*(2), 122–126.

Conwell, Y., & Thompson, C. (2008). Suicidal behavior in elders. *Psychiatric Clinics of North America, 31*(2), 333–356.

Cooper, D.C., & Bates, M.J. (2019). Military health provider training and evaluation of a problem-solving intervention to reduce distress and enhance readiness among service members. *Military Medicine, 184*(5–6), e303–e311.

Cooperman, N.A., & Simoni, J.M. (2005). Suicidal ideation and attempted suicide among women living with HIV/AIDS. *Journal of Behavioral Medicine, 28*, 149–156.

Copersino, M.L., Jones, H., Tuten, M., & Svikis, D. (2008). Suicidal ideation among drug-dependent treatment-seeking inner-city pregnant women. *Journal of Maintenance in the Addictions, 3*(2–4), 53–64.

Coryell, W., & Schlesser, M. (2001). The dexamethasone suppression test and suicide prediction. *American Journal of Psychiatry, 158*, 748–753.

Costanza, A., Prelati, M., & Pompili, M. (2019). The meaning in life in suicidal patients: The presence and the search for constructs. A systematic review. *Medicina, 55*(8), 465.

Cowden, R.G., & Meyer-Weitz, A. (2016). Self-reflection and self-insight predict resilience and stress in competitive tennis. *Social Behavior and Personality, 44*(7), 1133–1149.

Cox, G.R., Bailey, E., Jorm, A.F., Reavley, N.J., Templer, K., Parker, A., ... & Robinson, J. (2016). Development of suicide postvention guidelines for secondary schools: A Delphi study. *BMC Public Health*, *16*, 1–11.

Cox, A., Dudgeon, P., Holland, C., Kelly, K., Scrine, C., & Walker, R. (2014). Using participatory action research to prevent suicide in Aboriginal and Torres Strait Islander communities. *Australian Journal of Primary Health*, *20*(4), 345–349.

Cramer, R.J., & Kapusta, N.D. (2017). A social-ecological framework of theory, assessment, and prevention of suicide. *Frontiers in Psychology*, *8*, 1756.

Cunningham, R., Milner, A., Gibb, S., Rijnberg, V., Disney, G., & Kavanagh, A.M. (2021). Gendered experiences of unemployment, suicide and self-harm: A population-level record linkage study. *Psychological Medicine*, 1–9.

Currier, J.M., Holland, J.M., Jones, H.W., & Sheu, S. (2014). Involvement in abusive violence among Vietnam veterans: Direct and indirect associations with substance use problems and suicidality. *Psychological Trauma: Theory, Research, Practice, and Policy*, *6*(1), 73–82.

Curtin, S.C., Garnett, M.F., & Ahmad, F.B. (2022). Provisional numbers and rates of suicide by month and demographic characteristics: United States, 2021. *NVSS-Vital Statistics Rapid Release*, Report No. 24.

Curtin, S.C., Hedegaard, H., & Ahmad, F.B. (2021). Provisional numbers and rates of suicide by month and demographic characteristics: United States, 2020. *NVSS-Vital Statistics Rapid Release*, Report No. 16, 1–13.

Curtin, S.C. (2022). QuickStats: Age-adjusted suicide rates* for males and females, by race (†) and ethnicity-National Vital Statistics System, United States, 2000–2020. *Morbidity and Mortality Weekly Report*, *71*(8), 326–326.

Czyz, E.K., Arango, A., Healy, N., King, C.A., & Walton, M. (2020). Augmenting safety planning with text messaging support for adolescents at elevated suicide risk: Development and acceptability study. *JMIR Mental Health*, *7*(5), e17345.

Czyz, E.K., King, C.A., & Biermann, B.J. (2019). Motivational interviewing-enhanced safety planning for adolescents at high suicide risk: A pilot randomized controlled trial. *Journal of Clinical Child & Adolescent Psychology*, *48*(2), 250–262.

D'Alessio, L., Korman, G.P., Sarudiansky, M., Guelman, L.R., Scévola, L., Pastore, A., ... & Roldán, E.J. (2020). Reducing allostatic load in depression and anxiety disorders: Physical activity and yoga practice as add-on therapies. *Frontiers in Psychiatry*, *11*, 501.

D'Anci, K.E., Uhl, S., Giradi, G., & Martin, C. (2019). Treatments for the prevention and management of suicide: A systematic review. *Annals of Internal Medicine*, *171*(5), 334–342.

Daniel, A.E. (2006). Preventing suicide in prison: A collaborative responsibility of administrative, custodial, and clinical staff. *Journal of the American Academy of Psychiatry and the Law Online*, *34*(2), 165–175.

Davidson, L., Andres-Hyman, R., Bedregal, L., Tondora, J., Fry, J., & Kirk, T.A. (2008). From 'double trouble' to 'dual recovery': Integrating models of recovery in addiction and mental health. *Journal of Dual Diagnosis*, *4*(3), 273–290.

Davidson, C.L., Wingate, L.R., Rasmussen, K.A., & Slish, M.L. (2009). Hope as a predictor of interpersonal suicide risk. *Suicide and Life-Threatening Behavior*, *39*(5), 499–507.

Darwin, C. (1859; 2004). *On the origin of species*. Routledge.

Decker, S.E., Adams, L., Watkins, L.E., Sippel, L.M., Presnall-Shvorin, J., Sofuoglu, M., & Martino, S. (2019). Feasibility and preliminary efficacy of dialectical behaviour therapy skills groups for Veterans with suicidal ideation: Pilot. *Behavioural and Cognitive Psychotherapy*, *47*(5), 616–621.

De Giorgi, R. (2022). Ketamine for suicidal ideation. *BMJ*, 376, 1–2. DOI: 10.1136/bmj.074.

de Graaf R., Sandfort T.G., & Ten Have M. (2006). Suicidality and sexual orientation: Differences between men and women in a general population-based sample from the Netherlands. *Archives of Sexual Behavior*, *35*(3):253–262.

Deisenhammer, E.A., Ing, C.M., Strauss, R., Kemmler, G., Hinterhuber, H., & Weiss, E.M. (2009). The duration of the suicidal process: How much time is left for intervention between consideration and accomplishment of a suicide attempt? *Journal of Clinical Psychiatry*, *70*(1), 19.

De Jaegere, E., van Landschoot, R., Van Heeringen, K., van Spijker, B.A., Kerkhof, A.J., Mokkenstorm, J.K., & Portzky, G. (2019). The online treatment of suicidal ideation: A randomised controlled trial of an unguided web-based intervention. *Behaviour Research and Therapy*, *119*, 103406.

de Kloet, E.R., Joëls, M., & Holsboer, F. (2005). Stress and the brain: From adaptation to disease. *Nature Reviews Neuroscience*, *6*, 463–475.

de Lange, J., Baams, L., van Bergen, D.D., Bos, H.M., & Bosker, R.J. (2022). Minority stress and suicidal ideation and suicide attempts among LGBT adolescents and young adults: A meta-analysis. *LGBT Health*, *9*(4), 222–237.

De Leo, D. (2004). Suicide prevention is far more than a psychiatric business. *World Psychiatry*, *3*(3), 155–156.

Denning, D.G., Conwell, Y., King, D., & Cox, C. (2000). Method choice, intent, and gender in completed suicide. *Suicide and Life-Threatening Behavior*, *30*(3), 282–288.

Dervic, K., Oquendo, M.A., Grunebaum, M.F., Ellis, S., Burke, A.K., & Mann, J.J. (2004). Religious affiliation and suicide attempt. *American Journal of Psychiatry*, *161*(12), 2303–2308.

Dervic, K., Carballo, J.J., Baca-Garcia, E., Galfalvy, H.C., Mann, J.J., Brent, D.A., & Oquendo, M.A. (2011). Moral or religious objections to suicide may protect against suicidal behavior in bipolar disorder. *Journal of Clinical Psychiatry*, *72*(10), 1390–1396.

Devries, K.M., Mak, J.Y., Child, J.C., Falder, G., Bacchus, L.J., Astbury, J., & Watts, C.H. (2014). Childhood sexual abuse and suicidal behavior: A meta-analysis. *Pediatrics*, *133*(5), e1331–e1344.

Devries, K., Watts, C., Yoshihama, M., Kiss, L., Schraiber, L.B., Deyessa, N., ... & WHO Multi-Country Study Team. (2011). Violence against women is strongly associated with suicide attempts: Evidence from the WHO multi-country study on women's health and domestic violence against women. *Social Science & Medicine, 73*(1), 79–86.

Dhingra, K., Boduszek, D., & O'Connor, R.C. (2015). Differentiating suicide attempters from suicide ideators using the Integrated Motivational–Volitional model of suicidal behaviour. *Journal of Affective Disorders, 186*, 211–218.

Dhingra, K., Klonsky, E.D., & Tapola, V. (2019). An empirical test of the three-step theory of suicide in UK university students. *Suicide and Life-Threatening Behavior, 49*(2), 478–487.

d'Holbach, B. (1770). *The system of nature*, Vol. 2. www.public-library.uk/pdfs/2/118.pdf.

Diamond, G.S., O'Malley, A., Wintersteen, M.B., Peters, S., Yunghans, S., Biddle, V., ... & Schrand, S. (2012). Attitudes, practices, and barriers to adolescent suicide and mental health screening: A survey of Pennsylvania primary care providers. *Journal of Primary Care & Community Health, 3*(1), 29–35.

Di Carlo, F., Sociali, A., Picutti, E., Pettorruso, M., Vellante, F., Verrastro, V., ... & di Giannantonio, M. (2021). Telepsychiatry and other cutting-edge technologies in COVID-19 pandemic: Bridging the distance in mental health assistance. *International Journal of Clinical Practice, 75*(1). https://doi.org/10.1111/ijcp.13716.

Di Giacomo, E., Krausz, M., Colmegna, F., Aspesi, F., & Clerici, M. (2018). Estimating the risk of attempted suicide among sexual minority youths: A systematic review and meta-analysis. *JAMA Pediatrics, 172*(12), 1145–1152.

Dowman, J., Patel, A., & Rajput, K. (2005). Electroconvulsive therapy: Attitudes and misconceptions. *The Journal of ECT, 21*(2), 84–87.

Drapeau, C.W., & McIntosh, J.L. (2023). *U.S.A. suicide: 2021 Official final data*. Minneapolis, MN: Suicide Awareness Voices of Education (SAVE). https://save.org/about-suicide/suicidestatistics.

Draper, B.M. (2014). Suicidal behaviour and suicide prevention in later life. *Maturitas, 79*(2), 179–183.

Drogula, F.K. (2019). *Cato the Younger: Life and death at the end of the Roman Republic*. Oxford University Press.

Du, L., Shi, H.Y., Yu, H.R., Liu, X.M., Jin, X.H., Fu, X.L., ... & Chen, H.L. (2020). Incidence of suicide death in patients with cancer: A systematic review and meta-analysis. *Journal of Affective Disorders, 276*, 711–719.

Dube, S.R., Anda, R.F., Felitti, V.J., Chapman, D.P., Williamson, D.F., & Giles, W.H. (2001). Childhood abuse, household dysfunction, and the risk of attempted suicide throughout the life span: Findings from the Adverse Childhood Experiences Study. *JAMA, 286*(24), 3089–3096.

Ducasse, D., Dassa, D., Courtet, P., Brand-Arpon, V., Walter, A., Guillaume, S., ... & Olié, E. (2019). Gratitude diary for the management of suicidal inpatients: A randomized controlled trial. *Depression and Anxiety, 36*(5), 400–411.

Dumais, A., Lesage, A.D., Alda, M., Rouleau, G., Dumont, M., Chawky, N., ... & Turecki, G. (2005). Risk factors for suicide completion in major depression: A case-control study of impulsive and aggressive behaviors in men. *American Journal of Psychiatry, 162*(11), 2116–2124.

Dumser, T., Barocka, A., & Schubert, E. (1998). Weight of adrenal glands may be increased in persons who commit suicide. *The American Journal of Forensic Medicine and Pathology, 19*(1), 72–76.

Durkheim, E. (2005). *Suicide: A study in sociology.* Routledge.

Dwivedi, Y., Rizavi, H.S., Conley, R.R., Roberts, R.C., Tamminga, C.A., & Pandey, G.N. (2003). Altered gene expression of brain-derived neurotrophic factor and receptor tyrosine kinase B in postmortem brain of suicide subjects. *Archives of General Psychiatry, 60*(8), 804–815.

Dwivedi, Y., Rizavi, H.S., Zhang, H., Mondal, A.C., Roberts, R.C., Conley, R.R. & Pandey, G.N. (2009). Neurotrophin receptor activation and expression in human postmortem brain: Effect of suicide. *Biological Psychiatry, 65*(4), 319–328.

Dyregrov, K. (2011). What do we know about needs for help after suicide in different parts of the world? *Crisis, 32*(6):310–318.

D'Zurilla, T.J., & Nezu, A.M. (2010). Problem-solving therapy. *Handbook of Cognitive-Behavioral Therapies, 3,* 197–225.

Effinger, J.M., & Stewart, D.G. (2012). Classification of co-occurring depression and substance abuse symptoms predicts suicide attempts in adolescents. *Suicide and Life-Threatening Behavior, 42*(4), 353–358.

Egeland, B., Carlson, E., & Sroufe, L.A. (1993). Resilience as process. *Development and Psychopathology, 5*(4), 517–528.

Ehab, M., & Maged, V. (2022). The socio-economic determinants of suicide in selected MENA countries. *Modern Sciences and Arts Repository.* http://repository.msa.edu.eg/xmlui/handle/123456789/5104.

Ehlman, D.C., Yard, E., Stone, D.M., & Jones, C.M. (2022). Changes in suicide rates – United States, 2019 and 2020. *Morbidity and Mortality Weekly Report, 71*(8), 306–312.

Eiland, L., & Romeo, R.D. (2013). Stress and the developing adolescent brain. *Neuroscience 249,* 162–171.

Elnour, A.A., & Harrison, J. (2008). Lethality of suicide methods. *Injury Prevention, 14*(1), 39–45.

Englert, W. (1990). Seneca and the Stoic view of suicide. *The Society for Ancient Greek Philosophy Newsletter,* 184. https://orb.binghamton.edu/sagp/184.

Erickson, K.I., Voss, M.W., Prakash, R.S., Basak, C., Szabo, A., Chaddock, L., … & Kramer, A.F. (2011). Exercise training increases size of hippocampus and improves memory. *Proceedings of the National Academy of Sciences of United States of America, 108,* 3017–3022.

Ernst, C., Chen, E.S., & Turecki, G. (2009). Histone methylation and decreased expression of TrkB. T1 in orbital frontal cortex of suicide completers. *Molecular Psychiatry, 14*(9), 830–832.

Esang, M., & Ahmed, S. (2018). A closer look at substance use and suicide. *American Journal of Psychiatry Residents' Journal.* https://doi.org/10.1176/appi.ajp-rj.2018.130603.

Eskin, M., Sun, J.M., Abuidhail, J., Yoshimasu, K., Kujan, O., Janghorbani, M., … & Voracek, M. (2016). Suicidal behavior and psychological distress in university students: A 12-nation study. *Archives of Suicide Research, 20*(3), 369–388.

Espelage, D.L., Boyd, R.C., Renshaw, T.L., & Jimerson, S.R. (2022). Addressing youth suicide through school-based prevention and postvention: Contemporary scholarship advancing science, practice, and policy. *School Psychology Review*, *51*(3), 257–265.

Esquirol, J.E.D. (1845). *Mental maladies: A treatise on insanity* (E.K. Hunt, Trans.). Philadelphia: Lea and Blanchard.

Evans, E., Hawton, K., & Rodham, K. (2005). In what ways are adolescents who engage in self-harm or experience thoughts of self-harm different in terms of help-seeking, communication and coping strategies?. *Journal of Adolescence*, *28*(4), 573–587.

Falkowski, N. (2016). *Advocating a Stoic view on suicide*. Lambert Academic Publishing.

Farmer, P., & Stevenson, D. (2017). *Thriving at work: The independent review of mental health and employers*. Department for Work and Pensions and Department of Health. London, UK. www.gov.uk/government/publications/thriving-at-work-a-review-of-mental-health-and-employers.

Fava, G.A., McEwen, B.S., Guidi, J., Gostoli, S., Offidani, E., & Sonino, N. (2019). Clinical characterization of allostatic overload. *Psychoneuroendocrinology*, *108*, 94–101.

Fava, G.A., & Raffi, A.R. (2001). Obsessive-compulsive disorder and bulimia. *American Journal of Psychiatry*, *158*(3), 503–503.

Fazel, S., Cartwright, J., Norman-Nott, A., & Hawton, K. (2008). Suicide in prisoners: A systematic review of risk factors. *Journal of Clinical Psychiatry*, *69*(11), 1721–1731.

Feldman, R. (2020). What is resilience? An affiliative neuroscience approach. *World Psychiatry 19*, 132–150.

Fergus, S., & Zimmerman, M.A. (2005). Adolescent resilience: A framework for understanding healthy development in the face of risk. *Annual Review of Public Health*, *26*, 399–419.

Ferguson, M., Rhodes, K., Loughhead, M., McIntyre, H., & Procter, N. (2021). The effectiveness of the safety planning intervention for adults experiencing suicide-related distress: A systematic review. *Archives of Suicide Research*, 1–24.

Ferrari, A.J., Norman, R.E., Freedman, G., Baxter, A.J., Pirkis, J.E., Harris, M.G., … & Whiteford, H.A. (2014). The burden attributable to mental and substance use disorders as risk factors for suicide: Findings from the Global Burden of Disease Study 2010. *PloS One*, *9*(4), e91936.

Ferro, M.A., Rhodes, A.E., Kimber, M., Duncan, L., Boyle, M.H., Georgiades, K., … & MacMillan, H.L. (2017). Suicidal behaviour among adolescents and young adults with self-reported chronic illness. *The Canadian Journal of Psychiatry*, *62*(12), 845–853.

Figueroa, S., & Dalack, G.W. (2013). Exploring the impact of suicide on clinicians: A multidisciplinary retreat model. *Journal of Psychiatric Practice*, *19*(1), 72–77.

Fink, B.C., Uyttebrouck, O., & Larson, R.S. (2020). An effective intervention: Limiting opioid prescribing as a means of reducing opioid analgesic misuse, and overdose deaths. *Journal of Law, Medicine & Ethics*, *48*(2), 249–258.

Fink, D.S., Santaella-Tenorio, J., & Keyes, K.M. (2018). Increase in suicides the months after the death of Robin Williams in the US. *PLoS One*, *13*(2), e0191405.

Finlay, S., Rudd, D., McDermott, B., & Sarnyai, Z. (2021). Allostatic load in psychiatry: Systematic review and meta-analysis. *Psychoneuroendocrinology*, *131*, 105555.

Finlayson, B.T., Jones, E. & Pickens, J.C. (2023). Solution focused brief therapy telemental health suicide intervention. *Contemporary Family Therapy 45*, 49–60.

Fisher, P.A., Stoolmiller, M., Gunnar, M.R., & Burraston, B.O. (2007). Effects of a therapeutic intervention for foster preschoolers on diurnal cortisol activity. *Psychoneuroendocrinology*, *32*(8–10), 892–905.

Fiori, L.M., & Turecki, G. (2010). Genetic and epigenetic influences on expression of spermine synthase and spermine oxidase in suicide completers. *International Journal of Neuropsychopharmacology*, *13*(6), 725–736.

Fitzpatrick, S.J. (2016). Ethical and political implications of the turn to stories in suicide prevention. *Philosophy, Psychiatry, & Psychology*, *23*(3), 265–276.

Fitzpatrick, K.K., & Schmidt, N.B. (2005). Problem-solving and suicide ideation: A brief preventive intervention. In D. Roth & W.J. Lutz (Eds.), *New research in mental health*. Volume 16, (pp. 187–195). Ohio Department of Mental Health.

Fitzpatrick, K.K., Witte, T.K., & Schmidt, N.B. (2005). Randomized controlled trial of a brief problem-orientation intervention for suicidal ideation. *Behavior Therapy*, *36*(4), 323–333.

Flavin, P., & Radcliff, B. (2009). Public policies and suicide rates in the American states. *Social Indicators Research*, *90*(2), 195–209.

Fleegler, E.W., Lee, L.K., Monuteaux, M.C., Hemenway, D., & Mannix, R. (2013). Firearm legislation and firearm-related fatalities in the United States. *JAMA Internal Medicine*, *173*(9), 732–740.

Flynn, D., Kells, M., & Joyce, M. (2021). Dialectical behaviour therapy: Implementation of an evidence-based intervention for borderline personality disorder in public health systems. *Current Opinion in Psychology*, *37*, 152–157.

Fox, K.R., Huang, X., Guzmán, E.M., Funsch, K.M., Cha, C.B., Ribeiro, J.D., & Franklin, J.C. (2020). Interventions for suicide and self-injury: A meta-analysis of randomized controlled trials across nearly 50 years of research. *Psychological Bulletin*, *146*(12), 1117.

Frakt, A. (2021, September 10). What can be learned from differing rates of suicides among groups? *The New York Times*.

Franklin, J.C., Ribeiro, J.D., Fox, K.R., Bentley, K.H., Kleiman, E.M., Huang, X., … & Nock, M.K. (2017). Risk factors for suicidal thoughts and behaviors: A meta-analysis of 50 years of research. *Psychological Bulletin*, *143*(2), 187.

Fredrickson, B.L., & Joiner, T. (2018). Reflections on positive emotions and upward spirals. *Perspectives on Psychological Science*, *13*(2), 194–199.

Freud, S. (1938). *Psychopathology of everyday life* (Vol. 24). Penguin Group.

Freud, S. (1957). Contributions to a discussion on suicide. In S. Freud, J. Strachey, & A. Freud (Eds.), *The standard edition of the complete psychological works of Sigmund Freud, Volume XI (1910): Five lectures on Psycho-Analysis, Leonardo da Vinci and other works* (pp. 231–232). Hogarth Press and the Institute of Psychoanalysis.

Frey, R.G. (1999). Hume on suicide. *The Journal of Medicine and Philosophy*, *24*(4), 336–351.

Frey, L.M., Hans, J.D., & Cerel, J. (2016). Perceptions of suicide stigma: How do social networks and treatment providers compare? *Crisis*, *37*(2). https://doi.org/10.1027/0227-5910/a000358.

Friedman, M.J., & McEwen, B.S. (2004). Posttraumatic stress disorder, allostatic load, and medical illness. In P.P. Schnurr & B.L Green (Eds.), *Trauma and health: Physical health consequences of exposure to extreme stress* (pp. 157–188). Washington, DC: American Psychological Association.

Fries, E., Hesse, J., Hellhammer, J., & Hellhammer, D.H. (2005). A new view on hypocortisolism. *Psychoneuroendocrinology*, *30*, 1010–1016.

Frodl, T., Koutsouleris, N., Bottlender, R., Born, C., Jäger, M., Mörgenthaler, M., … & Meisenzahl, E. M. (2008). Reduced gray matter brain volumes are associated with variants of the serotonin transporter gene in major depression. *Molecular Psychiatry*, *13*(12), 1093–1101.

Gable, S.L., & Haidt, J. (2005). What (and why) is positive psychology? *Review of General Psychology*, *9*(2), 103–110.

Gallagher, S., Sumner, R., Creaven, A.M., O'Súilleabháin, P.S., & Howard, S. (2021). Allostatic load and mental health during COVID-19: The moderating role of neuroticism. *Brain, Behavior, & Immunity-Health*, *16*, 100311.

Gamarra, J.M., Luciano, M.T., Gradus, J.L., & Stirman, S.W. (2015). Assessing variability and implementation fidelity of suicide prevention safety planning in a regional VA healthcare system. *Crisis*, *36*(6), 433–439.

Gao, Q.Q., Wang, Y.X., Shi, J., Liang, X.J., Sun, Y.Y., Zhang, Q.Y., & Liu, P. (2020). The mediating role of psychological capital between occupational stress and suicidal ideation. *Chinese Journal of Preventive Medicine*, *54*(11), 1207–1212.

Garcia-Dia, M.J., DiNapoli, J.M., Garcia-Ona, L., Jakubowski, R., & O'Flaherty, D. (2013). Concept analysis: Resilience. *Archives of Psychiatric Nursing*, *27*(6), 264–270.

García-Moreno, C., Pallitto, C., Devries, K., Stöckl, H., Watts, C., & Abrahams, N. (2013). *Global and regional estimates of violence against women: Prevalence and health effects of intimate partner violence and non-partner sexual violence.* World Health Organization. https://apps.who.int/iris/bitstream/handle/10665/85239/?sequence=1.

Garner, M., Reith, W., & Krick, C. (2019). 10-week Hatha Yoga increases right hippocampal density compared to active and passive control groups: A controlled structural cMRI study. *Journal of Neuroimaging in Psychiatry & Neurology*, *4*(1), 1–11.

Gearing, R.E., & Alonzo, D. (2018). Religion and suicide: New findings. *Journal of Religion and Health*, *57*, 2478–2499.

Gearing, R.E., & Lizardi, D. (2009). Religion and suicide. *Journal of Religion and Health*, *48*(3), 332–341.

Gertner, A.K., Rotter, J.S., & Shafer, P.R. (2019). Association between state minimum wages and suicide rates in the US. *American Journal of Preventive Medicine*, *56*(5), 648–654.

Giovanetti, A.K., Punt, S.E., Nelson, E.L., & Ilardi, S.S. (2022). Teletherapy versus in-person psychotherapy for depression: A meta-analysis of randomized controlled trials. *Telemedicine and e-Health, 28*(8), 1077–1089.

Gilbert, P., & Allan, S. (1998). The role of defeat and entrapment (arrested flight) in depression: An exploration of an evolutionary view. *Psychological Medicine, 28*(3), 585–598.

Gillham, J.E., Shatté, A.J., Reivich, K.J., & Seligman, M.E.P. (2001). Optimism, pessimism, and explanatory style. In E.C. Chang (Ed.), *Optimism & pessimism: Implications for theory, research, and practice* (pp. 53–75). American Psychological Association.

Gilmore, A.K., & Ward-Ciesielski, E. (2019). Perceived risks and use of psychotherapy via telemedicine for patients at risk for suicide. *Journal of Telemedicine and Telecare, 25*(1), 59–63.

Gius, M. (2015). The impact of minimum age and child access prevention laws on firearm-related youth suicides and unintentional deaths. *The Social Science Journal, 52*(2), 168–175.

Glover, D.A. (2006). Allostatic load in women with and without PTSD symptoms. *Annals of the New York Academy of Sciences, 1071*, 442–447.

Glover, D.A., Stuber, M., & Poland, R.E. (2006). Allostatic load in women with and without PTSD symptoms. *Psychiatry, 69*(3), 191–203.

Glowinski, A.L., Bucholz, K.K., Nelson, E.C., Fu, Q., Madden, P.A., Reich, W., & Heath, A.C. (2001). Suicide attempts in an adolescent female twin sample. *Journal of the American Academy of Child & Adolescent Psychiatry, 40*(11), 1300–1307.

GLSEN. (2022). *The 2021 National School Climate Survey*. www.glsen.org/sites/default/files/2022-10/NSCS-2021-Full-Report.pdf.

Godleski, L., Cervone, D., Vogel, D., & Rooney, M. (2012). Home telemental health implementation and outcomes using electronic messaging. *Journal of Telemedicine and Telecare, 18*(1), 17–19.

Godleski, L., Nieves, J.E., Darkins, A., & Lehmann, L. (2008). VA telemental health: Suicide assessment. *Behavioral Sciences & The Law, 26*(3), 271–286.

Gogo, A., Osta, A., McClafferty, H., & Rana, D.T. (2019). Cultivating a way of being and doing: Individual strategies for physician well-being and resilience. *Current Problems in Pediatric and Adolescent Health Care, 49*(12), 100663.

Gold, L.H., & Frierson, R.L., (Eds.). (2020). *The American Psychiatric Association Publishing textbook of suicide risk assessment and management*. American Psychiatric Publishing.

Goldman-Mellor, S.J., Caspi, A., Harrington, H., Hogan, S., Nada-Raja, S., Poulton, R., & Moffitt, T.E. (2014). Suicide attempt in young people: A signal for long-term health care and social needs. *JAMA Psychiatry, 71*(2), 119–127.

Goldstein, E.V., & Wilson, F.A. (2022). Hispanic immigrants and suicide: Overcoming data challenges in an anti-immigrant climate. *AJPM Focus, 1*(2): 1–4.

Goodall, J., & Abrahams, D. (2021). *The book of hope*. Findaway World, LLC.

Goodman, M., Banthin, D., Blair, N.J., Mascitelli, K.A., Wilsnack, J., Chen, J., ... & New, A.S. (2016). A randomized trial of dialectical behavior therapy in high-risk suicidal veterans. *The Journal of Clinical Psychiatry*, *77*(12), 4031.

Goodman, M., Sullivan, S.R., Spears, A.P., Dixon, L., Sokol, Y., Kapil-Pair, K.N., ... & Stanley, B. (2021). An open trial of a suicide safety planning group treatment: "Project Life Force." *Archives of Suicide Research*, *25*(3), 690–703.

Goodwill, J.R., Taylor, R.J., & Watkins, D.C. (2021). Everyday discrimination, depressive symptoms, and suicide ideation among African American men. *Archives of Suicide Research*, *25*(1), 74–93.

Gothe, N.P., Keswani, R.K., & McAuley, E. (2016). Yoga practice improves executive function by attenuating stress levels. *Biological Psychology*, *121*, 109–116.

Gøtzsche, P.C., & Gøtzsche, P.K. (2017). Cognitive behavioural therapy halves the risk of repeated suicide attempts: Systematic review. *Journal of the Royal Society of Medicine*, *110*(10), 404–410.

Gould, M.S. (2001). Suicide and the media. *Annals of the New York Academy of Sciences*, *932*(1), 200–224.

Gould, M.S., Marrocco, F.A., Kleinman, M., Thomas, J.G., Mostkoff, K., Cote, J., & Davies, M. (2005). Evaluating iatrogenic risk of youth suicide screening programs: A randomized controlled trial. *JAMA*, *293*(13), 1635–1643.

Gould, M.S., Velting, D., Kleinman, M., Lucas, C., Thomas, J.G., & Chung, M. (2004). Teenagers' attitudes about coping strategies and help-seeking behavior for suicidality. *Journal of the American Academy of Child & Adolescent Psychiatry*, *43*(9), 1124–1133.

Gradus, J.L., Qin, P., Lincoln, A.K., Miller, M., Lawler, E., Sørensen, H.T., & Lash, T.L. (2012). Sexual victimization and completed suicide among Danish female adults. *Violence Against Women*, *18*(5), 552–561.

Gradus, J.L., Rosellini, A.J., Horváth-Puhó, E., Street, A.E., Galatzer-Levy, I., Jiang, T., ... & Sørensen, H.T. (2020). Prediction of sex-specific suicide risk using machine learning and single-payer health care registry data from Denmark. *JAMA Psychiatry*, *77*(1), 25–34.

Grattidge, L., Purton, T., Auckland, S., Lees, D., & Mond, J. (2021). Participatory action research in suicide prevention program evaluation: Opportunities and challenges from the National Suicide Prevention Trial, Tasmania. *Australian and New Zealand Journal of Public Health*, 1–4.

Gray, J.M., Wilson, C.D., Lee, T.T., Pittman, Q.J., Deussing, J.M., Hillard, C.J., ... & Hill, M.N. (2016). Sustained glucocorticoid exposure recruits cortico-limbic CRH signaling to modulate endocannabinoid function. *Psychoneuroendocrinology*, *66*, 151–158.

Green, J.D., Kearns, J.C., Rosen, R.C., Keane, T.M., & Marx, B.P. (2018). Evaluating the effectiveness of safety plans for military veterans: Do safety plans tailored to veteran characteristics decrease suicide risk? *Behavior Therapy*, *49*(6), 931–938.

Greening, L., & Stoppelbein, L. (2002). Religiosity, attributional style, and social support as psychosocial buffers for African American and White adolescents' perceived risk for suicide. *Suicide and Life-Threatening Behavior*, *32*(4), 404–417.

Gressier, F., Guillard, V., Cazas, O., Falissard, B., Glangeaud-Freudenthal, N.M., & Sutter-Dallay, A.L. (2017). Risk factors for suicide attempt in pregnancy and the post-partum period in women with serious mental illnesses. *Journal of Psychiatric Research, 84*, 284–291.

Greydanus, D., Patel, D., & Pratt, H. (2010). Suicide risk in adolescents with chronic illness: Implications for primary care and specialty pediatric practice: A review. *Developmental Medicine & Child Neurology, 52*(12), 1083–1087.

Grossman, D.C., Mueller, B.A., Riedy, C., Dowd, M.D., Villaveces, A., Prodzinski, J., … & Harruff, R. (2005). Gun storage practices and risk of youth suicide and unintentional firearm injuries. *JAMA, 293*(6), 707–714.

Grover, S., Sahoo, S., Rabha, A., & Koirala, R. (2019). ECT in schizophrenia: A review of the evidence. *Acta Neuropsychiatrica, 31*(3), 115–127.

Guille, C., Zhao, Z., Krystal, J., Nichols, B., Brady, K., & Sen, S. (2015). Web-based cognitive behavioral therapy intervention for the prevention of suicidal ideation in medical interns: A randomized clinical trial. *JAMA Psychiatry, 72*(12), 1192–1198.

Guidi, J., Lucente, M., Sonino, N., & Fava, G.A. (2021). Allostatic load and its impact on health: A systematic review. *Psychotherapy and Psychosomatics, 90*(1), 11–27.

Gunnar, M.R., Wewerka, S., Frenn, K., Long, J.D., & Griggs, C. (2009). Developmental changes in hypothalamus–pituitary–adrenal activity over the transition to adolescence: Normative changes and associations with puberty. *Development and Psychopathology, 21*(1), 69–85.

Gürhan, N., Beşer, N.G., Polat, Ü., & Koç, M. (2019). Suicide risk and depression in individuals with chronic illness. *Community Mental Health Journal, 55*, 840–848.

Gustavson, K.A., Alexopoulos, G.S., Niu, G.C., McCulloch, C., Meade, T., & Areán, P.A. (2016). Problem-solving therapy reduces suicidal ideation in depressed older adults with executive dysfunction. *The American Journal of Geriatric Psychiatry, 24*(1), 11–17.

Gvion, Y., & Apter, A. (2011). Aggression, impulsivity, and suicide behavior: A review of the literature. *Archives of Suicide Research, 15*(2), 93–112.

Gysin-Maillart, A., Schwab, S., Soravia, L., Megert, M., & Michel, K. (2016). A novel brief therapy for patients who attempt suicide: A 24-months follow-up randomized controlled study of the attempted suicide short intervention program (ASSIP). *PLoS Medicine, 13*(3), e1001968.

Gysin-Maillart, A.C., Soravia, L.M., Gemperli, A., & Michel, K. (2017). Suicide ideation is related to therapeutic alliance in a brief therapy for attempted suicide. *Archives of Suicide Research, 21*(1), 113–126.

Haas, A.P., Eliason, M., Mays, V.M., Mathy, R.M., Cochran, S.D., D'Augelli, A.R., … & Clayton, P.J. (2010). Suicide and suicide risk in lesbian, gay, bisexual, and transgender populations: Review and recommendations. *Journal of Homosexuality, 58*(1), 10–51.

Ha, H., & Tu, W. (2018). An ecological study of the spatially varying relationship between county-level suicide rates and altitude in the United States. *International Journal of Environmental Research and Public Health, 15*(4), 671.

Hagedoorn P., Groenewegen P.P., Roberts H., & Helbich M. (2020). Is suicide mortality associated with neighbourhood social fragmentation and deprivation? A Dutch register-based case-control study using individualised neighbourhoods. *Journal of Epidemiology and Community Health, 74,* 197–202.

Hageman, I., Andersen, H.S., & Jorgensen, M.B. (2001). Post-traumatic stress disorder: A review of psychobiology and pharmacotherapy. *Acta Psychiatrica Scandinavica, 104,* 411–422.

Hammond, M. (2018). Mad like me: Travels in bipolar country. Consultancy for Alternative Education (CAE Canada).

Hariprasad, V.R., Varambally, S., Shivakumar, V., Kalmady, S.V., Venkatasubramanian, G., & Gangadhar, B.N. (2013). Yoga increases the volume of the hippocampus in elderly subjects. *Indian Journal of Psychiatry, 55*(Suppl 3), S394–S396.

Harkness, K.L., Stewart, J.G., & Wynne-Edwards, K.E. (2011). Cortisol reactivity to social stress in adolescents: Role of depression severity and child maltreatment. *Psychoneuroendocrinology, 36,* 173–181.

Harris, K.M., Carpenter, C., & Bao, Y. (2006). The effects of state parity laws on the use of mental health care. *Medical Care,* 499–505.

Harriss, L., Hawton, K., & Zahl, D. (2005). Value of measuring suicidal intent in the assessment of people attending hospital following self-poisoning or self-injury. *British Journal of Psychiatry, 186*(1), 60–66.

Hatcher, S., Sharon, C., Parag, V., & Collins, N. (2011). Problem-solving therapy for people who present to hospital with self-harm: Zelen randomised controlled trial. *British Journal of Psychiatry, 199*(4), 310–316.

Haw, C., Hawton, K., Gunnell, D., & Platt, S. (2015). Economic recession and suicidal behaviour: Possible mechanisms and ameliorating factors. *International Journal of Social Psychiatry, 61*(1), 73–81.

Haws, C.A., Gray, D.D., Yurgelun-Todd, D.A., Moskos, M., Meyer, L.J., & Renshaw, P.F. (2009). The possible effect of altitude on regional variation in suicide rates. *Medical Hypotheses, 73*(4), 587–590.

Hawton, K. (1987). Assessment of suicide risk. *British Journal of Psychiatry, 150*(2), 145–153.

Hawton, K., Arensman, E., Townsend, E., Bremner, S., Feldman, E., Goldney, R., … & Träskman-Bendz, L. (1998). Deliberate self harm: Systematic review of efficacy of psychosocial and pharmacological treatments in preventing repetition. *BMJ (Clinical Research Ed.), 317*(7156), 441–447.

Hawton, K., Simkin, S., Deeks, J., Cooper, J., Johnston, A., Waters, K., … & Simpson, K. (2004). UK legislation on analgesic packs: Before and after study of long term effect on poisonings. *BMJ, 329*(7474), 1076.

Hawton, K., Sutton, L., Haw, C., Sinclair, J., & Harriss, L. (2005). Suicide and attempted suicide in bipolar disorder: A systematic review of risk factors. *Journal of Clinical Psychiatry, 66*(6), 693–704.

Hawton, K., Witt, K.G., Salisbury, T.L.T., Arensman, E., Gunnell, D., Hazell, P., … & van Heeringen, K. (2016). Psychosocial interventions following self-harm in adults: A systematic review and meta-analysis. *The Lancet Psychiatry,* *3*(8), 740–750.

Hedegaard, H., Curtin, S.C., & Warner, M. (2018). *Suicide rates in the United* *States continue to increase (Vol. 309).* US Department of Health and Human Services, Centers for Disease Control and Prevention, National Center for Health Statistics.

Hedegaard, H., Curtin, S.C., Warner, M. (2021). Suicide mortality in the United States, 1999–2019. *NCHS Data Brief,* (398), 1–8.

Hefferon, K., & Boniwell, I. (2011). *Positive psychology: Theory, research and appli-* *cations.* McGraw-Hill Education (UK).

Hegerl, U., Althaus, D., Schmidtke, A., & Niklewski, G. (2006). The alliance against depression: 2-year evaluation of a community-based intervention to reduce suicidality. *Psychological Medicine, 36*(9), 1225–1233.

Hegerl, U., Mergl, R., Havers, I., Schmidtke, A., Lehfeld, H., Niklewski, G., & Althaus, D. (2010). Sustainable effects on suicidality were found for the Nuremberg alliance against depression. *European Archives of Psychiatry and* *Clinical Neuroscience, 260,* 401–406.

Hegerl, U., Rummel-Kluge, C., Värnik, A., Arensman, E., & Koburger, N. (2013). Alliances against depression: A community-based approach to target depression and to prevent suicidal behaviour. *Neuroscience & Biobehavioral* *Reviews, 37*(10), 2404–2409.

Heisel, M.J., Neufeld, E., & Flett, G.L. (2016). Reasons for living, meaning in life, and suicide ideation: Investigating the roles of key positive psychological factors in reducing suicide risk in community-residing older adults. *Aging &* *Mental Health, 20*(2), 195–207.

Helmreich, I., Kunzler, A., Chmitorz, A., König, J., Binder, H., Wessa, M., & Lieb, K. (2017). Psychological interventions for resilience enhancement in adults. *Cochrane Database of Systematic Reviews, 2,* CD012527.

Hempstead, K.A., & Phillips, J.A. (2015). Rising suicide among adults aged 40–64 years: The role of job and financial circumstances. *American Journal of* *Preventive Medicine, 48*(5), 491–500.

Hendin, H. (1991). Psychodynamics of suicide, with particular reference to the young. *The American Journal of Psychiatry, 148*(9), 1150–1158.

Herman, J.P., McKlveen, J.M., Solomon, M.B., Carvalho-Netto, E., & Myers, B. (2012). Neural regulation of the stress response: Glucocorticoid feedback mechanisms. *Brazilian Journal of Medical and Biological Research, 45,* 292–298.

Herrenkohl, T. I. (2013). Person–environment interactions and the shaping of resilience. *Trauma, Violence, & Abuse,* 14(3), 191–194.

Heron, M. (2021). Deaths: Leading causes for 2019. *National Vital Statistics* *Reports, 70,* 9. www.cdc.gov/nchs/data/nvsr/nvsr70/nvsr70-09-508.pdf.

Hetrick, S.E., Yuen, H.P., Bailey, E., Cox, G.R., Templer, K., Rice, S.M., … & Robinson, J. (2017). Internet-based cognitive behavioural therapy for young people with suicide-related behaviour (Reframe-IT): A randomised controlled trial. *BMJ Mental Health, 20*(3), 76–82.

Hill, M.N., Patel, S., Carrier, E.J., Rademacher, D.J., Ormerod, B.K., Hillard, C.J., & Gorzalka, B.B. (2005). Downregulation of endocannabinoid signaling in the hippocampus following chronic unpredictable stress. *Neuropsychopharmacology*, *30*(3), 508–515.

Hill, R.M., & Pettit, J.W. (2013). The role of autonomy needs in suicidal ideation: Integrating the interpersonal-psychological theory of suicide and self-determination theory. *Archives of Suicide Research*, *17*(3), 288–301.

Hirsch, J.K. (2006). A review of the literature on rural suicide. *Crisis*, *27*(4), 189–199.

Hirsch, J., Chang, E., & Kelliher Rabon, J. (2018). *A positive psychological approach to suicide. Advances in mental health and addiction*. Cham: Springer.

Hirsch, J.K., Duberstein, P.R., Conner, K.R., Heisel, M.J., Beckman, A., Franus, N., & Conwell, Y. (2006). Future orientation and suicide ideation and attempts in depressed adults ages 50 and over. *The American Journal of Geriatric Psychiatry*, *14*(9), 752–757.

Holmes, G., Clacy, A., Hermens, D.F., & Lagopoulos, J. (2021). The long-term efficacy of suicide prevention gatekeeper training: A systematic review. *Archives of Suicide Research*, *25*(2), 177–207.

Hölzel, B.K., Carmody, J., Vangel, M., Congleton, C., Yerramsetti, S.M., Gard, T., & Lazar, S.W. (2011). Mindfulness practice leads to increases in regional brain gray matter density. *Psychiatry Research*, *191*(1), 36–43.

Hopko, D.R., Funderburk, J.S., Shorey, R.C., McIndoo, C.C., Ryba, M.M., File, A.A., … & Vitulano, M. (2013). Behavioral activation and problem-solving therapy for depressed breast cancer patients: Preliminary support for decreased suicidal ideation. *Behavior Modification*, *37*(6), 747–767.

Horwitz, A.G., Hill, R.M., & King, C.A. (2011). Specific coping behaviors in relation to adolescent depression and suicidal ideation. *Journal of Adolescence*, *34*(5), 1077–1085.

Huffman, J.C., Boehm, J.K., Beach, S.R., Beale, E.E., DuBois, C.M., & Healy, B.C. (2016). Relationship of optimism and suicidal ideation in three groups of patients at varying levels of suicide risk. *Journal of Psychiatric Research*, *77*, 76–84.

Huffman, J.C., DuBois, C.M., Healy, B.C., Boehm, J.K., Kashdan, T.B., Celano, C.M., … & Lyubomirsky, S. (2014). Feasibility and utility of positive psychology exercises for suicidal inpatients. *General Hospital Psychiatry*, *36*(1), 88–94.

Huffman, J.C., Legler, S.R., & Boehm, J.K. (2017). Positive psychological well-being and health in patients with heart disease: A brief review. *Future Cardiology*, *13*(5), 443–450.

Hughes, B., Durran, A., Langford, N.J., & Mutimer, D. (2003). Paracetamol poisoning: Impact of pack size restrictions. *Journal of Clinical Pharmacy and Therapeutics*, *28*(4), 307–310.

Hull-Blanks, E.E., Kerr, B.A., & Robinson Kurpius, S.E. (2004). Risk factors of suicidal ideations and attempts in talented, at-risk girls. *Suicide and Life-Threatening Behavior*, *34*(3), 267–276.

Hutchison, C. (1999). Social support: Factors to consider when designing studies that measure social support. *Journal of Advanced Nursing*, *29*(6), 1520–1526.

Hwang, A.C., Peng, L.N., Wen, Y.W., Tsai, Y.W., Chang, L.C., Chiou, S.T., & Chen, L.K. (2014). Predicting all-cause and cause-specific mortality by static and dynamic measurements of allostatic load: A 10-year population-based cohort study in Taiwan. *Journal of the American Medical Directors Association, 15*(7), 490–496.

Hybholt, L., Higgins, A., Buus, N., Berring, L.L., Connolly, T., Erlangsen, A., & Morrissey, J. (2022). The spaces of peer-led support groups for suicide bereaved in Denmark and the Republic of Ireland: A focus group study. *International Journal of Environmental Research and Public Health, 19*(16), 9898.

Iasiello, M., & Van Agteren, J. (2020). Mental health and/or mental illness: A scoping review of the evidence and implications of the dual-continua model of mental health. *Evidence Base: A Journal of Evidence Reviews in Key Policy Areas*, (1), 1–45.

Ilgen, M.A., Czyz, E.K., Welsh, D.E., Zeber, J.E., Bauer, M.S. & Kilbourne, A.M. (2009). A collaborative therapeutic relationship and risk of suicidal ideation in patients with bipolar disorder. *Journal of Affective Disorders, 115*(1–2), 246–251.

Ilgen, M.A., Bohnert, A.S., Ganoczy, D., Bair, M.J., McCarthy, J.F., & Blow, F.C. (2016). Opioid dose and risk of suicide. *Pain, 157*(5), 1079.

Infurna, F.J., Gerstorf, D., & Lachman, M.E. (2020). Midlife in the 2020s: Opportunities and challenges. *American Psychologist, 75*(4), 470.

Interian, A., Chesin, M., Kline, A., St. Hill, L., King, A., Miller, R., ... & Stanley, B. (2021). Coping with suicidal urges: An important factor for suicide risk assessment and Intervention. *Archives of Suicide Research, 25*(2), 224–237.

Irwin, J.A., Coleman, J.D., Fisher, C.M., & Marasco, V.M. (2014). Correlates of suicide ideation among LGBT Nebraskans. *Journal of Homosexuality, 61*(8), 1172–1191.

Isaac, M., Elias, B., Katz, L.Y., Belik, S.L., Deane, F.P., Enns, M.W., ... & Swampy Cree Suicide Prevention Team. (2009). Gatekeeper training as a preventative intervention for suicide: A systematic review. *The Canadian Journal of Psychiatry, 54*(4), 260–268.

Isacsson, G. (1997). Depression, antidepressants, and suicide: Pharmacoepidemiological evidence for suicide prevention. In R.W. Maris, M.M. Silverman, & S.S. Canetto (Eds.), *Review of suicidology* (pp. 168–201). Guilford Press.

Isgor, C., Kabbaj, M., Akil, H., & Watson, S.J. (2004). Delayed effects of chronic variable stress during peripubertal-juvenile period on hippocampal morphology and on cognitive and stress axis functions in rats. *Hippocampus, 14*(5), 636–648.

Ivey-Stephenson, A.Z., Crosby, A.E., Jack, S.P., Haileyesus, T., & Kresnow-Sedacca, M. (2017). Suicide trends among and within urbanization levels by sex, race/ethnicity, age group, and mechanism of death – United States, 2001–2015. *MMWR Surveillance Summaries, 66*(SS-18), 1–16.

Ivey-Stephenson, A.Z., Demissie, Z., Crosby, A.E., Stone, D.M., Gaylor, E., Wilkins, N., ... & Brown, M. (2020). Suicidal ideation and behaviors among high school students: Youth risk behavior survey, United States, 2019. *MMWR Supplements, 69*(1), 47.

Jacobson, J.M., Osteen, P., Jones, A., & Berman, A. (2012). Evaluation of the recognizing and responding to suicide risk training. *Suicide and Life-Threatening Behavior*, *42*(5), 471–485.

Jamison, K.R. (2011). *Night falls fast: Understanding suicide*. Vintage.

Jamison, E.C., Bol, K.A., & Mintz, S.N. (2019). Analysis of the effects on time between divorce decree and suicide. *Crisis*, *40*(5), 309–316.

Jamison, E.C., Mintz, S., Bol, K.A., & Herndon, K. (2017). *Suicide in Colorado, 2011–2015: A summary from the Colorado violent death reporting system.* Colorado Department of Public Health and Environment, Vital Records & Statistics Branch.

Janeček, M., & Dabrowska, J. (2019). Oxytocin facilitates adaptive fear and attenuates anxiety responses in animal models and human studies: Potential interaction with the corticotropin-releasing factor (CRF) system in the bed nucleus of the stria terminalis (BNST). *Cell and Tissue Research*, *375*, 143–172.

Jardim, G.B.G., Novelo, M., Spanemberg, L., von Gunten, A., Engroff, P., Nogueira, E.L., & Neto, A.C. (2018). Influence of childhood abuse and neglect subtypes on late-life suicide risk beyond depression. *Child Abuse & Neglect*, *80*, 249–256.

Jenike, M.A. (1989). Treatment of affective illness in the elderly with drugs and electroconvulsive therapy. *Journal of Geriatric Psychiatry*, *22*(1), 77–112.

Jia, C.X., & Zhang, J. (2012). Global functioning and suicide among Chinese rural population aged 15–34 years: A psychological autopsy case-control study. *Journal of Forensic Sciences*, *57*(2), 391–397.

Jiménez-Muñoz, L., Peñuelas-Calvo, I., Díaz-Oliván, I., Gutiérrez-Rojas, L., Baca-García, E., & Porras-Segovia, A. (2022). Suicide prevention in your pocket: A systematic review of ecological momentary interventions for the management of suicidal thoughts and behaviors. *Harvard Review of Psychiatry*, *30*(2), 85–99.

Jobes, D.A., & Chalker, S.A. (2019). One size does not fit all: A comprehensive clinical approach to reducing suicidal ideation, attempts, and deaths. *International Journal of Environmental Research and Public Health*, *16*(19), 3606.

Jobes, D.A. (2006). *Managing suicidal risk: A collaborative approach*. Guilford.

Jobes, D.A., Au, J.S., & Siegelman, A. (2015). Psychological approaches to suicide treatment and prevention. *Current Treatment Options in Psychiatry*, *2*(4), 363–370.

Johnson, R.M., Barber, C., Azrael, D., Clark, D.E., & Hemenway, D. (2010). Who are the owners of firearms used in adolescent suicides? *Suicide and Life-Threatening Behavior*, *40*(6), 609–611.

Johnson, J., Panagioti, M., Bass, J., Ramsey, L., & Harrison, R. (2017). Resilience to emotional distress in response to failure, error or mistakes: A systematic review. *Clinical Psychology Review*, *52*, 19–42.

Joiner, T.E. (2005). *Why people die by suicide*. Harvard University Press.

Joiner Jr, T.E., Pettit, J.W., Perez, M., Burns, A.B., Gencoz, T., Gencoz, F., & Rudd, M.D. (2001). Can positive emotion influence problem-solving attitudes among suicidal adults? *Professional Psychology: Research and Practice*, *32*(5), 507.

Joiner, T.E., Van Orden, K.A., Witte, T.K., Selby, E.A., Ribeiro, J.D., Lewis, R., & Rudd, M.D. (2009). Main predictions of the interpersonal-psychological theory of suicidal behavior: Empirical tests in two samples of young adults. *Journal of Abnormal Psychology, 118*(3), 634–646.

Jokinen, J., Chatzittofis, A., Hellström, C., Nordström, P., Uvnäs-Moberg, K., & Åsberg, M. (2012). Low CSF oxytocin reflects high intent in suicide attempters. *Psychoneuroendocrinology, 37*(4), 482–490.

Jokinen, J., Ouda, J., & Nordström, P. (2010). Noradrenergic function and HPA axis dysregulation in suicidal behaviour. *Psychoneuroendocrinology, 35*, 1536–1542.

Jones, N., Marks, R., Ramiex, R., & Rios-Vargas, M. (2021). *Improved race and ethnicity measures reveal U.S. population is much more multiracial.* www.census.gov/library/stories/2021/08/improved-race-ethnicity-measures-reveal-united-states-population-much-more-multiracial.html.

Jordan, J.R., & McIntosh, J.L. (2010). *Grief after suicide: Understanding the consequences and caring for the survivors.* Routledge.

Juster, R.P., de Torre, M.B., Kerr, P., Kheloui, S., Rossi, M., & Bourdon, O. (2019). Sex differences and gender diversity in stress responses and allostatic load among workers and LGBT people. *Current Psychiatry Reports, 21*, 1–11.

Juster, R.P., McEwen, B.S., & Lupien, S.J. (2010). Allostatic load biomarkers of chronic stress and impact on health and cognition. *Neuroscience & Biobehavioral Reviews, 35*, 2–16.

Juster, R., Russell, J., Almeida, D., & Picard, M. (2016). Allostatic load and comorbidities: A mitochondrial, epigenetic, and evolutionary perspective. *Development and Psychopathology, 28*(4pt1), 1117–1146.

Juster, R.P., Sasseville, M., Giguère C.É., Consortium, S., & Lupien, S.J. (2018). Elevated allostatic load in individuals presenting at psychiatric emergency services. *Journal of Psychosomatic Research, 115*, 101–109.

Juster, R.P., Marin, M.F., Sindi, S., Nair, N. V., Ng, Y. K., Pruessner, J. C., & Lupien, S. J. (2011). Allostatic load associations to acute, 3-year and 6-year prospective depressive symptoms in healthy older adults. *Physiology & Behavior, 104*(2), 360–364.

Juster, R.P., Vencill, J.A., & Johnson, P.J. (2017). Impact of stress and strain on current LGBT health disparities. In K. Eckstrand & J. Potter (Eds.), *Trauma, resilience, and health promotion in LGBT patients* (pp. 35–48). Springer.

Kalesan, B., Zhao, S., Poulson, M., Neufeld, M., Dechert, T., Siracuse, J.J., ... & Li, F. (2020). Intersections of firearm suicide, drug-related mortality, and economic dependency in rural America. *Journal of Surgical Research, 256*, 96–102.

Kanat, M., Heinrichs, M., Mader, I., Van Elst, L.T., & Domes, G. (2015). Oxytocin modulates amygdala reactivity to masked fearful eyes. *Neuropsychopharmacology, 40*(11), 2632–2638.

Kandola, A., Hendrikse, J., Lucassen, P.J., Yücel, M., & Nolan, Y. (2016). Aerobic exercise as a tool to improve hippocampal plasticity and function in humans: Practical implications for mental health treatment. *Frontiers in Human Neuroscience, 10*, 1–25.

Kann, L., McManus, T., Harris, W.A., Shanklin, S.L., Flint, K.H., Queen, B., ... & Ethier, K.A. (2018). Youth risk behavior surveillance – United States, 2017. *MMWR Surveillance Summaries, 67*(8), 1.

Kapczinski, F., Vieta, E., Andreazza, A.C., Frey, B.N., Gomes, F.A., Tramontina, J., & Post, R.M. (2008). Allostatic load in bipolar disorder: Implications for pathophysiology and treatment. *Neuroscience & Biobehavioral Reviews 32*, 675–692.

Kapusta, N.D., Etzersdorfer, E., Krall, C., & Sonneck, G. (2007). Firearm legislation reform in the European Union: Impact on firearm availability, firearm suicide and homicide rates in Austria. *The British Journal of Psychiatry, 191*(3), 253–257.

Karlamangla, A.S., Singer, B.H., & Seeman, T.E. (2006). Reduction in allostatic load in older adults is associated with lower all-cause mortality risk: MacArthur studies of successful aging. *Psychosomatic Medicine, 68*, 500–507.

Kaslow, N.J., Garcia-Williams, A., Moffitt, L., McLeod, M., Zesiger, H., Ammirati, R., ... & Emory Cares 4U Coalition. (2012). Building and maintaining an effective campus-wide coalition for suicide prevention. *Journal of College Student Psychotherapy, 26*(2), 121–139.

Katz, I., Barry, C.N., Cooper, S.A., Kasprow, W.J., & Hoff, R.A. (2020). Use of the Columbia-Suicide Severity Rating Scale (C-SSRS) in a large sample of Veterans receiving mental health services in the Veterans Health Administration. *Suicide and Life-Threatening Behavior, 50*(1), 111–121.

Katz, L.Y., Cox, B.J., Gunasekara, S., & Miller, A.L. (2004). Feasibility of dialectical behavior therapy for suicidal adolescent inpatients. *Journal of the American Academy of Child & Adolescent Psychiatry, 43*(3), 276–282.

Katz, I.R., Rogers, M.P., Lew, R., Thwin, S.S., Doros, G., Ahearn, E., ... & Li+ plus Investigators. (2022). Lithium treatment in the prevention of repeat suicide-related outcomes in veterans with major depression or bipolar disorder: A randomized clinical trial. *JAMA Psychiatry, 79*(1), 24–32.

Kaufman, J.A., Salas-Hernández, L.K., Komro, K.A., & Livingston, M.D. (2020). Effects of increased minimum wages by unemployment rate on suicide in the USA. *Journal of Epidemiology and Community Health, 74*(3), 219–224.

Kawashima, D., Koga, Y., & Yoshioka, M. (2022). Feasibility of brief online gatekeeper training for Japanese university students: A randomized controlled trial. *Death Studies, 47*, 1–10.

Kegler, S.R., Simon, T.R., Zwald, M.L., Chen, M.S., Mercy, J.A., Jones, C.M., ... & Dills, J. (2022). Vital signs: Changes in firearm homicide and suicide rates – United States, 2019–2020. *Morbidity and Mortality Weekly Report, 71*(19), 656.

Kegler, S.R., Stone, D.M., & Holland, K.M. (2017). Trends in suicide by level of urbanization – United States, 1999–2015. *Morbidity and Mortality Weekly Report, 66*(10), 270.

Keilp, J.G., Stanley, B.H., Beers, S.R., Melhem, N.M., Burke, A.K., Cooper, T.B., ... & Mann, J.J. (2016). Further evidence of low baseline cortisol levels in suicide attempters. *Journal of Affective Disorders, 190*, 187–192.

Keller, S., Sarchiapone, M., Zarrilli, F., Videtic, A., Ferraro, A., Carli, V., & Chiariotti, L., 2010. Increased BDNF promoter methylation in the Wernicke area of suicide subjects. *Archives of General Psychiatry, 67*(3), 258–267.

Kellner, C.H., Fink, M., Knapp, R., Petrides, G., Husain, M., Rummans, T., ... & Malur, C. (2005). Relief of expressed suicidal intent by ECT: A consortium for research in ECT study. *American Journal of Psychiatry, 162*(5), 977–982.

Kessler, R.C., Stein, M.B., Petukhova, M.V., Bliese, P., Bossarte, R.M., Bromet, E.J., ... & Bell, A.M. (2017). Predicting suicides after outpatient mental health visits in the Army Study to Assess Risk and Resilience in Servicemembers (Army STARRS). *Molecular Psychiatry, 22*(4), 544–551.

Khazem, L.R. (2018). Physical disability and suicide: Recent advancements in understanding and future directions for consideration. *Current Opinion in Psychology, 22*, 18–22.

Khubchandani, J., & Price, J.H. (2022). Suicides among non-elderly adult Hispanics, 2010–2020. *Journal of Community Health 47*, 966–973.

Kidd, S., & Shahar, G. (2008). Resilience in homeless youth: The key role of self-esteem. *American Journal of Orthopsychiatry, 78*(2), 163–172.

Kim, S., Lee, H.K., & Lee, K. (2021). Which PHQ-9 items can effectively screen for suicide? Machine learning approaches. *International Journal of Environmental Research and Public Health, 18*(7), 3339.

Kim, N., Mickelson, J.B., Brenner, B.E., Haws, C.A., Yurgelun-Todd, D.A., & Renshaw, P.F. (2011). Altitude, gun ownership, rural areas, and suicide. *American Journal of Psychiatry, 168*(1), 49–54.

King, C.A., & Merchant, C.R. (2008). Social and interpersonal factors relating to adolescent suicidality: A review of the literature. *Archives of Suicide Research, 12*(3), 181–196.

King, M., Semlyen, J., Tai, S.S., Killaspy, H., Osborn, D., Popelyuk, D., & Nazareth, I. (2008). A systematic review of mental disorder, suicide, and deliberate self-harm in lesbian, gay and bisexual people. *BMC Psychiatry, 8*, 1–17.

Kinman, G., & Torry, R. (2021). Developing a suicide postvention framework for staff in primary healthcare. *Occupational Medicine, 71*(4–5), 171–173.

Kiosses, D.N., Szanto, K., Alexopoulos, G.S. (2014). Suicide in older adults: The role of emotions and cognition. *Current Psychiatry Reports, 16*, 495.

Kirby, T. (2015). Ketamine for depression: The highs and lows. *The Lancet Psychiatry, 2*(9), 783–784.

Kirkham, J.G., & Seitz, D.P. (2022). More evidence for problem-solving therapy: Improving access is still a problem in need of solving. *International Psychogeriatrics, 34*(2), 105–107.

Kirsch, P., Esslinger, C., Chen, Q., Mier, D., Lis, S., Siddhanti, S., ... & Meyer-Lindenberg, A. (2005). Oxytocin modulates neural circuitry for social cognition and fear in humans. *Journal of Neuroscience, 25*, 11489–11493.

Kivisto, A.J., & Phalen, P.L. (2018). Effects of risk-based firearm seizure laws in Connecticut and Indiana on suicide rates, 1981–2015. *Psychiatric Services, 69*(8), 855–862.

Kleck, G. (2019). Macro-level research on the effect of firearms prevalence on suicide rates: A systematic review and new evidence. *Social Science Quarterly*, *100*(3), 936–950.

Kleck, G. (2022). The cross-national association of gun ownership rates and suicide rates: An analysis of 194 nations. *Archives of Suicide Research*, *26*(3), 1478–1486.

Kleiman, E.M., & Liu, R.T. (2013). Social support as a protective factor in suicide: Findings from two nationally representative samples. *Journal of Affective Disorders*, *150*(2), 540–545.

Kleiman, E.M., & Riskind, J.H. (2013). Utilized social support and self-esteem mediate the relationship between perceived social support and suicide ideation: A test of a multiple mediator model. *Crisis*, *34*(1), 42–49.

Kleiman, E.M., Riskind, J.H., & Schaefer, K.E. (2014). Social support and positive events as suicide resiliency factors: Examination of synergistic buffering effects. *Archives of Suicide Research*, *18*(2), 144–155.

Kleiman, E.M., Riskind, J.H., Schaefer, K.E., & Weingarden, H. (2012). The moderating role of social support on the relationship between impulsivity and suicide risk. *Crisis*, *33*(5), 273–279.

Klonsky, E.D., & May, A.M. (2014). Differentiating suicide attempters from suicide ideators: A critical frontier for suicidology research. *Suicide and Life-Threatening Behavior*, *44*(1), 1–5.

Klonsky, E.D., & May, A.M. (2015). The three-step theory (3ST): A new theory of suicide rooted in the "ideation-to-action" framework. *International Journal of Cognitive Therapy*, *8*(2), 114–129.

Klonsky, E.D., Pachkowski, M.C., Shahnaz, A., & May, A.M. (2021). The three-step theory of suicide: Description, evidence, and some useful points of clarification. *Preventive Medicine*, *152*, 106549.

Klonsky, E.D., Saffer, B.Y., & Bryan, C.J. (2018). Ideation-to-action theories of suicide: A conceptual and empirical update. *Current Opinion in Psychology*, *22*, 38–43.

Knipe, D.W., Chang, S.S., Dawson, A., Eddleston, M., Konradsen, F., Metcalfe, C., & Gunnell, D. (2017). Suicide prevention through means restriction: Impact of the 2008–2011 pesticide restrictions on suicide in Sri Lanka. *PloS One*, *12*(3), e0172893.

Knipe, D.W., Chang, S.S., Dawson, A., Eddleston, M., Konradsen, F., Metcalfe, C., & Gunnell, D. (2017). Suicide prevention through means restriction: Impact of the 2008–2011 pesticide restrictions on suicide in Sri Lanka. *PloS One*, *12*(3), e0172893.

Knox, K. (2014). Approaching suicide as a public health issue. *Annals of Internal Medicine*, *161*(2), 151–152.

Knox, K.L., Conwell, Y., & Caine, E.D. (2004). If suicide is a public health problem, what are we doing to prevent it? *American Journal of Public Health*, *94*(1), 37–45.

Knox, K.L., Kemp, J., McKeon, R., & Katz, I.R. (2012). Implementation and early utilization of a suicide hotline for veterans. *American Journal of Public Health*, *102*(S1), S29–S32.

Knox, K.L., Litts, D.A., Talcott, G.W., Feig, J.C., & Caine, E.D. (2003). Suicide risk and related adverse outcomes after exposure to a suicide prevention programme in the US Air Force: Cohort study. *BMJ, 327*(7428), 1376.

Kobrosly, R.W., van Wijngaarden, E., Seplaki, C.L., Cory-Slechta, D.A., & Moynihan, J. (2014). Depressive symptoms are associated with allostatic load among community-dwelling older adults. *Physiology & Behavior, 123*, 223–230.

Koenig, H.G. (2009). Research on religion, spirituality, and mental health: A review. *Canadian Journal of Psychiatry, 54*(5), 283–291.

Koenig, H.G. (2012). Religion, spirituality, and health: The research and clinical implications. *International Scholarly Research Notices.* doi:10.5402/2012/278730.

Koenig, H., Koenig, H.G., King, D., & Carson, V.B. (2012). *Handbook of religion and health.* Oxford University Press.

Koenig Kellas, J., Horstman, H.K., Willer, E.K., & Carr, K. (2015). The benefits and risks of telling and listening to stories of difficulty over time: Experimentally testing the expressive writing paradigm in the context of interpersonal communication between friends. *Health Communication, 30*(9), 843–858.

Komiti, A., Judd, F., Grech, P., Mijch, A., Hoy, J., Lloyd, J.H., & Street, A. (2001). Suicidal behaviour in people with HIV/AIDS: A review. *Australian & New Zealand Journal of Psychiatry, 35*(6), 747–757.

Kposowa, A.J. (2003). Divorce and suicide risk. *Journal of Epidemiology & Community Health, 57*(12), 993–993.

Kposowa, A., Hamilton, D., & Wang, K. (2016). Impact of firearm availability and gun regulation on state suicide rates. *Suicide and Life-Threatening Behavior, 46*(6), 678–696.

Kral, M.J., & Idlout, L. (2016). Indigenous best practices: Community-based suicide prevention in Nunavut, Canada. In J. White, I. Marsh, M.J. Kral, & J. Morris (Eds.), *Critical suicidology: Transforming suicide research and prevention for the 21st century* (pp. 229–243). University of British Columbia Press.

Kramer, J., Boon, B., Schotanus-Dijkstra, M., van Ballegooijen, W., Kerkhof, A., & Van Der Poel, A. (2015). The mental health of visitors of web-based support forums for bereaved by suicide. *Crisis, 36*(1), 38–45.

Krause, N., Ellison, C.G., Shaw, B.A., Marcum, J.P., & Boardman, J.D. (2001). Church-based social support and religious coping. *Journal for the Scientific Study of Religion, 40*(4), 637–656.

Kreibich, A., Hennecke, M., & Brandstätter, V. (2020). The effect of self-awareness on the identification of goal-related obstacles. *European Journal of Personality, 34*(2), 215–233.

Kroenke, K., Spitzer, R.L., & Williams, J.B. (2001). The PHQ-9: Validity of a brief depression severity measure. *Journal of General Internal Medicine, 16*, 606–613.

Krystal, J.H., Abdallah, C.G., Sanacora, G., Charney, D.S., & Duman, R S. (2019). Ketamine: A paradigm shift for depression research and treatment. *Neuron, 101*(5), 774–778.

Krysinska, K., Lester, D., Lyke, J., & Corveleyn, J. (2015). Trait gratitude and suicidal ideation and behavior. *Crisis, 36*, 291–296.

Kubzansky, L.D., Huffman, J.C., Boehm, J.K., Hernandez, R., Kim, E.S., Koga, H.K., ... & Labarthe, D.R. (2018). Positive psychological well-being and cardiovascular disease: JACC health promotion series. *Journal of the American College of Cardiology*, *72*(12), 1382–1396.

Kuhn, M., Scharfenort, R., Schümann, D., Schiele, M.A., Münsterkötter, A.L., Deckert, J., ... & Lonsdorf, T.B. (2016). Mismatch or allostatic load? Timing of life adversity differentially shapes gray matter volume and anxious temperament. *Social Cognitive and Affective Neuroscience*, *11*(4), 537–547.

Kyriopoulos, I., Vandoros, S., & Kawachi, I. (2022). Police killings and suicide among Black Americans. *Social Science & Medicine*, *305*, 114964.

Labelle, R., Breton, J.J., Pouliot, L., Dufresne, M.J., & Berthiaume, C. (2013). Cognitive correlates of serious suicidal ideation in a community sample of adolescents. *Journal of Affective Disorders*, *145*(3), 370–377.

Labouliere, C.D., Stanley, B., Lake, A.M., & Gould, M.S. (2020). Safety planning on crisis lines: Feasibility, acceptability, and perceived helpfulness of a brief intervention to mitigate future suicide risk. *Suicide and Life-Threatening Behavior*, *50*(1), 29–41.

Labuschagne, I., Phan, K.L., Wood, A., Angstadt, M., Chua, P., Heinrichs, M., ... & Nathan, P.J. (2010). Oxytocin attenuates amygdala reactivity to fear in generalized social anxiety disorder. *Neuropsychopharmacology*, *35*(12), 2403–2413.

Lachman, M.E., Teshale, S., & Agrigoroaei, S. (2015). Midlife as a pivotal period in the life course: Balancing growth and decline at the crossroads of youth and old age. *International Journal of Behavioral Development*, *39*(1), 20–31.

Lambert, S.F., Copeland-Linder, N., & Ialongo, N.S. (2008). Longitudinal associations between community violence exposure and suicidality. *Journal of Adolescent Health*, *43*(4), 380–386.

Lambert, M.T., & Silva, P.S. (1998). An update on the impact of gun control legislation on suicide. *Psychiatric Quarterly*, *69*(2), 127–134.

Landes, S.J., Matthieu, M.M., Smith, B.N., McBain, S.A., & Ray, E.S. (2021). Challenges and potential solutions to implementing phone coaching in dialectical behavior therapy. *Cognitive and Behavioral Practice*, *28*(1), 66–76.

Lane, T.J. (2022). Associations between firearm and suicide rates: A replication of Kleck (2021). *Archives of Suicide Research*, 1–16.

Lang M. (2013). The impact of mental health insurance laws on state suicide rates. *Health Economics*, *22*(1), 73–88.

Lapierre, S., Dubé, M., Bouffard, L., & Alain, M. (2007). Addressing suicidal ideations through the realization of meaningful personal goals. *Crisis*, *28*(1), 16–25.

Large, M., Kaneson, M., Myles, N., Myles, H., Gunaratne, P., & Ryan, C. (2016). Meta-analysis of longitudinal cohort studies of suicide risk assessment among psychiatric patients: Heterogeneity in results and lack of improvement over time. *PloS One*, *11*(6), e0156322.

Large, M., Myles, N., Myles, H., Corderoy, A., Weiser, M., Davidson, M., & Ryan, C.J. (2018). Suicide risk assessment among psychiatric inpatients: A systematic review and meta-analysis of high-risk categories. *Psychological Medicine*, *48*(7), 1119–1127.

Large, M.M., Soper, C.A., & Ryan, C.J. (2022). Suicide risk assessment. *The Lancet Psychiatry*, *9*(12), 938–939.

Larsen, M.E., Nicholas, J., & Christensen, H. (2016). A systematic assessment of smartphone tools for suicide prevention. *PloS One*, *11*(4), e0152285.

Lavretsky, H. (2018). Resilience and amygdala function in older healthy and depressed adults. *Journal of Affective Disorders*, *237*, 27–34.

Law, K.C., & Anestis, M.D. (2021). Testing whether suicide capability has a dynamic propensity: The role of affect and arousal on momentary fluctuations in suicide capability. *Frontiers in Psychology*, *12*, 1–17.

Leaver, A.M., Yang, H., Siddarth, P., Vlasova, R.M., Krause, B., Cyr, N.S., ... & Hawkins, R. (2017). Is cognitive behavioural therapy effective in reducing suicidal ideation and behaviour when delivered face-to-face or via e-health? A systematic review and meta-analysis. *Cognitive Behaviour Therapy*, *46*(5), 353–374.

Leaver, A. M., Yang, H., Siddarth, P., Vlasova, R. M., Krause, B., Cyr, N. S., ... & Lavretsky, H. (2018). Resilience and amygdala function in older healthy and depressed adults. *Journal of Affective Disorders*, *237*, 27–34.

Leaune, E., Cuvillier, B., Vieux, M., Pacaut-Troncin, M., Chalancon, B., Perez, A.F., ... & Durif-Bruckert, C. (2020). The SUPPORT-S protocol study: A postvention program for professionals after patient or user suicide. *Frontiers in Psychology*, *11*, 805.

Leavey, K., & Hawkins, R. (2017). Is cognitive behavioural therapy effective in reducing suicidal ideation and behaviour when delivered face-to-face or via e-health? A systematic review and meta-analysis. *Cognitive Behaviour Therapy*, *46*(5), 353–374.

Lee, D.J., Bryan, C.J., & Rudd, M.D. (2020). Longitudinal suicide ideation trajectories in a clinical trial of brief CBT for US military personnel recently discharged from psychiatric hospitalization. *Psychiatry Research*, *293*, 113335.

Lee, D.J., Kearns, J.C., Wisco, B.E., Green, J.D., Gradus, J.L., Sloan, D.M., ... & Marx, B.P. (2018). A longitudinal study of risk factors for suicide attempts among Operation Enduring Freedom and Operation Iraqi Freedom veterans. *Depression and Anxiety*, *35*(7), 609–618.

Leong, F.T., Leach, M.M., Yeh, C., & Chou, E. (2007). Suicide among Asian Americans: What do we know? What do we need to know? *Death Studies*, *31*(5), 417–434.

Levi-Belz, Y., Peleg, D., & Ifrah, K. (2022). An integrative psychological model of risk factors for suicidal ideation and behavior among Israeli LGBT individuals. *OMEGA-Journal of Death and Dying*, 00302228221087504.

Lewinsohn, P.M., Rohde, P., & Seeley, J.R. (1994). Psychosocial risk factors for future adolescent suicide attempts. *Journal of Consulting and Clinical Psychology*, *62*(2), 297.

Lewis, S. (2011). *Positive psychology at work: How positive leadership and appreciative inquiry create inspiring organizations*. John Wiley & Sons.

Lewis, D.C., Flores, A.R., Haider-Markel, D.P., Miller, P.R., & Taylor, J.K. (2022). Transitioning opinion? Assessing the dynamics of public attitudes toward transgender rights. *Public Opinion Quarterly*, *86*(2), 343–368.

Li, R., Cai, Y., Wang, Y., Gan, F., & Shi, R. (2016). Psychological pathway to suicidal ideation among men who have sex with men in Shanghai, China: A structural equation model. *Journal of Psychiatric Research, 83*, 203–210.

Li, H., Glecia, A., Kent-Wilkinson, A., Leidl, D., Kleib, M., & Risling, T. (2022). Transition of mental health service delivery to telepsychiatry in response to COVID-19: A literature review. *Psychiatric Quarterly, 93*(1), 181–197.

Li, Z., & Zhang, Z. (2012). Coping skills, mental disorders, and suicide among rural youths in China. *The Journal of Nervous and Mental Disease, 200*, 885–890.

Lim, J.S., Buckley, N.A., Chitty, K.M., Moles, R.J., & Cairns, R. (2021). Association between means restriction of poison and method-specific suicide rates: A systematic review. *JAMA Health Forum, 2*(10), e213042–e213042.

Lin, Y.T., Chen, C.C., Huang, C.C., Nishimori, K., & Hsu, K.S. (2017). Oxytocin stimulates hippocampal neurogenesis via oxytocin receptor expressed in CA3 pyramidal neurons. *Nature Communications, 8*, 1–16.

Lin, T., Heckman, T.G., & Anderson, T. (2022). The efficacy of synchronous teletherapy versus in-person therapy: A meta-analysis of randomized clinical trials. *Clinical Psychology: Science and Practice, 29*(2), 167.

Lindqvist, D., Isaksson, A., & Brundin, L. (2008). Salivary cortisol and suicidal behavior – A follow-up study. *Psychoneuroendocrinology, 33*(8), 1061–1068.

Linehan, M.M. (1993). *Cognitive-behavioral treatment of borderline personality disorder*. Guilford Publications.

Linehan, M.M., Armstrong, H.E., Suarez, A., Allmon, D., & Heard, H.L. (1991). Cognitive-behavioral treatment of chronically parasuicidal borderline patients. *Archives of General Psychiatry, 48*(12), 1060–1064.

Linehan, M.M., Comtois, K.A., Murray, A.M., Brown, M.Z., Gallop, R.J., Heard, H.L., … & Lindenboim, N. (2006). Two-year randomized controlled trial and follow-up of dialectical behavior therapy vs. therapy by experts for suicidal behaviors and borderline personality disorder. *Archives of General Psychiatry, 63*(7), 757–766.

Linehan, M.M., Goodstein, J.L., Nielsen, S.L., & Chiles, J.A. (1983). Reasons for staying alive when you are thinking of killing yourself: The reasons for living inventory. *Journal of Consulting and Clinical Psychology, 51*(2), 276.

Linehan, M.M., Korslund, K.E., Harned, M.S., Gallop, R.J., Lungu, A., Neacsiu, A.D., … & Murray-Gregory, A.M. (2015). Dialectical behavior therapy for high suicide risk in individuals with borderline personality disorder: A randomized clinical trial and component analysis. *JAMA Psychiatry, 72*(5), 475–482.

Linthicum, K.P., Schafer, K.M., & Ribeiro, J.D. (2019). Machine learning in suicide science: Applications and ethics. *Behavioral Sciences & the Law, 37*, 214–222.

Liston, C., McEwen, B.S., & Casey, B.J. (2009). Psychosocial stress reversibly disrupts prefrontal processing and attentional control. *Proceedings of the National Academy of Sciences, 106*(3), 912–917.

Liu, X., Gentzler, A.L., George, C.J., & Kovacs, M. (2009). Responses to depressed mood and suicide attempt in young adults with a history of childhood-onset mood disorder. *Journal of Clinical Psychiatry, 70*(5), 644.

Liu, X., & Tein, J.Y. (2005). Life events, psychopathology, and suicidal behavior in Chinese adolescents. *Journal of Affective Disorders, 86,* 195–203.

Liu, C.H., Wang, J.H., Weng, S.C., Cheng, Y.H., Yeh, M.K., Bai, M.Y., & Chang, J.C. (2018). Is heart failure associated with suicide risk? *Journal of Cardiac Failure, 24*(11), 795–800.

Lizardi, D., Dervic, K., Grunebaum, M.F., Burke, A., Mann, J.J., & Oquendo, M.A. (2008). The role of moral objections to suicide in the assessment of suicidal patients. *Journal of Psychiatric Research, 42*(10), 815–821.

Lohr, J.B., Chang, H., Sexton, M., & Palmer, B.W. (2020). Allostatic load and the cannabinoid system: Implications for the treatment of physiological abnormalities in post-traumatic stress disorder (PTSD). *CNS Spectrums 25,* 743–749.

Lopez, J.F., Vazquez, D.M., Chalmers, D.T., & Watson, S.J. (1997). Regulation of 5-HT receptors and the hypothalamic-pituitary-adrenal axis: Implications for the neurobiology of suicide. *Annals of the New York Academy of Sciences, 836*(1), 106–134.

Louzon, S.A., Bossarte, R., McCarthy, J.F., & Katz, I.R. (2016). Does suicidal ideation as measured by the PHQ-9 predict suicide among VA patients? *Psychiatric Services, 67*(5), 517–522.

Lucassen, P.J., Meerlo, P., Naylor, A.S., Van Dam, A.M., Dayer, A.G., Fuchs, E., ... & Czeh, B. (2010). Regulation of adult neurogenesis by stress, sleep disruption, exercise and inflammation: Implications for depression and antidepressant action. *European Neuropsychopharmacology, 20*(1), 1–17.

Luecken, L.J., Hagan, M.J., Sandler, I.N., Tein, J.Y., Ayers, T.S., & Wolchik, S.A. (2010). Cortisol levels six-years after participation in the Family Bereavement Program. *Psychoneuroendocrinology, 35,* 785–789.

Luethi, M., Meier, B., & Sandi, C. (2009). Stress effects on working memory, explicit memory, and implicit memory for neutral and emotional stimuli in healthy men. *Frontiers in Behavioral Neuroscience, 2,* 5.

Lunde, C.E., & Sieberg, C.B. (2020). Walking the tightrope: A proposed model of chronic pain and stress. *Frontiers in Neuroscience, 14,* 270.

Lupien, S.J., McEwen, B.S., Gunnar, M.R., & Heim, C. (2009). Effects of stress throughout the lifespan on the brain, behaviour and cognition. *Nature Reviews Neuroscience, 10,* 434–445.

Luthans, F., & Avolio, B.J. (2014). Brief summary of psychological capital and introduction to the special issue. *Journal of Leadership & Organizational Studies, 21*(2), 125–129.

Luthans, F., & Broad, J.D. (2022). Positive psychological capital to help combat the mental health fallout from the pandemic and VUCA environment. *Organizational Dynamics, 51*(2), 100817.

Luthans, F., & Youssef-Morgan, C.M. (2017). Psychological capital: An evidence-based positive approach. *Annual Review of Organizational Psychology and Organizational Behavior, 4,* 339–366.

Luthans, F., & Youssef-Morgan, C.M. (2021). Positive workplaces. In C.R. Snyder, S.J. Lopez, L.M. Edwards, & S.C. Marques (Eds.), *The Oxford handbook of positive psychology* (pp. 820–831). Oxford University Press.

Lytle, M.C., Silenzio, V.M., & Caine, E.D. (2016). Are there still too few suicides to generate public outrage? *JAMA Psychiatry, 73*(10), 1003–1004.

Ma, J., Batterham, P.J., Calear, A.L., & Han, J. (2016). A systematic review of the predictions of the Interpersonal–Psychological Theory of Suicidal Behavior. *Clinical Psychology Review, 46*, 34–45.

MacDonald, K., & Feifel, D. (2014). Oxytocin's role in anxiety: A critical appraisal. *Brain Research, 1580*, 22–56.

Mac Giollabhui, N., Nielsen, J., Seidman, S., Olino, T.M., Abramson, L.Y., & Alloy, L.B. (2018). The development of future orientation is associated with faster decline in hopelessness during adolescence. *Journal of Youth and Adolescence, 47*, 2129–2142.

Mackenzie, C.S., Reynolds, K., Cairney, J., Streiner, D.L., & Sareen, J. (2012). Disorder-specific mental health service use for mood and anxiety disorders: Associations with age, sex, and psychiatric comorbidity. *Depression and Anxiety, 29*(3), 234–242.

Macintyre, V.G., Mansell, W., Pratt, D., & Tai, S.J. (2021). The psychological pathway to suicide attempts: A strategy of control without awareness. *Frontiers in Psychology, 12*, 588683.

MacIsaac, M.B., Bugeja, L.C., & Jelinek, G.A. (2017). The association between exposure to interpersonal violence and suicide among women: A systematic review. *Australian and New Zealand Journal of Public Health, 41*(1), 61–69.

Maghbouleh, N., Schachter, A., & Flores, R.D. (2022). Middle Eastern and North African Americans may not be perceived, nor perceive themselves, to be White. *Proceedings of the National Academy of Sciences, 119*(7), e2117940119.

Malakouti, S.K., Rasouli, N., Rezaeian, M., Nojomi, M., Ghanbari, B., & Mohammadi, A.S. (2020). Effectiveness of self-help mobile telephone applications (apps) for suicide prevention: A systematic review. *Medical Journal of the Islamic Republic of Iran, 34*, 85.

Malberg, J.E., Eisch, A.J., Nestler, E.J., & Duman, R.S. (2000). Chronic antidepressant treatment increases neurogenesis in adult rat hippocampus. *Journal of Neuroscience, 20*, 9104–9110.

Malhi, G. S., Gessler, D., & Outhred, T. (2017). The use of lithium for the treatment of bipolar disorder: Recommendations from clinical practice guidelines. *Journal of Affective Disorders, 217*, 266–280.

Mallory, C., & Sears, B. (2020). *LGBT discrimination, subnational public policy, and law in the United States.* https://doi.org/10.1093/acrefore/9780190228637.013.1200.

Malone, K.M., Oquendo, M.A., Haas, G.L., Ellis, S.P., Li, S., & Mann, J.J. (2000). Protective factors against suicidal acts in major depression: Reasons for living. *American Journal of Psychiatry, 157*, 1084–1088.

Mangla, K., Hoffman, M.C., Trumpff, C., O'Grady, S., & Monk, C. (2019). Maternal self-harm deaths: An unrecognized and preventable outcome. *American Journal of Obstetrics and Gynecology, 221*(4), 295–303.

Mann, J.J., Apter, A., Bertolote, J., Beautrais, A., Currier, D., Haas, A., … & Hendin, H. (2005). Suicide prevention strategies: A systematic review. *JAMA, 294*(16), 2064–2074.

Mann, J.J., & Currier, D. (2007). A review of prospective studies of biologic predictors of suicidal behavior in mood disorders. *Archives of Suicide Research, 11*, 3–16.

Mann, J.J., Currier, D., Stanley, B., Oquendo, M.A., Amsel, L.V., & Ellis, S.P. (2006). Can biological tests assist prediction of suicide in mood disorders? *International Journal of Neuropsychopharmacology, 9*, 465–474.

Mann, J.J., & Michel, C.A. (2016). Prevention of firearm suicide in the United States: What works and what is possible? *American Journal of Psychiatry, 173*(10), 969–979.

Mann, J.J., Stanley, M., McBride, P.A., & McEwen, B.S. (1986). Increased serotonin2 and β-adrenergic receptor binding in the frontal cortices of suicide victims. *Archives of General Psychiatry, 43*, 954–959.

Mann, J.J., Waternaux, C., Haas, G.L., & Malone, K.M. (1999). Toward a clinical model of suicidal behavior in psychiatric patients. *American Journal of Psychiatry, 156*(2), 181–189.

Maussion, G., Yang, J., Yerko, V., Barker, P., Mechawar, N., Ernst, C., & Turecki, G. (2012). Regulation of a truncated form of tropomyosin-related kinase B (TrkB) by Hsa-miR-185* in frontal cortex of suicide completers. *PLoS One, 7*(6):e39301.

Markowitz, S., Chatterji, P., & Kaestner, R. (2003). Estimating the impact of alcohol policies on youth suicides. *Journal of Mental Health Policy and Economics, 6*(1), 37–46.

Martinengo, L., Van Galen, L., Lum, E., Kowalski, M., Subramaniam, M., & Car, J. (2019). Suicide prevention and depression apps' suicide risk assessment and management: A systematic assessment of adherence to clinical guidelines. *BMC Medicine, 17*(1), 1–12.

Martinez-Ales, G., Hernandez-Calle, D., Khauli, N., & Keyes, K.M. (2020). Why are suicide rates increasing in the United States? Towards a multilevel reimagination of suicide prevention. In E. Baca-Garcia (Ed.), *Behavioral neurobiology of suicide and self-harm. Current topics in behavioral neurosciences* (pp. 1–23). Springer.

Martínez-Alés, G., Jiang, T., Keyes, K.M., & Gradus, J.L. (2022). The recent rise of suicide mortality in the United States. *Annual Review of Public Health, 43*, 99–116.

Martínez-Martí, M.L., & Ruch, W. (2017). Character strengths predict resilience over and above positive affect, self-efficacy, optimism, social support, self-esteem, and life satisfaction. *The Journal of Positive Psychology, 12*(2), 110–119.

Masdrakis, V. G., & Baldwin, D. S. (2023). Prevention of suicide by clozapine in mental disorders: Systematic review. *European Neuropsychopharmacology, 69*, 4–23.

Maser, J.D., Akiskal, H.S., Schettler, P., Scheftner, W., Mueller, T., Endicott, J., … & Clayton, P. (2002). Can temperament identify affectively ill patients who engage in lethal or near-lethal suicidal behavior? A 14-year prospective study. *Suicide and Life-Threatening Behavior, 32*(1), 10–32.

Matarazzo, B.B., Homaifar, B.Y., & Wortzel, H.S. (2014). Therapeutic risk management of the suicidal patient: Safety planning. *Journal of Psychiatric Practice, 20*(3), 220–224.

Mato, S., Pilar-Cuéllar, F., Valdizán, E.M., González-Maeso, J., Rodríguez-Puertas, R., Meana, J., Sallés, J., … & Pazos, Á. (2018). Selective up-regulation of cannabinoid CB1 receptor coupling to Go-proteins in suicide victims with mood disorders. *Biochemical Pharmacology, 157*, 258–265.

Matsubayashi, T., & Ueda, M. (2012). Government partisanship and human well-being. *Social Indicators Research*, 107, 127–148.

Mattson, M.P., Maudsley, S., & Martin, B. (2004). BDNF and 5-HT: A dynamic duo in age-related neuronal plasticity and neurodegenerative disorders. *Trends in Neurosciences, 27*(10), 589–594.

Mayer, L., Rüsch, N., Frey, L.M., Nadorff, M.R., Drapeau, C.W., Sheehan, L., & Oexle, N. (2020). Anticipated suicide stigma, secrecy, and suicidality among suicide attempt survivors. *Suicide and Life-Threatening Behavior, 50*(3), 706–713.

McDaid, D., Bonin, E., Park, A., Hegerl, U., Arensman, E., Kopp, M., & Gusmao, R. (2010). Making the case for investing in suicide prevention interventions: Estimating the economic impact of suicide and non-fatal self-harm events. *Injury Prevention, 16*(Suppl 1), A257–A258.

McDaid C., Trowman R., Golder S., Hawton K., & Sowden A. (2008). Interventions for people bereaved through suicide: Systematic review. *The British Journal of Psychiatry, 193*(6), 438–443.

McEwen, B.S. (1998). Stress, adaptation, and disease: Allostasis and allostatic load. *Annals of the New York Academy of Sciences, 840*, 33–44.

McEwen, B.S. (2000). The neurobiology of stress: From serendipity to clinical relevance. *Brain Research, 886*, 172–89.

McEwen, B.S. (2003). Mood disorders and allostatic load. *Biological Psychiatry, 54*, 200–207.

McEwen, B.S. (2004). Protection and damage from acute and chronic stress: Allostasis and allostatic overload and relevance to the pathophysiology of psychiatric disorders. *Annals of the New York Academy of Sciences, 1032*, 1–7.

McEwen, B.S. (2007). Physiology and neurobiology of stress and adaptation: Central role of the brain. *Physiological Reviews, 87*(3), 873–904.

McEwen, B.S. (2016). Central role of the brain in stress and adaptation: Allostasis, biological embedding, and cumulative change. In G. Fink (Ed.), *Stress: Concepts, cognition, emotion, and behavior* (pp. 39–55). Academic Press.

McEwen, B.S. (2017). Neurobiological and systemic effects of chronic stress. *Chronic Stress, 1*, 1–17.

McEwen, C.A. (2022). Connecting the biology of stress, allostatic load and epigenetics to social structures and processes. *Neurobiology of Stress, 17*, 100426.

McEwen, B.S., Gray, J.D., & Nasca, C. (2015). Recognizing resilience: Learning from the effects of stress on the brain. *Neurobiology of Stress, 1*, 1–11.

McEwen, C.A., & McEwen, B.S. (2017). Social structure, adversity, toxic stress, and intergenerational poverty: An early childhood model. *Annual Review of Sociology, 43*, 445–472.

McEwen, B.S., & Morrison, J.H. (2013). The brain on stress: Vulnerability and plasticity of the prefrontal cortex over the life course. *Neuron, 79*(1), 16–29.

McEwen, B.S., & Stellar, E. (1993). Stress and the individual: Mechanisms leading to disease. *Archives of Internal Medicine, 153*(18), 2093–2101.

McEwen, B.S., & Wingfield, J.C. (2003). The concept of allostasis in biology and biomedicine. *Hormones and Behavior, 43*, 2–15.

McGhee, L.M. (2020). *Mitigating suicide risk post-discharge from inpatient crisis stabilization: Safety planning intervention* (Doctoral dissertation, University of Missouri-Saint Louis).

McGill, K., Bhullar, N., Batterham, P.J., Carrandi, A., Wayland, S., & Maple, M. (2023). Key issues, challenges, and preferred supports for those bereaved by suicide: Insights from postvention experts. *Death Studies, 47*(5), 624.

McGinn, M.M., Roussev, M.S., Shearer, E.M., McCann, R.A., Rojas, S.M., & Felker, B.L. (2019). Recommendations for using clinical video telehealth with patients at high risk for suicide. *Psychiatric Clinics, 42*(4), 587–595.

McGowan, P.O., Sasaki, A., D'Alessio, A.C., Dymov, S., Labonte, B., Szyf, M., & Meaney, M.J. (2009). Epigenetic regulation of the glucocorticoid receptor in human brain associates with childhood abuse. *Nature Neuroscience, 12*, 342–348.

McHugh, C.M., & Large, M.M. (2020). Can machine-learning methods really help predict suicide? *Current Opinion in Psychiatry, 33*(4), 369–374.

McKenzie, K., Van Os, J., Samele, C., Van Horn, E., Tattan, T., & Murray, R. (2003). Suicide and attempted suicide among people of Caribbean origin with psychosis living in the UK. *The British Journal of Psychiatry, 183*(1), 40–44.

McKoy, J. (2022). *U.S. suicide rates are stagnant or rising among many groups, despite overall national decline.* Available at: www.bu.edu/sph/news/articles/2022/us-suicides-are-stagnant-or-on-the-rise-among-many-groups/.

McLeavey, B.C., Daly, R.J., Ludgate, J.W., & Murray, C.M. (1994). Interpersonal Problem-Solving skills training in the treatment of self-poisoning patients. *Suicide and Life-Threatening Behavior, 24*(4), 382–394.

McMain, S.F., Guimond, T., Barnhart, R., Habinski, L., & Streiner, D.L. (2017). A randomized trial of brief dialectical behaviour therapy skills training in suicidal patients suffering from borderline disorder. *Acta Psychiatrica Scandinavica, 135*(2), 138–148.

McMain, S.F., Links, P.S., Gnam, W.H., Guimond, T., Cardish, R.J., Korman, L., & Streiner, D.L. (2009). A randomized trial of dialectical behavior therapy versus general psychiatric management for borderline personality disorder. *American Journal of Psychiatry, 166*(12), 1365–1374.

Meerwijk, E.L., Parekh, A., Oquendo, M.A., Allen, I.E., Franck, L.S., & Lee, K.A. (2016). Direct versus indirect psychosocial and behavioural interventions to prevent suicide and suicide attempts: A systematic review and meta-analysis. *The Lancet Psychiatry, 3*(6), 544–554.

Melhem, N.M., Keilp, J.G., Porta, G., Oquendo, M.A., Burke, A., Stanley, B., ... & Brent, D.A. (2016). Blunted HPA axis activity in suicide attempters compared to those at high risk for suicidal behavior. *Neuropsychopharmacology, 41*(6), 1447–1456.

Melia, R., Francis, K., Hickey, E., Bogue, J., Duggan, J., O'Sullivan, M., & Young, K. (2020). Mobile health technology interventions for suicide prevention: Systematic review. *JMIR mHealth and uHealth*, *8*(1), e12516.

Meltzer, H.Y., Alphs, L., Green, A.I., Altamura, A.C., Anand, R., Bertoldi, A., … & InterSePT Study Group. (2003). Clozapine treatment for suicidality in schizophrenia: International suicide prevention trial (InterSePT). *Archives of General Psychiatry*, *60*(1), 82–91.

Melvin, G.A., Gresham, D., Beaton, S., Coles, J., Tonge, B.J., Gordon, M.S., & Stanley, B. (2019). Evaluating the feasibility and effectiveness of an Australian safety planning smartphone application: A pilot study within a tertiary mental health service. *Suicide and Life-Threatening Behavior*, *49*(3), 846–858.

Memiah, P., Biadgilign, S., Kuhlman, J., Cook, C., Mburia, P., Kingori, C., … & Hawkins, M. (2022). Allostatic load, single, and dual chronic conditions: Evidence from the National Health and Nutrition Examination Survey. *Metabolic Syndrome and Related Disorders*, *20*(2), 104–113.

Méndez-Bustos, P., Calati, R., Rubio-Ramírez, F., Olié, E., Courtet, P., & Lopez-Castroman, J. (2019). Effectiveness of psychotherapy on suicidal risk: A systematic review of observational studies. *Frontiers in Psychology*, *10*, 277.

Menninger, K.A. (1938; 1989). *Man against himself. Deutsch: Selbstzerstörung. Psychoanalyse des Selbstmordes*. Frankfurt am.

Merali, Z., Du, L., Hrdina, P., Palkovits, M., Faludi, G., Poulter, M.O., & Anisman, H. (2004). Dysregulation in the suicide brain: mRNA expression of corticotropin-releasing hormone receptors and GABAA receptor subunits in frontal cortical brain region. *Journal of Neuroscience, 24*, 1478–1485.

Mewton, L., & Andrews, G. (2015). Cognitive behaviour therapy via the internet for depression: A useful strategy to reduce suicidal ideation. *Journal of Affective Disorders, 170*, 78–84.

Meyer, I.H., & Frost, D.M. (2013). Minority stress and the health of sexual minorities. In C.J. Patterson & A.R. D'Augelli (Eds.), *Handbook of psychology and sexual orientation* (pp. 252–266). Oxford University Press.

Meyer, I.H., Russell, S.T., Hammack, P.L., Frost, D.M., & Wilson, B.D. (2021). Minority stress, distress, and suicide attempts in three cohorts of sexual minority adults: A U.S. probability sample. *PLoS One*, *16*(3), e0246827.

Michel, K. (2021). Suicide models and treatment models are separate entities. What does it mean for clinical suicide prevention? *International Journal of Environmental Research and Public Health*, *18*(10), 5301.

Micol, V.J., Prouty, D., & Czyz, E.K. (2022). Enhancing motivation and self-efficacy for safety plan use: Incorporating motivational interviewing strategies in a brief safety planning intervention for adolescents at risk for suicide. *Psychotherapy*, *59*(2), 174.

Miller, J.N., & Black, D.W. (2020). Bipolar disorder and suicide: A review. *Current Psychiatry Reports*, *22*, 1–10.

Miller, G.E., Chen, E., & Zhou, E.S. (2007). If it goes up, must it come down? Chronic stress and the hypothalamic-pituitary-adrenocortical axis in humans. *Psychological Bulletin*, *133*, 25–45.

Miller, C.L., & Druss, B. (2001). Datapoints: Suicide and access to care. *Psychiatric Services, 52*(12), 1566–1566.

Miller, H.N., LaFave, S., Marineau, L., Stephens, J., & Thorpe Jr., R.J. (2021). The impact of discrimination on allostatic load in adults: An integrative review of literature. *Journal of Psychosomatic Research*, 110434.

Millner, A.J., Robinaugh, D.J., & Nock, M.K. (2020). Advancing the understanding of suicide: The need for formal theory and rigorous descriptive research. *Trends in Cognitive Sciences, 24*(9), 704–716.

Milner, A., Page, A., & LaMontagne, A.D. (2013). Long-term unemployment and suicide: A systematic review and meta-analysis. *PLoS ONE, 8*(1), e51333.

Milner, A., Page, A., & LaMontagne, A.D. (2014). Cause and effect in studies on unemployment, mental health and suicide: A meta-analytic and conceptual review. *Psychological Medicine, 44*(5), 909–917.

Milner, A., Scovelle, A.J., Hewitt, B., Maheen, H., Ruppanner, L., & King, T.L. (2020). Shifts in gender equality and suicide: A panel study of changes over time in 87 countries. *Journal of Affective Disorders, 276*, 495–500.

Miranda-Mendizabal, A., Castellví, P., Parés-Badell, O., Alayo, I., Almenara, J., Alonso, I., … & Alonso, J. (2019). Gender differences in suicidal behavior in adolescents and young adults: systematic review and meta-analysis of longitudinal studies. *International Journal of Public Health, 64*, 265–283.

Minoiu, C., & Andres, A.R. (2008). The effect of public spending on suicide: Evidence from U.S. state data. *The Journal of Socio-Economics, 37*(1), 237–261.

Mirkovic, B., Labelle, R., Guilé, J.M., Belloncle, V., Bodeau, N., Knafo, A., … & Gérardin, P. (2015). Coping skills among adolescent suicide attempters: Results of a multisite study. *Canadian Journal of Psychiatry, 60*(2 Suppl 1), S37.

Miranda, R., Scott, M., Hicks, R., Wilcox, H.C., Munfakh, J.L.H., & Shaffer, D. (2008). Suicide attempt characteristics, diagnoses, and future attempts: Comparing multiple attempters to single attempters and ideators. *Journal of the American Academy of Child & Adolescent Psychiatry, 47*(1), 32–40.

Miron, O., Yu, K.H., Wilf-Miron, R., & Kohane, I.S. (2019). Suicide rates among adolescents and young adults in the United States, 2000–2017. *JAMA, 321*(23), 2362–2364.

Misiak, B., Kotowicz, K., Loska, O., Stramecki, F., Beszłej, J.A., Samochowiec, J., … & Piotrowski, P. (2018). Decreased use of active coping styles contributes to elevated allostatic load index in first-episode psychosis. *Psychoneuroendocrinology, 96*, 166–172.

Mo, P.K.H., Ko, T.T., & Xin, M.Q. (2018). School-based gatekeeper training programmes in enhancing gatekeepers' cognitions and behaviours for adolescent suicide prevention: A systematic review. *Child and Adolescent Psychiatry and Mental Health, 12*, 29.

Mohatt, N.V. (2014). Forward to ecological description of a multi-level community-based cultural intervention: Reflections on culturally-situated participatory research. *American Journal of Community Psychology, 54*, 81–82 (2014).

Mohatt, N.V., Kreisel, C.J., Hoffberg, A.S., & Beehler, S.J. (2021). A systematic review of factors impacting suicide risk among rural adults in the United States. *The Journal of Rural Health, 37*(3), 565–575.

Mollan, K.R., Tierney, C., Hellwege, J.N., Eron, J.J., Hudgens, M.G., Gulick, R.M., ... & AIDS Clinical Trials Group. (2017). Race/ethnicity and the pharmacogenetics of reported suicidality with efavirenz among clinical trials participants. *The Journal of Infectious Diseases, 216*(5), 554–564.

Monnat, S.M. (2020). Opioid crisis in the rural U.S. In J. Glick, S. McHale, & V. King (Eds.), Rural families and communities in the United States. *National symposium on family issues* (vol 10, pp. 117–143). Springer.

Monte, L.M., & Shin, H.B. (2022). *20.6 million people in the US identify as Asian, Native Hawaiian or Pacific Islander.* www.census.gov/library/stories/2022/05/aanhpi-population-diverse-geographically-dispersed.html#:~:text=20.6%20Million%20People%20in%20the,Native%20Hawaiian%20or%20Pacific%20Islander&text=There%20are%2020.6%20million%20people,according%20to%20the%202020%20Census.

Morres, I.D., Hatzigeorgiadis, A., Stathi, A., Comoutos, N., Arpin-Cribbie, C., Krommidas, C., & Theodorakis, Y. (2019). Aerobic exercise for adult patients with major depressive disorder in mental health services: A systematic review and meta-analysis. *Depression and Anxiety, 36*(1), 39–53.

Mueller, A.S., & Abrutyn, S. (2015). Suicidal disclosures among friends: Using social network data to understand suicide contagion. *Journal of Health and Social Behavior, 56*(1), 131–148.

Mueller, A.S., & Abrutyn, S. (2016). Adolescents under pressure: A new Durkheimian framework for understanding adolescent suicide in a cohesive community. *American Sociological Review, 81*(5), 877–899.

Mueller, A.S., Abrutyn, S., Pescosolido, B., & Diefendorf, S. (2021). The social roots of suicide: Theorizing how the external social world matters to suicide and suicide prevention. *Frontiers in Psychology, 12*(763), 1–14.

Mueller, A.S., Abrutyn, S., & Stockton, C. (2015). Can social ties be harmful? Examining the spread of suicide in early adulthood. *Sociological Perspectives, 58*(2), 204–222.

Müller, M.B., Zimmermann, S., Sillaber, I., Hagemeyer, T.P., Deussing, J.M., Timpl, P., ... & Holsboer, F. (2003). Limbic corticotropin-releasing hormone receptor 1 mediates anxiety-related behavior and hormonal adaptation to stress. *Nature Neuroscience, 6*(10), 1100–1107.

Mustanski, B., & Liu, R.T. (2013). A longitudinal study of predictors of suicide attempts among lesbian, gay, bisexual, and transgender youth. *Archives of Sexual Behavior, 42*, 437–448.

Myers, W., Turanovic, J.J., Lloyd, K.M., & Pratt, T.C. (2020). The victimization of LGBTQ students at school: A meta-analysis. *Journal of School Violence, 19*(4), 421–432.

Naghavi, M. (2019). Global, regional, and national burden of suicide mortality 1990 to 2016: Systematic analysis for the Global Burden of Disease Study 2016. *BMJ, 364*, l94.

Nanayakkara, S., Misch, D., Chang, L., & Henry, D. (2013). Depression and exposure to suicide predict suicide attempt. *Depression and Anxiety, 30*(10), 991–996.

National Academies of Sciences, Engineering, and Medicine. (2021). *High and rising mortality rates among working-age adults.* The National Academies Press.

National Action Alliance for Suicide Prevention. (2015). *Responding to grief, trauma, and distress after a suicide: U.S. National Guidelines.* www.sprc.org/resources-programs/responding-grief-trauma-and-distress-after-suicide-us-national-guidelines.

NCAI Policy Research Center. (2016). *Disaggregating American Indian & Alaska Native data: A review of literature.* National Congress of American Indians.

Nearchou, F., Flinn, C., Niland, R., Subramaniam, S.S., & Hennessy, E. (2020). Exploring the impact of COVID-19 on mental health outcomes in children and adolescents: A systematic review. *International Journal of Environmental Research and Public Health, 17*(22), 8479.

Neeleman, J., de Graaf, R., & Vollebergh, W. (2004). The suicidal process: Prospective comparison between early and later stages. *Journal of Affective Disorders, 82*(1), 43–52.

Neeleman, J., Halpern, D., Leon, D., & Lewis, G. (1997). Tolerance of suicide, religion and suicide rates: An ecological and individual study in 19 Western countries. *Psychological Medicine, 27*(5), 1165–1171.

Nemeroff, C.B., Widerlöv, E., Bissette, G., Walleus, H., Karlsson, I., Eklund, K., ... & Vale, W. (1984). Elevated concentrations of CSF corticotropin-releasing factor-like immunoreactivity in depressed patients. *Science, 226*(4680), 1342–1344.

Nestadt, P.S., Triplett, P., Fowler, D.R., & Mojtabai, R. (2017). Urban–rural differences in suicide in the state of Maryland: The role of firearms. *American Journal of Public Health, 107*(10), 1548–1553.

Neufeld, E., & O'Rourke, N. (2009). Impulsivity and hopelessness as predictors of suicide-related ideation among older adults. *The Canadian Journal of Psychiatry, 54*(10), 684–692.

Newman, R. (2005). APA's resilience initiative. *Professional Psychology: Research and Practice, 36*(3), 227.

Nezu, A.M., & Nezu, C.M. (2001). Problem solving therapy. *Journal of Psychotherapy Integration, 11*(2), 187.

Ng, Q.X., Yong, B.Z.J., Ho, C.Y.X., Lim, D.Y., & Yeo, W.S. (2018). Early life sexual abuse is associated with increased suicide attempts: An update meta-analysis. *Journal of Psychiatric Research, 99*, 129–141.

Nicholas, A., Haregu, T., Henderson, C., & Armstrong, G. (2022). Suicide stigma measures: A scoping review. *Journal of Affective Disorders, 321*, 114–125.

Niederhoffer, K.G., & Pennebaker, J.W. (2009). Sharing one's story: On the benefits of writing or talking about emotional experience. In S.J. Lopez & C.R. Snyder (Eds.), *Oxford handbook of positive psychology* (pp. 621–632). Oxford University Press.

Niederkrotenthaler, T., Braun, M., Pirkis, J., Till, B., Stack, S., Sinyor, M., ... & Spittal, M.J. (2020). Association between suicide reporting in the media and suicide: Systematic review and meta-analysis. *BMJ, 368*.

Niederkrotenthaler, T., Reidenberg, D.J., Till, B., & Gould, M.S. (2014). Increasing help-seeking and referrals for individuals at risk for suicide by decreasing stigma: The role of mass media. *American Journal of Preventive Medicine, 47*(3), S235–S243.

Niederkrotenthaler, T., Stack, S., Till, B., Sinyor, M., Pirkis, J., Garcia, D., ... & Tran, U.S. (2019). Association of increased youth suicides in the United States with the release of "13 Reasons Why." *JAMA Psychiatry*, *76*(9), 933–940.

Nietzsche, F. (1964). Thus spoke Zarathustra. tr. Thomas Common. In O. Levy (Ed.), *The complete works of Friedrich Nietzsche* (pp. 82–85). Russell & Russell, Inc.

NIMH. (2022). *Suicide.* www.nimh.nih.gov/health/statistics/suicide#:~:text= Figure%202%20shows%20the%20crude,older%20(40.5%20per%20100% 2C000).

Nock, M.K., Borges, G., Bromet, E.J., Alonso, J., Angermeyer, M., Beautrais, A., ... & Williams, D. (2008). Cross-national prevalence and risk factors for suicidal ideation, plans and attempts. *The British Journal of Psychiatry*, *192*(2), 98–105.

Nock, M.K., Green, J.G., Hwang, I., McLaughlin, K.A., Sampson, N.A., Zaslavsky, A.M., & Kessler, R.C. (2013). Prevalence, correlates, and treatment of lifetime suicidal behavior among adolescents: Results from the National Comorbidity Survey Replication Adolescent Supplement. *JAMA Psychiatry*, *70*(3), 300–310.

Nock, M.K., Millner, A.J, Joiner, T.E., Gutierrez, P.M., Han, G., Hwang, I., ... & Kessler, R.C. (2018). Risk factors for the transition from suicide ideation to suicide attempt: Results from the Army Study to Assess Risk and Resilience in Servicemembers (Army STARRS). *Journal of Abnormal Psychology*, *127*(2), 139.

Notredame, C.E., Chawky, N., Beauchamp, G., Vaiva, G., & Séguin, M. (2020). Life trajectories towards suicide: Developmental role and specificities of adolescence. *bioRxiv* 2020.01.18.911230.

Novak, S. (2022). Suicides among black people may be vastly undercounted. *Scientific American.* www.scientificamerican.com/article/suicides-among-black-people-may-be-vastly-undercounted/.

Novella, J.K., Ng, K.M., & Samuolis, J. (2022). A comparison of online and in-person counseling outcomes using solution-focused brief therapy for college students with anxiety. *Journal of American College Health*, *70*(4), 1161–1168.

Nrugham, L., Holen, A., & Sund, A.M. (2012). Suicide attempters and repeaters: Depression and coping: A prospective study of early adolescents followed up as young adults. *The Journal of Nervous and Mental Disease, 200,* 197–203.

Nugent, A.C., Ballard, E.D., Park, L.T., & Zarate, C.A. (2019). Research on the pathophysiology, treatment, and prevention of suicide: Practical and ethical issues. *BMC Psychiatry*, *19*(1), 1–12.

Nugent, K.L., Chiappelli, J., Rowland, L.M., & Hong, L.E. (2015). Cumulative stress pathophysiology in schizophrenia as indexed by allostatic load. *Psychoneuroendocrinology*, *60*, 120–129.

Nuij, C., van Ballegooijen, W., De Beurs, D., Juniar, D., Erlangsen, A., Portzky, G., ... & Riper, H. (2021). Safety planning-type interventions for suicide prevention: Meta-analysis. *The British Journal of Psychiatry*, *219*(2), 419–426.

Nuij, C., van Ballegooijen, W., Ruwaard, J., De Beurs, D., Mokkenstorm, J., van Duijn, E., ... & Kerkhof, A. (2018). Smartphone-based safety planning and self-monitoring for suicidal patients: Rationale and study protocol of the CASPAR (Continuous Assessment for Suicide Prevention and Research) study. *Internet Interventions, 13*, 16–23.

Nuño, V., Siu, A., Deol, N., & Juster, R.P. (2019). Osteopathic manipulative treatment for allostatic load lowering. *Journal of Osteopathic Medicine, 119*, 646–654.

O'Connor, D.B., Green, J.A., Ferguson, E., O'Carroll, R.E., & O'Connor, R.C. (2017). Cortisol reactivity and suicidal behavior: Investigating the role of hypothalamic-pituitary-adrenal axis responses to stress in suicide attempters and ideators. *Psychoneuroendocrinology, 75*, 183–191.

O'Connor, D.B., Ferguson, E., Green, J., O'Carroll, R.E., & O'Connor, R.C. (2016). Cortisol and suicidal behavior: A meta-analysis. *Psychoneuroendocrinology, 63*, 370–379.

O'Connor, R.C., & Kirtley, O.J. (2018). The integrated motivational–volitional model of suicidal behaviour. *Philosophical Transactions of the Royal Society B: Biological Sciences*, 373 (1754), 20170268., 1–10

O'Connor, S.S., Mcclay, M.M., Choudhry, S., Shields, A.D., Carlson, R., Alonso, Y., … & Nicolson, S.E. (2020). Pilot randomized clinical trial of the Teachable Moment Brief Intervention for hospitalized suicide attempt survivors. *General Hospital Psychiatry, 63*, 111–118.

Office of Management and Budget. (1997). Revisions to the standards for the classification of federal data on race and ethnicity. *Federal Register, 62*(210), 58781–58790.

Office of Minority Health. (2021). *Mental and behavioral health – Hispanics.* Available at: https://minorityhealth.hhs.gov/omh/browse.aspx?lvl=4&lvlid=69#1.

Offidani, E., & Ruini, C. (2012). Psychobiological correlates of allostatic overload in a healthy population. *Brain, Behavior, and Immunity, 26*(2), 284–291.

Oh, H., Du, J., Smith, L., & Koyanagi, A. (2022). Mental health differences between multiracial and monoracial college students in the United States: Emerging racial disparities. *International Journal of Social Psychiatry,* 00207640221135817.

Okşak, Y., Koyuncu, C., & Yilmaz, R. (2021). *The impact of macroeconomic variables on suicides: Are they related in the long-run?* Available at https://papers.ssrn.com/sol3/papers.cfm?abstract_id=3987989.

Olfson, M., Marcus, S.C., & Bridge, J.A. (2014). Focusing suicide prevention on periods of high risk. *JAMA, 311*(11), 1107–1108.

Oliffe, J.L., Broom, A., Rossnagel, E., Kelly, M.T., Affleck, W., & Rice, S.M. (2020). Help-seeking prior to male suicide: Bereaved men perspectives. *Social Science & Medicine, 261*, 113173.

Ong, A.D., Bergeman, C.S., Bisconti, T.L., & Wallace, K.A. (2006). Psychological resilience, positive emotions, and successful adaptation to stress in later life. *Journal of Personality and Social Psychology, 91*(4), 730–749.

Ong, E., & Thompson, C. (2019). The importance of coping and emotion regulation in the occurrence of suicidal behavior. *Psychological Reports, 122*(4), 1192–1210.

Ono, Y., Sakai, A., Otsuka, K., Uda, H., Oyama, H., Ishizuka, N., ... & Yonemoto, N. (2013). Effectiveness of a multimodal community intervention program to prevent suicide and suicide attempts: A quasi-experimental study. *PLoS One, 8*(10), e74902.

Ostiguy, C.S., Ellenbogen, M.A., Walker, C.D., Walker, E.F., & Hodgins, S. (2011). Sensitivity to stress among the offspring of parents with bipolar disorder: A study of daytime cortisol levels. *Psychological Medicine, 41*(11), 2447–2457.

Oquendo, M.A., Dragatsi, D., Harkavy-Friedman, J., Dervic, K., Currier, D., Burke, A.K., ... & Mann, J.J. (2005). Protective factors against suicidal behavior in Latinos. *The Journal of Nervous and Mental Disease, 193*(7), 438–443.

O'Toole, M.S., Arendt, M.B., & Pedersen, C.M. (2019). Testing an app-assisted treatment for suicide prevention in a randomized controlled trial: Effects on suicide risk and depression. *Behavior Therapy, 50*(2), 421–429.

Owens, D., Horrocks, J., & House, A. (2002). Fatal and non-fatal repetition of self-harm: Systematic review. *British Journal of Psychiatry, 181*, 193–199.

Oyesanya, M., Lopez-Morinigo, J., & Dutta, R. (2015). Systematic review of suicide in economic recession. *World J Psychiatry, 5*(2), 243–254.

Ozanne-Smith, J., Ashby, K., Newstead, S., Stathakis, V.Z., & Clapperton, A. (2004). Firearm related deaths: The impact of regulatory reform. *Injury Prevention, 10*(5), 280–286.

Padesky, C.A., & Mooney, K.A. (2012). Strengths-based cognitive–behavioural therapy: A four-step model to build resilience. *Clinical Psychology & Psychotherapy, 19*(4), 283–290.

Page, A., Morrell, S., & Taylor, R. (2002). Suicide and political regime in New South Wales and Australia during the 20th century. *Journal of Epidemiology & Community Health, 56*(10), 766–772.

Palladino, C.L., Singh, V., Campbell, J., Flynn, H., & Gold, K. (2011). Homicide and suicide during the perinatal period: Findings from the National Violent Death Reporting System. *Obstetrics and Gynecology, 118*(5), 1056.

Pandey, G.N., Dwivedi, Y., Rizavi, H.S., Ren, X., Pandey, S.C., Pesold, C., & Tamminga, C.A. (2002). Higher expression of serotonin 5-HT2A receptors in the postmortem brains of teenage suicide victims. *American Journal of Psychiatry, 159*(3), 419–429.

Pandey, G.N., Ren, X., Rizavi, H.S., Conley, R.R., Roberts, R.C., & Dwivedi, Y. (2008). Brain-derived neurotrophic factor and tyrosine kinase B receptor signalling in post-mortem brain of teenage suicide victims. *The International Journal of Neuropsychopharmacology, 11*(8), 1047–1061.

Parcover, J., Mays, S., & McCarthy, A. (2015). Implementing a public health approach to addressing mental health needs in a university setting: Lessons and challenges. *Journal of College Student Psychotherapy, 29*(3), 197–210.

Park, S.M. (2019). Effects of work conditions on suicidal ideation among middle-aged adults in South Korea. *International Journal of Social Psychiatry, 65*(2), 144–150.

Parker, K., Menasce Horowitz, J., Igielnik, R., Oliphant, J.B., & Brown, A. (2017). *America's complex relationship with guns.* Pew Research Center,

www.pewresearch.org/social-trends/wp-content/uploads/sites/3/2017/06/
Guns-Report-FOR-WEBSITE-PDF-6-21.pdf.

Parker, K.J., Schatzberg, A.F., & Lyons, D.M. (2003). Neuroendocrine aspects of hypercortisolism in major depression. *Hormones and Behavior, 43*(1), 60–66.

Pascoe, M.C., Thompson, D.R., & Ski, C.F. (2017). Yoga, mindfulness-based stress reduction and stress-related physiological measures: A meta-analysis. *Psychoneuroendocrinology, 86,* 152–168.

Patel, M., Patel, S., Hardy, D.W., Benzies, B.J., & Tare, V. (2006). Should electroconvulsive therapy be an early consideration for suicidal patients?. *The Journal of ECT, 22*(2), 113–115.

Patten, M., Carmichael, H., Moore, A., & Velopulos, C. (2022). Circumstances of suicide among lesbian, gay, bisexual and transgender individuals. *Journal of Surgical Research, 270,* 522–529.

Patten, M., Carmichael, H., Moore, A., & Velopulos, C. (2022). Circumstances of suicide among lesbian, gay, bisexual and transgender individuals. *Journal of Surgical Research, 270,* 522–529.

Paul, J.P., Catania, J., Pollack, L., Moskowitz, J., Canchola, J., Mills, T., ... & Stall, R. (2002). Suicide attempts among gay and bisexual men: Lifetime prevalence and antecedents. *American Journal of Public Health, 92*(8), 1338–1345.

Pelton, M., Ciarletta, M., Wisnousky, H., Lazzara, N., Manglani, M., Ba, D.M., ... & Ssentongo, P. (2021). Rates and risk factors for suicidal ideation, suicide attempts and suicide deaths in persons with HIV: A systematic review and meta-analysis. *General Psychiatry, 34*(2), e100247.

Peltzman, T., Shiner, B., & Watts, B.V. (2020). Effects of electroconvulsive therapy on short-term suicide mortality in a risk-matched patient population. *The Journal of ECT, 36*(3), 187–192.

Perlis, R.H., & Fihn, S.D. (2020). Hard truths about suicide prevention. *JAMA Network Open, 3*(10), e2022713.

Perlman, W.R., Webster, M.J., Herman, M.M., Kleinman, J.E., & Weickert, C.S. (2007). Age-related differences in glucocorticoid receptor mRNA levels in the human brain. *Neurobiology of Aging, 28*(3), 447–458.

Perepletchikova, F., Axelrod, S.R., Kaufman, J., Rounsaville, B.J., Douglas-Palumberi, H., & Miller, A.L. (2011). Adapting Dialectical Behaviour Therapy for children: Towards a new research agenda for paediatric suicidal and non-suicidal self-injurious behaviours. *Child and Adolescent Mental Health, 16*(2), 116–121.

Perez-Rodriguez, M.M., Baca-Garcia, E., Oquendo, M.A., Wang, S., Wall, M.M., Liu, S.M., & Blanco, C. (2014). Relationship between acculturation, discrimination, and suicidal ideation and attempts among US Hispanics in the National Epidemiologic Survey of Alcohol and Related Conditions. *The Journal of Clinical Psychiatry, 75*(4), 17272.

Perron, S., Burrows, S., Fournier, M., Perron, P.A., & Ouellet, F. (2013). Installation of a bridge barrier as a suicide prevention strategy in Montréal, Québec, Canada. *American Journal of Public Health, 103*(7), 1235–1239.

Peters, K., Staines, A., Cunningham, C., & Ramjan, L. (2015). The lifekeeper memory quilt: Evaluation of a suicide postvention program. *Death Studies*, *39*(6), 353–359.

Peterson, C., Sussell, A., Li, J., Schumacher, P.K., Yeoman, K., & Stone, D.M. (2020). Suicide rates by industry and occupation – National Violent Death Reporting System, 32 states, 2016. *Morbidity and Mortality Weekly Report*, *69*(3), 57.

Phillips, J.A., Robin, A.V., Nugent, C.N., & Idler, E.L. (2010). Understanding recent changes in suicide rates among the middle-aged: Period or cohort effects? *Public Health Reports*, *125*(5), 680–688.

Pierre, J.M. (2015). Culturally sanctioned suicide: Euthanasia, seppuku, and terrorist martyrdom. *World Journal of Psychiatry*, *5*(1), 4–14.

Piotrowski, P., Kotowicz, K., Rymaszewska, J., Beszłej, J.A., Plichta, P., Samochowiec, J., … & Misiak, B. (2019). Allostatic load index and its clinical correlates at various stages of psychosis. *Schizophrenia Research*, *210*, 73–80.

Pirkis, J., San Too, L., Spittal, M.J., Krysinska, K., Robinson, J., & Cheung, Y.T.D. (2015). Interventions to reduce suicides at suicide hotspots: A systematic review and meta-analysis. *The Lancet Psychiatry*, *2*(11), 994–1001.

Piscopo, K.D. (2017). Suicidality and death by suicide among middle-aged adults in the United States. *The CBHSQ Report: September 27, 2017*. Center for Behavioral Health Statistics and Quality, Substance Abuse and Mental Health Services Administration. Rockville, MD.

Pollak, O.H., Guzmán, E.M., Shin, K.E., & Cha, C.B. (2021). Defeat, entrapment, and positive future thinking: Examining key theoretical predictors of suicidal ideation among adolescents. *Frontiers in Psychology*, *12*, 590388.

Pompili, M., Serafini, G., Innamorati, M., Möller-Leimkühler, A.M., Giupponi, G., Girardi, P., Tatarelli, R., & Lester, D. (2010). The hypothalamic-pituitary-adrenal axis and serotonin abnormalities: A selective overview for the implications of suicide prevention. *European Archives of Psychiatry and Clinical Neuroscience*, *260*(8), 583–600.

Pope, W. (1976). *Durkheim's suicide: A classic analyzed*. University of Chicago Press.

Posner, K., Brent, D., Lucas, C., Gould, M., Stanley, B., Brown, G., … & Mann, J. (2008). *Columbia-suicide severity rating scale (C-SSRS)*. Columbia University.

Poulter, M.O., Du, L., Weaver, I.C., Palkovits, M., Faludi, G., Merali, Z., … & Anisman, H. (2008). GABAA receptor promoter hypermethylation in suicide brain: Implications for the involvement of epigenetic processes. *Biological Psychiatry*, *64*(8), 645–652.

Poushter, J., & Kent, N. (2020). *The global divide on homosexuality persists*. Pew Research Center, 25.

Powell, J., Geddes, J., Deeks, J., Goldacre, M., & Hawton, K. (2000). Suicide in psychiatric hospital in-patients: Risk factors and their predictive power. *The British Journal of Psychiatry*, *176*(3), 266–272.

Power, M.L. (2004). Commentary: Viability as opposed to stability: An evolutionary perspective on physiological regulation. In J. Schulkin: (Ed.) *Allostasis, homeostasis, and the costs of physiological adaptation* (pp. 343–364). Cambridge.

Powers, W.T. (1973). *Behavior: The control of perception.* Aldine.

Pratt, D., Piper, M., Appleby, L., Webb, R., & Shaw, J. (2006). Suicide in recently released prisoners: A population-based cohort study. *The Lancet, 368*(9530), 119–123.

Powsner, S., Goebert, D., Richmond, J.S., & Takeshita, J. (2023). Suicide risk assessment, management, and mitigation in the emergency setting. *Focus, 21*(1), 8–17.

Price, M., Albaugh, M., Hahn, S., Juliano, A.C., Fani, N., Brier, Z.M., ... & Garavan, H. (2021). Examination of the association between exposure to childhood maltreatment and brain structure in young adults: A machine learning analysis. *Neuropsychopharmacology, 46*(11), 1888–1894.

Price, J.H., & Khubchandani, J. (2021). Firearm suicides in the elderly: A narrative review and call for action. *Journal of Community Health, 46,* 1050–1058.

Prudic, J., & Sackeim, H.A. (1999). Electroconvulsive therapy and suicide risk. *Journal of Clinical Psychiatry, 60*(2), 104–110.

Pruitt, Z., Chapin, K.P., Eakin, H., & Glover, A.L. (2022). Telehealth during COVID-19: Suicide prevention and American Indian communities in Montana. *Telemedicine and e-Health, 28*(3), 325–333.

Pruitt, L.D., Luxton, D.D., & Shore, P. (2014). Additional clinical benefits of home-based telemental health treatments. *Professional Psychology: Research and Practice, 45*(5), 340.

Public Health England. (2016). *Support after a suicide: A guide to providing local services: a practice resource.* http://assets.publishing.service.gov.uk/government/uploads/system/uploads/attachment_data/file/590838/support_after_a_suicide.pdf.

Purba, J.S., Hoogendijk, W.J., Hofman, M.A., & Swaab, D.F. (1996). Increased number of vasopressin- and oxytocin-expressing neurons in the paraventricular nucleus of the hypothalamus in depression. *Archives of General Psychiatry, 53,* 137–143.

Qin, P., Agerbo, E., & Mortensen, P.B. (2003). Suicide risk in relation to socioeconomic, demographic, psychiatric, and familial factors: A national register–based study of all suicides in Denmark, 1981–1997. *American Journal of Psychiatry, 160*(4), 765–772.

Qin, S., Hermans, E.J., Van Marle, H.J., Luo, J., & Fernández, G. (2009). Acute psychological stress reduces working memory-related activity in the dorsolateral prefrontal cortex. *Biological Psychiatry, 66*(1), 25–32.

Quinlan, K., Nickerson, K., Ebin, J., Humphries-Wadsworth, T., Stout, E., & Frankini, E. (2021). Supporting a public health approach to suicide prevention: Recommendations for state infrastructure. *Suicide and Life-Threatening Behavior, 51*(2), 352–357.

Quintana-Orts, C., & Rey, L. (2018). Traditional bullying, cyberbullying and mental health in early adolescents: Forgiveness as a protective factor of peer victimisation. *International Journal of Environmental Research and Public Health, 15*(11), 2389. 1–14.

Raifman, J., Charlton, B.M., Arrington-Sanders, R., Chan, P.A., Rusley, J., Mayer, K.H., … & McConnell, M. (2020). Sexual orientation and suicide attempt disparities among US adolescents: 2009–2017. *Pediatrics, 145*(3), 1–11.

Ram, D., Chandran, S., Sadar, A., & Gowdappa, B. (2019). Correlation of cognitive resilience, cognitive flexibility and impulsivity in attempted suicide. *Indian Journal of Psychological Medicine, 41*(4), 362–367.

Rambotti, S. (2020). Is there a relationship between welfare-state policies and suicide rates? Evidence from the US states, 2000–2015. *Social Science & Medicine, 246*, 112778.

Ramchand, R. (2022). *Personal Firearm storage in the United States: Recent estimates, patterns, and effectiveness of interventions.* RAND Corporation. www.rand.org/pubs/research_reports/RRA243-5.html.

Ramchand, R., Ayer, L., Fisher, G., Osilla, K.C., Barnes-Proby, D., & Wertheimer, S. (2015). Suicide postvention in the Department of Defense: Evidence, policies and procedures, and perspectives of loss survivors. *Rand Health Quarterly, 5*(2), 20.

Randall, J.R., Nickel, N.C., & Colman, I. (2015). Contagion from peer suicidal behavior in a representative sample of American adolescents. *Journal of Affective Disorders, 186*, 219–225.

Randle, A.A., & Graham, C.A. (2011). A review of the evidence on the effects of intimate partner violence on men. *Psychology of Men & Masculinity, 12*(2), 97.

Ray, C. (2020). *Psychological capital: An exploration of its usefulness in police departments* (Doctoral dissertation, The Chicago School of Professional Psychology).

Reeves, A., McKee, M., Gunnell, D., Chang, S.S., Basu, S., Barr, B., & Stuckler, D. (2015). Economic shocks, resilience, and male suicides in the Great Recession: Cross-national analysis of 20 EU countries. *The European Journal of Public Health, 25*(3), 404–409.

Reid, W.H. (2009). Prognosis after suicide attempt: Standard of care and the consequences of not meeting it. *Journal of Psychiatric Practice, 15*(2), 141–144.

Reifels, L., Morgan, A., Too, L.S., Schlichthorst, M., Williamson, M., & Jordan, H. (2021). What works in community-led suicide prevention: Perspectives of Wesley LifeForce network coordinators. *International Journal of Environmental Research and Public Health, 18*(11), 6084.

Resnick, S.G., & Leddy, M.A. (2015). Building recovery-oriented service systems through positive psychology. In S. Joseph (Ed.), *Positive psychology in practice: Promoting human flourishing in work, health, education, and everyday life* (pp. 695–710). John Wiley & Sons.

Rhee, T.G., Sint, K., Olfson, M., Gerhard, T., Busch, S.H., & Wilkinson, S.T. (2021). Association of ECT with risks of all-cause mortality and suicide in older Medicare patients. *American Journal of Psychiatry, 178*(12), 1089–1097.

Riblet, N.B., Shiner, B., Young-Xu, Y., & Watts, B.V. (2017). Strategies to prevent death by suicide: Meta-analysis of randomised controlled trials. *British Journal of Psychiatry, 210*(6), 396–402.

Richards, J.E., Whiteside, U., Ludman, E.J., Pabiniak, C., Kirlin, B., Hidalgo, R., & Simon, G. (2019). Understanding why patients may not report suicidal ideation at a health care visit prior to a suicide attempt: A qualitative study. *Psychiatric Services, 70*(1), 40–45.

Richardson, T., Elliott, P., & Roberts, R. (2013). The relationship between personal unsecured debt and mental and physical health: A systematic review and meta-analysis. *Clinical Psychology Review, 33*(8), 1148–1162.

Rieger, S.J., Peter, T., & Roberts, L.W. (2015). 'Give me a reason to live!' Examining reasons for living across levels of suicidality. *Journal of Religion and Health, 54*(6), 2005–2019.

Rigg, K.K., Monnat, S.M., & Chavez, M.N. (2018). Opioid-related mortality in rural America: Geographic heterogeneity and intervention strategies. *International Journal of Drug Policy, 57*, 119–129.

Rihmer, Z. (2001). Can better recognition and treatment of depression reduce suicide rates? A brief review. *European Psychiatry, 16*(7), 406–409.

Robin, L., Brener, N.D., Donahue, S.F., Hack, T., Hale, K., & Goodenow, C. (2002). Associations between health risk behaviors and opposite-, same-, and both-sex sexual partners in representative samples of Vermont and Massachusetts high school students. *Archives of Pediatrics & Adolescent Medicine, 156*(4), 349–355.

Robins, A., & Fiske, A. (2009). Explaining the relation between religiousness and reduced suicidal behavior: Social support rather than specific beliefs. *Suicide and Life-Threatening Behavior, 39*(4), 386–395.

Robinson, J.P., & Espelage, D.L. (2013). Peer victimization and sexual risk differences between lesbian, gay, bisexual, transgender, or questioning and nontransgender heterosexual youths in grades 7–12. *American Journal of Public Health, 103*(10), 1810–1819.

Robinson, W.L., Whipple, C.R., Keenan, K., Flack, C.E., & Wingate, L. (2022). Suicide in African American adolescents: Understanding risk by studying resilience. *Annual Review of Clinical Psychology, 18*, 359–385.

Rogers, M.L., Gai, A.R., Lieberman, A., Musacchio Schafer, K., & Joiner, T.E. (2022). Why does safety planning prevent suicidal behavior? *Professional Psychology: Research and Practice, 53*(1), 33.

Rogers, M.L., Gallyer, A.J., & Joiner, T.E. (2021). The relationship between suicide-specific rumination and suicidal intent above and beyond suicidal ideation and other suicide risk factors: A multilevel modeling approach. *Journal of Psychiatric Research, 137*, 506–513.

Rojas, S.M., Carter, S.P., McGinn, M.M., & Reger, M.A. (2020). A review of telemental health as a modality to deliver suicide-specific interventions for rural populations. *Telemedicine and e-Health, 26*(6), 700–709.

Romeo, R.D. (2017). The impact of stress on the structure of the adolescent brain: Implications for adolescent mental health. *Brain Research, 1654*, 185–191.

Rosario-Williams, B., Rowe-Harriott, S., Ray, M., Jeglic, E., & Miranda, R. (2022). Factors precipitating suicide attempts vary across race. *Journal of American College Health, 70*(2), 568–574.

Rosemberg, M.A.S., Granner, J., Li, Y., & Seng, J.S. (2020). A scoping review of interventions targeting allostatic load. *Stress, 23*, 519–528.

Rosen, J.B., & Schulkin, J. (1998). From normal fear to pathological anxiety. *Psychological Review, 105*, 325–350.

Rosen, J.B., & Schulkin, J. (2022). Hyperexcitability: From normal fear to pathological anxiety and trauma. *Frontiers in Systems Neuroscience*, 80, Article 727054.

Rosmarin, D.H., Bigda-Peyton, J.S., Öngur, D., Pargament, K.I., & Björgvinsson, T. (2013). Religious coping among psychotic patients: Relevance to suicidality and treatment outcomes. *Psychiatry Research, 210*(1), 182–187.

Ross, L.D. (1977). The intuitive psychologist and his shortcomings: Distortions in the attribution process. In L. Berkowitz (Ed.), *Advances in experimental social psychology* (Vol. 10, pp. 174–221). Academic Press.

Ross, J.F., Hewitt, W.L., Wahl, C.W., Okun, R., Shapiro, B.J., Slawson, P.F., & Shneidman, E.S. (1971). The management of the presuicidal, suicidal, and postsuicidal patient. *Annals of Internal Medicine, 75*(3), 441–458.

Ross, J.M., Yakovlev, P.A., & Carson, F. (2012). Does state spending on mental health lower suicide rates? *The Journal of Socio-Economics, 41*(4), 408–417.

Rowhani A., Simonetti J.A., & Rivara F.P. (2016). Effectiveness of interventions to promote safe firearm storage. *Epidemiologic Reviews, 38*, 111–124.

Roy, A., Segal, N.L., Centerwall, B.S., & Robinette, C.D. (1991). Suicide in twins. *Archives of General Psychiatry, 48*(1), 29–32.

Rozek, D. C., Keane, C., Sippel, L. M., Stein, J. Y., Rollo-Carlson, C., & Bryan, C. J. (2019). Short-term effects of crisis response planning on optimism in a US Army sample. *Early Intervention in Psychiatry, 13*(3), 682–685.

Ruch, D.A., Sheftall, A.H., Schlagbaum, P., Rausch, J., Campo, J.V., & Bridge, J.A. (2019). Trends in suicide among youth aged 10 to 19 years in the United States, 1975 to 2016. *JAMA Network Open, 2*(5), e193886–e193886.

Rudd, M.D. (2012). Brief cognitive behavioral therapy (BCBT) for suicidality in military populations. *Military Psychology, 24*(6), 592–603.

Rudd, M. D. (2014). Core competencies, warning signs, and a framework for suicide risk assessment in clinical practice. In M.K. Nock (Ed.), *The Oxford handbook of suicide and self-injury* (pp. 323–336). New York: Oxford University Press.

Rudd, M.D., Berman, A.L., Joiner Jr, T.E., Nock, M.K., Silverman, M.M., Mandrusiak, M., … & Witte, T. (2006). Warning signs for suicide: Theory, research, and clinical applications. *Suicide and Life-Threatening Behavior, 36*(3), 255–262.

Rudd, M.D., Bryan, C.J., Wertenberger, E.G., Peterson, A.L., Young-McCaughan, S., Mintz, J., … & Bruce, T.O. (2015). Brief cognitive-behavioral therapy effects on post-treatment suicide attempts in a military sample: Results of a randomized clinical trial with 2-year follow-up. *American Journal of Psychiatry, 172*(5), 441–449.

Rudd, B.N., George, J.M., Snyder, S.E., Whyte, M., Cliggitt, L., Weyler, R., & Brown, G. (2022). Harnessing quality improvement and implementation science to support the implementation of suicide prevention practices in juvenile detention. *Psychotherapy, 59*(2), 150.

Rudd, M.D., Joiner, T.E., & Rajab, M.H. (2001). *Treating suicidal behavior: An effective, time-limited approach.* Guilford Press.

Rudd, K.L., & Yates, T.M. (2020). The health implications of resilience. In K. Sweeny, Megan L. Robbins, & Lee M. Cohen (Eds.), *The Wiley encyclopedia of health psychology* (pp. 269–277). Wiley.

Ruff, C.A. (1974). *The complexity of Roman suicide.* Master's Theses, University of Richmond. https://scholarship.richmond.edu/cgi/viewcontent.cgi?article=1956&context=masters-theses.

Runeson, B., & Åsberg, M. (2003). Family history of suicide among suicide victims. *American Journal of Psychiatry, 160*(8), 1525–1526.

Runeson, B., Odeberg, J., Pettersson, A., Edbom, T., Jildevik Adamsson, I., & Waern, M. (2017). Instruments for the assessment of suicide risk: A systematic review evaluating the certainty of the evidence. *PLoS One, 12*(7), e0180292.

Ruocco, K.A., Patton, C.S., Burditt, K., Carroll, B., & Mabe, M. (2022). TAPS Suicide Postvention ModelTM: A comprehensive framework of healing and growth. *Death Studies, 46*(8), 1897–1908.

Ruskin, R., Sakinofsky, I., Bagby, R.M., Dickens, S., & Sousa, G. (2004). Impact of patient suicide on psychiatrists and psychiatric trainees. *Academic Psychiatry, 28*(2), 104–110.

Russell, S. T., & Joyner, K. (2001). Adolescent sexual orientation and suicide risk: Evidence from a national study. *American Journal of Public Health, 91*(8), 1276–1281.

Russell S.T., & Toomey R.B. (2010). Men's sexual orientation and suicide: Evidence for adolescent-specific risk. *Social Science and Medicine, 74*(4), 523–529.

Sachar, E. J., Hellman, L., Fukushima, D. K., & Gallagher, T. F. (1970). Cortisol production in depressive illness: A clinical and biochemical clarification. *Archives of General Psychiatry, 23*(4), 289–298.

Saks, E. (2007). *The center cannot hold: My journey through madness.* Hachette Books.

Salkovskis, P.M., Atha, C., & Storer, D. (1990). Cognitive-behavioural problem solving in the treatment of patients who repeatedly attempt suicide: A controlled trial. *The British Journal of Psychiatry, 157*, 871–876.

Sall, J., Brenner, L., Millikan Bell, A.M., & Colston, M.J. (2019). Assessment and management of patients at risk for suicide: Synopsis of the 2019 U.S. Department of Veterans Affairs and U.S. Department of Defense clinical practice guidelines. *Annals of Internal Medicine, 171*(5), 343–353.

SAMHSA. (2020). *Results from the 2020 National Survey on Drug Use and Health: Detailed tables, Appendix A: Key Definitions for the 2020 National Survey on Drug Use and Health.* www.samhsa.gov/data/sites/default/files/reports/rpt35323/NSDUHDetailedTabs2020v25/NSDUHDetailedTabs2020v25/NSDUHDetTabsAppA2020.htm.

SAMHSA. (2022). *People at Greater Suicide risk.* www.samhsa.gov/data/sites/default/files/reports/rpt35323/NSDUHDetailedTabs2020v25/NSDUHDetailedTabs2020v25/NSDUHDetTabsAppA2020.htm.

SAMHSA. (2023). *Help prevent suicide*. www.samhsa.gov/suicide.

Sareen, J., Isaak, C., Bolton, S.L., Enns, M.W., Elias, B., Deane, F., ... & Katz, L.Y. (2013). Gatekeeper training for suicide prevention in First Nations community members: A randomized controlled trial. *Depression and Anxiety, 30*(10), 1021–1029.

Sapolsky, R.M., Romero, L.M., & Munck, A.U. (2000). How do glucocorticoids influence stress responses? Integrating permissive, suppressive, stimulatory, and preparative actions. *Endocrine Reviews, 21*, 55–89.

Savransky, A., Chiappelli, J., Fisseha, F., Wisner, K.M., Xiaoming, D., Mirmomen, S.M., ... & Hong, L.E. (2018). Elevated allostatic load early in the course of schizophrenia. *Translational Psychiatry, 8*, 1–7.

Saxbe, D.E., Beckes, L., Stoycos, S.A., & Coan, J.A. (2020). Social allostasis and social allostatic load: A new model for research in social dynamics, stress, and health. *Perspectives on Psychological Science, 15*(2), 469–482.

Schenk, H.M., Jeronimus, B.F., van der Krieke, L., Bos, E.H., de Jonge, P., & Rosmalen, J.G. (2017). Associations of positive affect and negative affect with allostatic load: A lifelines cohort study. *Psychosomatic Medicine, 80*, 160–166.

Schlagbaum, P., Tissue, J.L., Sheftall, A.H., Ruch, D.A., Ackerman, J.P., & Bridge, J.A. (2021). The impact of peer influencing on adolescent suicidal ideation and suicide attempts. *Journal of Psychiatric Research, 140*, 529–532.

Schmitz, W.M., Allen, M.H., Feldman, B.N., Gutin, N.J., Jahn, D.R., Kleespies, P.M., ... & Simpson, S. (2012). Preventing suicide through improved training in suicide risk assessment and care: An American Association of Suicidology Task Force report addressing serious gaps in US mental health training. *Suicide and Life-Threatening Behavior, 42*(3), 292–304.

Schopenhauer, A. (1893). *Studies in pessimism: A series of essays*. S. Sonnenschein. https://babel.hathitrust.org/cgi/pt?id=uva.x002153349&view=1up&seq=13&q1=suicide.

Schulkin, J. (2003). *Rethinking homeostasis: Allostatic regulation in physiology and pathophysiology*. MIT Press.

Schulkin, J. (2011). Social allostasis: Anticipatory regulation of the internal milieu. *Frontiers in Evolutionary Neuroscience, 2*, 111.

Schulkin, J., Gold, P.W., & McEwen, B.S. (1998). Induction of corticotropin-releasing hormone gene expression by glucocorticoids: Implication for understanding the states of fear and anxiety and allostatic load. *Psychoneuroendocrinology, 23*(3), 219–243.

Schulkin, J., McEwen, B.S., & Gold, P.W. (1994). Allostasis, amygdala, and anticipatory angst. *Neuroscience & Biobehavioral Reviews, 18*, 385–396.

Schulkin, J., Morgan, M.A., & Rosen, J.B. (2005). A neuroendocrine mechanism for sustaining fear. *Trends in Neurosciences, 28*(12), 629–635.

Schwarzer, R., & Warner, L.M. (2013). Perceived self-efficacy and its relationship to resilience. In S. Prince-Embury & D. Saklofske (Eds.), *Resilience in children, adolescents, and adults: Translating research into practice* (pp. 139–150). Springer.

Scocco, P., Zerbinati, L., Preti, A., Ferrari, A., & Totaro, S. (2019). Mindfulness-based weekend retreats for people bereaved by suicide (*Panta Rhei*): A pilot feasibility study. *Psychology and Psychotherapy, 92*(1), 39–56.

Seeman, T., Epel, E., Gruenewald, T., Karlamangla, A., & McEwen, B.S. (2010). Socio-economic differentials in peripheral biology: Cumulative allostatic load. *Annals of the New York Academy of Sciences, 1186*, 223–239.

Seeman, T.E., Singer, B.H., Rowe, J.W., Horwitz, R.I., & McEwen, B.S. (1997). Price of adaptation – Allostatic load and its health consequences: MacArthur studies of successful aging. *Archives of Internal Medicine, 157*(19), 2259–2268.

Seeman, T.E., Singer, B.H., Ryff, C.D., Love, G.D., & Levy-Storms, L. (2002). Social relationships, gender, and allostatic load across two age cohorts. *Psychosomatic Medicine, 64*, 395–406.

Seery, M.D. (2011). Resilience: A silver lining to experiencing adverse life events? *Current Directions in Psychological Science, 20*(6), 390–394.

Séguin, M., Beauchamp, G., Robert, M., DiMambro, M., & Turecki, G. (2014). Developmental model of suicide trajectories. *The British Journal of Psychiatry, 205*(2), 120–126.

Seligman, M.E. (2002). Positive psychology, positive prevention, and positive therapy. *Handbook of Positive Psychology, 2*(2002), 3–12.

Seligman, M.E., & Csikszentmihalyi, M. (2000). *Positive psychology: An introduction* (Vol. 55, No. 1, p. 5). American Psychological Association.

Seligman, M. E., Steen, T. A., Park, N., & Peterson, C. (2005). Positive psychology progress: Empirical validation of interventions. *American psychologist, 60*(5), 410–421.

Serafini, G., Muzio, C., Piccinini, G., Flouri, E., Ferrigno, G., Pompili, M., … & Amore, M. (2015). Life adversities and suicidal behavior in young individuals: A systematic review. *European Child & Adolescent Psychiatry, 24*, 1423–1446.

Shaygan, M., Sheybani Negad, S., & Motazedian, S. (2022). The effect of combined sertraline and positive psychotherapy on hopelessness and suicidal ideation among patients with major depressive disorder: A randomized controlled trial. *The Journal of Positive Psychology, 17*(5), 655–664.

Sheline, Y.I., Sanghavi, M., Mintun, M.A., & Gado, M.H. (1999). Depression duration but not age predicts hippocampal volume loss in medically healthy women with recurrent major depression. *Journal of Neuroscience, 19*(12), 5034–5043.

Shen, X., Yang, Y.L., Wang, Y., Liu, L., Wang, S., & Wang, L. (2014). The association between occupational stress and depressive symptoms and the mediating role of psychological capital among Chinese university teachers: A cross-sectional study. *BMC Psychiatry, 14*(1), 1–8

Sher, L. (2019). Resilience as a focus of suicide research and prevention. *Acta Psychiatrica Scandinavica, 140*(2), 169–180.

Sher, L., Grunebaum, M.F., Sullivan, G.M., Burke, A.K., Cooper, T.B., Mann, J.J., & Oquendo, M.A. (2014). Association of testosterone levels and future suicide attempts in females with bipolar disorder. *Journal of Affective Disorders, 166*, 98–102.

Sher, L., & Mann, J.J. (2003). Psychiatric pathophysiology: Mood disorders. In A. Tasman, J. Kay, & J.A. Lieberman (Eds.). *Psychiatry* (pp. 300–315). John Wiley & Sons.

Shin, L.M., Orr, S.P., Carson, M.A., Rauch, S.L., Macklin, M.L., Lasko, N.B., … & Alpert, N.M. (2004). Regional cerebral blood flow in the amygdala and medial prefrontal cortex during traumatic imagery in male and female Vietnam veterans with PTSD. *Archives of General Psychiatry*, *61*(2), 168–176.

Shorter, E. (2009). The history of lithium therapy. *Bipolar Disorders*, *11*, 4–9.

Shneidman, E.S. (1981). A psychological theory of suicide. *Suicide and Life-Threatening Behavior*, *11*, 221–231.

Shneidman, E.S. (1993). *Suicide as psychache: A clinical approach to self-destructive behavior*. Jason Aronson – Rowman & Littlefield Publishers.

Sidhartha, T., & Jena, S. (2006). Suicidal behaviors in adolescents. *The Indian Journal of Pediatrics*, *73*, 783–788.

Sierra Hernandez, C.A., Han, C., Oliffe, J.L., & Ogrodniczuk, J.S. (2014). Understanding help-seeking among depressed men. *Psychology of Men & Masculinity*, *15*(3), 346.

Silva, C., & Van Orden, K.A. (2018). Suicide among Hispanics in the United States. *Current Opinion in Psychology*, *22*, 44–49.

Silverman, J.J., Galanter, M., Jackson-Triche, M., Jacobs, D.G., Lomax, J.W., Riba, M.B., … & Yager, J. (2015). The American Psychiatric Association practice guidelines for the psychiatric evaluation of adults. *American Journal of Psychiatry*, *172*(8), 798–802.

Simon, R.I. (2012). Suicide risk assessment: Gateway to treatment and management. In R.I. Simon & R.E. Hales (Eds.), *The American Psychiatric Publishing textbook of suicide assessment and management, second edition* (pp. 3–28). American Psychiatric Publishing.

Simon, G.E., Johnson, E., Lawrence, J.M., Rossom, R.C., Ahmedani, B., Lynch, F.L., … & Shortreed, S.M. (2018). Predicting suicide attempts and suicide deaths following outpatient visits using electronic health records. *American Journal of Psychiatry*, *175*(10), 951–960.

Simon, G.E., Rutter, C.M., Peterson, D., Oliver, M., Whiteside, U., Operskalski, B., & Ludman, E.J. (2013). Does response on the PHQ-9 Depression Questionnaire predict subsequent suicide attempt or suicide death? *Psychiatric Services*, *64*(12), 1195–1202.

Simon, G.E., Specht, C., & Doederlein, A. (2016). Coping with suicidal thoughts: A survey of personal experience. *Psychiatric Services*, *67*(9), 1026–1029.

Simon, T.R., Swann, A.C., Powell, K.E., Potter, L.B., Kresnow, M.J., & O'Carroll, P.W. (2001). Characteristics of impulsive suicide attempts and attempters. *Suicide and Life-Threatening Behavior*, *32*(Supplement to Issue 1), 49–59.

Simpson, S.A., Goans, C., Loh, R., Ryall, K., Middleton, M.C., & Dalton, A. (2021). Suicidal ideation is insensitive to suicide risk after emergency department discharge: Performance characteristics of the Columbia-Suicide Severity Rating Scale Screener. *Academic Emergency Medicine*, *28*(6), 621–629.

Sinha, R., Lacadie, C., Skudlarski, P., & Wexler, B.E. (2004). Neural circuits underlying emotional distress in humans. *Annals of the New York Academy of Sciences*, *1032*(1), 254–257.

Sisask, M., Värnik, A., lves, K., Bertolote, J.M., Bolhari, J., Botega, N.J., ... & Wasserman, D. (2010). Is religiosity a protective factor against attempted suicide: A cross-cultural case-control study. *Archives of Suicide Research*, *14*(1), 44–55.

Sisto, A., Vicinanza, F., Campanozzi, L.L., Ricci, G., Tartaglini, D., & Tambone, V. (2019). Towards a transversal definition of psychological resilience: A literature review. *Medicina*, *55*(11), 745.

Skogman, K., Alsén, M., & Öjehagen, A. (2004). Sex differences in risk factors for suicide after attempted suicide. *Social Psychiatry and Psychiatric Epidemiology*, *39*, 113–120.

Skovgaard Larsen, J.L., Frandsen, H., & Erlangsen, A. (2016). MYPLAN: A mobile phone application for supporting people at suicide risk. *Crisis*, *37*(3), 236.

Smith P.N., Stanley I.H., Joiner T.E., Sachs-Ericsson N.J., & Van Orden K.A. (2016). An aspect of the capability for suicide – Fearlessness of the pain involved in dying – Amplifies the association between suicide ideation and attempts. *Archives of Suicide Research*, *20*, 650–662.

Soria, C.A., Rcmcdi, C., D'Alessio, L., & Roldán, E.J. (2018). Sex and age-related differences in neuroticism and allostatic load index in urban patients with general anxiety disorder treated with alprazolam. *Open Journal of Psychiatry*, *8*, 212–232.

Spark, T.L., Wright-Kelly, E., Ma, M., James, K.A., Reid, C.E., & Brooks-Russell, A. (2021). Assessment of rural-urban and geospatial differences in perceived handgun access and reported suicidality among youth in Colorado. *JAMA Network Open*, *4*(10), e2127816–e2127816.

Speckens, A.E., & Hawton, K. (2005). Social problem solving in adolescents with suicidal behavior: A systematic review. *Suicide and Life-Threatening Behavior*, *35*(4), 365–387.

SPRC. (2017). *Problem-solving therapy*. Available at: https://sprc.org/online-library/problem-solving-therapy-pst.

SPRC. (2022). *Scope of the problem*. Retrieved March 19, 2023, from: https://sprc.org/about-suicide/scope-of-the-problem/.

Stack, S. (2002). Political regime and suicide: Some relevant variables to be considered. *Journal of Epidemiology & Community Health*, *56*(10), 727–727.

Stack, S. (2003). Media coverage as a risk factor in suicide. *Journal of Epidemiology & Community Health*, *57*(4), 238–240.

Stack, S. (2005). Suicide in the media: A quantitative review of studies based on nonfictional stories. *Suicide and Life-Threatening Behavior*, *35*(2), 121–133.

Stack, S. (2021). Contributing factors to suicide: Political, social, cultural and economic. *Preventive Medicine*, *152*, 106498.

Stack, S., & Bowman, B. (2017). Why men choose firearms more than women: Gender and the portrayal of firearm suicide in film, 1900–2013. In T. Niederkrotenthaler & S. Stack (Eds.), *Media and suicide: International perspectives on research, theory, and policy* (pp. 27–36). Routledge.

Stacy, M., Dwyer, E., Kremer, M., & Schulkin, J. (2022). Obstetrician/gynecologists' knowledge, attitudes, and practice regarding suicide screening among women. *Journal of Women's Health*, *31*(10), 1481–1489.

Stacy, M., Kremer, M., & Schulkin, J. (2022). Suicide among women and the role of women's health care providers. *Obstetrical & Gynecological Survey, 77*(5), 293–301.

Stanley, B., & Brown, G.K. (2012). Safety planning intervention: A brief intervention to mitigate suicide risk. *Cognitive and Behavioral Practice, 19*(2), 256–264.

Stanley, B., Brown, G.K., Brenner, L.A., Galfalvy, H.C., Currier, G.W., Knox, K.L., ... & Green, K.L. (2018). Comparison of the safety planning intervention with follow-up vs. usual care of suicidal patients treated in the emergency department. *JAMA Psychiatry, 75*(9), 894–900.

Stanley, B., Brown, G., Brent, D.A., Wells, K., Poling, K., Curry, J., ... & Hughes, J. (2009). Cognitive-behavioral therapy for suicide prevention (CBT-SP): Treatment model, feasibility, and acceptability. *Journal of the American Academy of Child & Adolescent Psychiatry, 48*(10), 1005–1013.

Stanley, B., Brown, G.K., Karlin, B., Kemp, J.E., & VonBergen, H.A. (2008). *Safety plan treatment manual to reduce suicide risk: Veteran version.* Washington, DC: United States Department of Veterans Affairs.

Stanley, B., Green, K.L., Ghahramanlou-Holloway, M., Brenner, L.A., & Brown, G.K. (2017). The construct and measurement of suicide-related coping. *Psychiatry Research, 258*, 189–193.

Statham, D.J., Heath, A.C., Madden, P.A., Bucholz, K.K., Bierut, L., Dinwiddie, S.H., ... & Martin, N.G. (1998). Suicidal behaviour: An epidemiological and genetic study. *Psychological Medicine, 28*(4), 839–855.

Steele, I.H., Thrower, N., Noroian, P., & Saleh, F.M. (2018). Understanding suicide across the lifespan: A United States perspective of suicide risk factors, assessment & management. *Journal of Forensic Sciences, 63*(1), 162–171.

Steelesmith, D.L., Fontanella, C.A., Campo, J.V., Bridge, J.A., Warren, K.L., & Root, E.D. (2019). Contextual factors associated with county-level suicide rates in the United States, 1999 to 2016. *JAMA Network Open, 2*(9), e1910936–e1910936.

Steinberg, L.J., & Mann, J.J. (2020). Abnormal stress responsiveness and suicidal behavior: A risk phenotype. *Biomarkers in Neuropsychiatry, 2*, 100011.

Sterling, P. (2020). *What is health?: Allostasis and the evolution of human design.* MIT Press.

Sterling, P., & Eyer, J. (1988). Allostasis: A new paradigm to explain arousal pathology. In S. Fisher & J. Reason (Eds.), *Handbook of life stress, cognition and health* (pp. 629–649). John Wiley & Sons.

Sterling, P., & Platt, M.L. (2022). Why deaths of despair are increasing in the US and not other industrial nations: Insights from neuroscience and anthropology. *JAMA Psychiatry, 79*(4), 368–374.

Stevenson, J.R., McMahon, E.K., Boner, W., & Haussmann, M.F. (2019). Oxytocin administration prevents cellular aging caused by social isolation. *Psychoneuroendocrinology, 103*, 52–60.

Stewart, S.M., Eaddy, M., Horton, S.E., Hughes, J., & Kennard, B. (2017). The validity of the interpersonal theory of suicide in adolescence: A review. *Journal of Clinical Child & Adolescent Psychology, 46*(3), 437–449.

Stewart, C.D., Quinn, A., Plever, S., & Emmerson, B. (2009). Comparing cognitive behavior therapy, problem solving therapy, and treatment as usual in a high-risk population. *Suicide and Life-Threatening Behavior, 39*(5), 538–547.

Stickley, T., & Wright, N. (2011). The British research evidence for recovery, papers published between 2006 and 2009 (inclusive). Part One: A review of the peer-reviewed literature using a systematic approach. *Journal of Psychiatric and Mental Health Nursing, 18*(3), 247–256.

Stone, D.M., Holland, K.M., Bartholow, B.N., Crosby, A.E., Davis, S.P., & Wilkins, N. (2017). *Preventing suicide: A technical package of policies, programs, and practice.* National Center for Injury Prevention and Control, Centers for Disease Control and Prevention.

Stone, D.M., Jones, C.M., & Mack, K.A. (2021). Changes in suicide rates: United States, 2018–2019. *Morbidity and Mortality Weekly Report, 70*(8), 261.

Stone, L.B., Liu, R.T., & Yen, S. (2014). Adolescent inpatient girls' report of dependent life events predicts prospective suicide risk. *Psychiatry Research, 219,* 137–142.

Stone, D.M., Simon, T.R., Fowler, K.A., Kegler, S.R., Yuan, K., Holland, K.M., … & Crosby, A.E. (2018). Vital signs: Trends in state suicide rates – United States, 1999–2016 and circumstances contributing to suicide – 27 states, 2015. *Morbidity and Mortality Weekly Report, 67,* 617.

Stone, D., Trinh, E., Zhou, H., Welder, L., End of Horn, P., Fowler, K., & Ivey-Stephenson, A. (2022). Suicides among American Indian or Alaska Native persons – National Violent Death Reporting System, United States, 2015–2020. *Morbidity and Mortality Weekly Report, 71,* 1161–1168.

Stuart-Maver, S.L., Foley Nicpon, M., Stuart-Maver, C.I.M., & Mahatmya, D. (2021). Trends and disparities in suicidal behaviors for heterosexual and sexual minority youth 1995–2017. *Psychology of Sexual Orientation and Gender Diversity.* https://doi.org/10.1037/sgd0000525.

Su, C., Aseltine, R., Doshi, R., Chen, K., Rogers, S.C., & Wang, F. (2020). Machine learning for suicide risk prediction in children and adolescents with electronic health records. *Translational Psychiatry, 10*(1), 413.

Subica, A.M., & Wu, L.T. (2018). Substance use and suicide in Pacific Islander, American Indian, and multiracial youth. *American Journal of Preventive Medicine, 54*(6), 795–805.

Sublette, M.E. (2020). Lipids and suicide risk. In E. Baca-Garcia (Ed.), *Behavioral neurobiology of suicide and self harm* (pp. 155–177). Springer.

Sullivan, E.M., Annest, J.L., & Luo, F. (2013). Suicide among adults aged 35–64 years – United States, 1999–2010. *Morbidity and Mortality Weekly Report, 62*(17), 321–325.

Sullivan, S.R., Monahan, M.F., Mitchell, E.L., Spears, A P., Walsh, S., Szeszko, J.R., … & Goodman, M. (2021). Group treatments for individuals at risk for suicide: A PRISMA scoping review. *Psychiatry Research, 304,* 114108.

Sullivan, S.R., Myhre, K., Mitchell, E.L., Monahan, M., Khazanov, G., Spears, A.P., … & Goodman, M. (2022). Suicide and telehealth treatments: A PRISMA scoping review. *Archives of Suicide Research, 26*(4), 1794–1814.

Supiano, K.P., Haynes, L.B., & Pond, V. (2017). The transformation of the meaning of death in complicated grief group therapy for survivors of suicide: A treatment process analysis using the meaning of loss codebook. *Death Studies*, *41*(9), 553–561.

Swartz, J.R., Williamson, D.E., & Hariri, A.R. (2015). Developmental change in amygdala reactivity during adolescence: Effects of family history of depression and stressful life events. *American Journal of Psychiatry*, *172*(3), 276–283.

Sylvia, L.G., Ametrano, R.M., & Nierenberg, A.A. (2010). Exercise treatment for bipolar disorder: Potential mechanisms of action mediated through increased neurogenesis and decreased allostatic load. *Psychotherapy and Psychosomatics*, *79*, 87–96.

Taft, C.T., Bryant-Davis, T., Woodward, H.E., Tillman, S., & Torres, S.E. (2009). Intimate partner violence against African American women: An examination of the socio-cultural context. *Aggression and Violent Behavior*, *14*(1), 50–58.

Takayanagi, Y., & Onaka, T. (2022). Roles of oxytocin in stress responses, allostasis and resilience. *International Journal of Molecular Sciences*, *23*(1), 150.

Takeuchi, D.T., Gong, F., & Gee, G. (2012). The NLAAS story: Some reflections, some insights. *Asian American Journal of Psychology*, *3*(2), 121.

Tamir, C. (2021). *The growing diversity of Black America*. Pew Research Center. www.pewresearch.org/social-trends/2021/03/25/the-growing-diversity-of-black-america/.

Tan, M., Mamun, A., Kitzman, H., & Dodgen, L. (2019). Longitudinal changes in allostatic load during a randomized church-based, lifestyle intervention in African American women. *Ethnicity & Disease*, *29*, 297–308.

Tarrier, N., Taylor, K., & Gooding, P. (2008). Cognitive-behavioral interventions to reduce suicide behavior: A systematic review and meta-analysis. *Behavior Modification*, *32*(1), 77–108.

Tarullo, A.R., & Gunnar, M.R. (2006). Child maltreatment and the developing HPA axis. *Hormones and Behavior*, *50*, 632–639.

Tao, Y., Yang, J., & Chai, Y. (2020). The anatomy of health-supportive neighborhoods: A multilevel analysis of built environment, perceived disorder, social interaction and mental health in Beijing. *International Journal of Environmental Research and Public Health*, *17*(1), 13.

Taylor, S.E., Saphire-Bernstein, S., & Seeman, T.E. (2010). Are plasma oxytocin in women and plasma vasopressin in men biomarkers of distressed pair-bond relationships? *Psychological Science*, *21*, 3–7.

Tebbe, E.A., & Moradi, B. (2016). Suicide risk in trans populations: An application of minority stress theory. *Journal of Counseling Psychology*, *63*(5), 520.

Terpstra, S., Beekman, A., Abbing, J., Jaken, S., Steendam, M., & Gilissen, R. (2018). Suicide prevention gatekeeper training in the Netherlands improves gatekeepers' knowledge of suicide prevention and their confidence to discuss suicidality, an observational study. *BMC Public Health*, *18*(1), 1–8.

The Trevor Project. *2022 National Survey on LGBTQ Youth Mental Health*. Retrieved March 19, 2023, from: www.thetrevorproject.org/survey-2022/.

The White House. (2021). *Reducing military and veteran suicide: Advancing a comprehensive, cross-sector, evidence-informed public health strategy.* www.whitehouse.gov/wp-content/uploads/2021/11/Military-and-Veteran-Suicide-Prevention-Strategy.pdf.

The White House. (2022). *FACT SHEET: Biden-Harris administration actions to prevent suicide.* Retrieved March 19, 2023, from: www.whitehouse.gov/briefing-room/statements-releases/2022/09/30/fact-sheet-biden-harris-administration-actions-to-prevent-suicide/.

Tomba, E., & Offidani, E. (2012). A clinimetric evaluation of allostatic overload in the general population. *Psychotherapy and Psychosomatics,* 81(6), 378.

Thompson, M.P., Kingree, J.B., & Lamis, D. (2019). Associations of adverse childhood experiences and suicidal behaviors in adulthood in a US nationally representative sample. *Child: Care, Health and Development,* 45(1), 121–128.

Timpl, P., Spanagel, R., Sillaber, I., Kresse, A., Reul, J.M., Stalla, G.K., ... & Wurst, W. (1998). Impaired stress response and reduced anxiety in mice lacking a functional corticotropin-releasing hormone receptor 1. *Nature Genetics,* 19(2), 162–166.

Tomlinson, M.W. (2012). War, peace and suicide: The case of Northern Ireland. *International Sociology,* 27(4), 464–482.

Tomoda, A., Sheu, Y.S., Rabi, K., Suzuki, H., Navalta, C.P., Polcari, A., & Teicher, M.H. (2011). Exposure to parental verbal abuse is associated with increased gray matter volume in superior temporal gyrus. *Neuroimage,* 54, S280–S286.

Tomoda, A., Polcari, A., Anderson, C.M., & Teicher, M.H. (2012). Reduced visual cortex gray matter volume and thickness in young adults who witnessed domestic violence during childhood. *PloS One,* 7(12), e52528.

Torgler, B., & Schaltegger, C.A. (2012). *Suicide and religion: New evidence on the differences between Protestantism and Catholicism.* Center for Research in Economics, Management and the Arts (CREMA) Working Paper, No. 2012-12, CREMA, Basel. Retrieved March 19, 2023, from: www.crema-research.ch/wp-content/uploads/2022/01/suicide-and-religion-new-evidence-on-the-differences-between-protestantism-and-catholicism.pdf.

Torok, M., Han, J., Baker, S., Werner-Seidler, A., Wong, I., Larsen, M.E., & Christensen, H. (2020). Suicide prevention using self-guided digital interventions: A systematic review and meta-analysis of randomised controlled trials. *The Lancet Digital Health,* 2(1), e25–e36.

Torous, J., Bucci, S., Bell, I.H., Kessing, L.V., Faurholt-Jepsen, M., Whelan, P., ... & Firth, J. (2021). The growing field of digital psychiatry: Current evidence and the future of apps, social media, chatbots, and virtual reality. *World Psychiatry,* 20(3), 318–335.

Torous, J., Myrick, K.J., Rauseo-Ricupero, N., & Firth, J. (2020). Digital mental health and COVID-19: Using technology today to accelerate the curve on access and quality tomorrow. *JMIR Mental Health,* 7(3), e18848.

Treadway, M.T., Waskom, M.L., Dillon, D.G., Holmes, A.J., Park, M.T.M., Chakravarty, M.M., ... & Pizzagalli, D.A. (2015). Illness progression, recent stress, and morphometry of hippocampal subfields and medial prefrontal cortex in major depression. *Biological Psychiatry, 77*(3), 285–294.

Tripodianakis, J., Markianos, M., Rouvali, O., & Istikoglou, C. (2007). Gonadal axis hormones in psychiatric male patients after a suicide attempt. *European Archives of Psychiatry and Clinical Neuroscience, 257*, 135–139.

Tsai, M., Lari, H., Saffy, S., & Klonsky, E.D. (2021). Examining the three-step theory (3ST) of suicide in a prospective study of adult psychiatric inpatients. *Behavior Therapy, 52*(3), 673–685.

Tu, P.C., Yeh, D.C., & Hsieh, H.C. (2020). Positive psychological changes after breast cancer diagnosis and treatment: The role of trait resilience and coping styles. *Journal of Psychosocial Oncology, 38*(2), 156–170.

Tunnard, C., Rane, L.J., Wooderson, S.C., Markopoulou, K., Poon, L., Fekadu, A., … & Cleare, A.J. (2014). The impact of childhood adversity on suicidality and clinical course in treatment-resistant depression. *Journal of Affective Disorders, 152*, 122–130.

Turner, R.M. (2000). Naturalistic evaluation of dialectical behavior therapy-oriented treatment for borderline personality disorder. *Cognitive and Behavioral Practice, 7*(4), 413–419.

Turecki, G., Brent, D.A., Gunnell, D., O'Connor, R.C., Oquendo, M.A., Pirkis, J., & Stanley, B.H. (2019). Suicide and suicide risk. *Nature Reviews Disease Primers, 5*(1), 1–22.

Turvey, C., Stromquist, A., Kelly, K., Zwerling, C., & Merchant, J. (2002). Financial loss and suicidal ideation in a rural community sample. *Acta Psychiatrica Scandinavica, 106*(5), 373–380.

Tuttle, J. (2018). Specifying the effect of social welfare expenditures on homicide and suicide: A cross-national, longitudinal examination of the stream analogy of lethal violence. *Justice Quarterly, 35*(1), 87–113.

Tyndal, T., Zhang, I., & Jobes, D.A. (2022). The Collaborative Assessment and Management of Suicidality (CAMS) stabilization plan for working with patients with suicide risk. *Psychotherapy, 59*(2), 143.

Uebelacker, L.A., German, N.M., Gaudiano, B.A., & Miller, I.W. (2011). Patient health questionnaire depression scale as a suicide screening instrument in depressed primary care patients: A cross-sectional study. *The Primary Care Companion for CNS Disorders, 13*(1), 27081.

U.S. Census Bureau. (2022). *About the topic of race.* Retrieved March 19, 2023, from: www.census.gov/topics/population/race/about.html.

U.S. Department of Veterans Affairs. (2018). *National strategy for preventing veteran suicide 2018–2028.* www.mentalhealth.va.gov/suicide_prevention/docs/Office-of-Mental-Health-and-Suicide-Prevention-National-Strategy-for-Preventing-Veterans-Suicide.pdf.

U.S. Department of Veterans Affairs. (2022). *National Veteran Suicide Prevention Annual Report.* www.mentalhealth.va.gov/docs/data-sheets/2022/2022-National-Veteran-Suicide-Prevention-Annual-Report-FINAL-508.pdf.

U.S. Department of Veterans Affairs and Department of Defense. (2019). *VA/DoD clinical practice guideline for the assessment and management of patients at risk for suicide.* www.healthquality.va.gov/guidelines/MH/srb/VADoDSuicideRiskFullCPGFinal5088212019.pdf.

U.S. Food and Drug Administration. (2022). *Information on clozapine.* www.fda.gov/drugs/postmarket-drug-safety-information-patients-and-providers/information-clozapine.

U.S. Office of the Surgeon General; *National strategy for suicide prevention: Goals and objectives for action: A Report of the U.S. Surgeon General and of the National Action Alliance for Suicide Prevention.* Washington, DC: US Department of Health & Human Services (US). PMID: 23136686.

U.S. Office of the Surgeon General; National Action Alliance for Suicide Prevention. (2021). *The Surgeon General's call to action to implement the national strategy for suicide prevention.* www.hhs.gov/sites/default/files/sprc-call-to-action.pdf.

Van Aalst, J., Ceccarini, J., Demyttenaere, K., Sunaert, S., & Van Laere, K. (2020). What has neuroimaging taught us on the neurobiology of yoga? A review. *Frontiers in Integrative Neuroscience, 14,* 34.

Van Der Feltz-Cornelis, C.M., Sarchiapone, M., Postuvan, V., Volker, D., Roskar, S., Grum, A.T., … & Hegerl, U. (2011). Best practice elements of multilevel suicide prevention strategies. *Crisis, 32*(6), 319–333.

Van Heeringen, C. (2001). The suicidal process and related concepts. In C. Van Heeringen (Ed.). *Understanding suicidal behaviour: The suicidal process approach to research, treatment and prevention* (pp. 1–15). Wiley.

van Heeringen, K. (2012). Stress-diathesis model of suicidal behavior. In Yogesh Dwivedi (Ed.). *The neurobiological basis of suicide* (pp. 113–123). CRC Press

van Heeringen, K., & Mann, J.J. (2014). The neurobiology of suicide. *The Lancet Psychiatry, 1,* 63–72.

Van Orden, K.A., Witte, T.K., Cukrowicz, K.C., Braithwaite, S.R., Selby, E.A., & Joiner Jr, T.E. (2010). The interpersonal theory of suicide. *Psychological Review, 117*(2), 575.

VanSickle, M., Werbel, A., Perera, K., Pak, K., DeYoung, K., & Ghahramanlou-Holloway, M. (2016). Perceived barriers to seeking mental health care among United States Marine Corps noncommissioned officers serving as gatekeepers for suicide prevention. *Psychological Assessment, 28*(8), 1020.

Vaynman, S., Ying, Z., & Gomez-Pinilla, F. (2004). Hippocampal BDNF mediates the efficacy of exercise on synaptic plasticity and cognition. *European Journal of Neuroscience, 20*(10), 2580–2590.

Velupillai, S., Hadlaczky, G., Baca-Garcia, E., Gorrell, G.M., Werbeloff, N., Nguyen, D., … & Dutta, R. (2019). Risk assessment tools and data-driven approaches for predicting and preventing suicidal behavior. *Frontiers in Psychiatry, 10,* 36.

Vespa, J. (2018). *The graying of America: More older adults than kids by 2035.* www.census.gov/library/stories/2018/03/graying-america.html#:~:text=By%202060%2C%20nearly%20one%20in,caregiving%20and%20assisted%20living%20facilities.

Vijayakumar, L., Mohanraj, R., Kumar, S., Jeyaseelan, V., Sriram, S., & Shanmugam, M. (2017). CASP: An intervention by community volunteers to reduce suicidal behaviour among refugees. *International Journal of Social Psychiatry, 63*(7), 589–597.

Villemure, C., Ceko, M., Cotton, V.A., & Bushnell, M.C. (2015). Neuroprotective effects of yoga practice: Age-, experience-, and frequency-dependent plasticity. *Frontiers in Human Neuroscience, 9*, 281.

Visser, V.S., Comans, T.A., & Scuffham, P.A. (2014). Evaluation of the effectiveness of a community-based crisis intervention program for people bereaved by suicide. *Journal of Community Psychology, 42*(1), 19–28.

Walker, E.F., Brennan, P.A., Esterberg, M., Brasfield, J., Pearce, B., & Compton, M.T. (2010). Longitudinal changes in cortisol secretion and conversion to psychosis in at-risk youth. *Journal of Abnormal Psychology, 119*(2), 401.

Walsh, C.G., Ribeiro, J.D., & Franklin, J.C. (2017). Predicting suicide risk attempts over time through machine learning. *Clinical Psychological Science, 5*(3), 457–469.

Walsh, C.G., Ribeiro, J.D., & Franklin, J.C. (2018). Predicting suicide attempts in adolescents with longitudinal clinical data and machine learning. *Journal of Child Psychology and Psychiatry, 59*, 1261–1270.

Wang, J., Brown, M.M., Ivey-Stephenson, A.Z., Xu, L., & Stone, D.M. (2022). Rural–urban comparisons in the rates of self-harm, US, 2018. *American Journal of Preventive Medicine, 63*(1), 117–120.

Wang, P.S., Lane, M., Olfson, M., Pincus, H.A., Wells, K.B., & Kessler, R.C. (2005). Twelve-month use of mental health services in the United States: Results from the National Comorbidity Survey Replication. *Archives of General Psychiatry, 62*(6), 629–640.

Warnez, S., & Alessi-Severini, S. (2014). Clozapine: A review of clinical practice guidelines and prescribing trends. *BMC Psychiatry 14*, 102.

Wasserman, I.M. (1983). Political business cycles, presidential elections, and suicide and mortality patterns. *American Sociological Review, 48*(5), 711–720.

Wasserman, D., Rihmer, Z., Rujescu, D., Sarchiapone, M., Sokolowski, M., Titelman, D., … & Carli, V. (2012). The European Psychiatric Association (EPA) guidance on suicide treatment and prevention. *European Psychiatry, 27*(2), 129–141.

Watts, S., Newby, J.M., Mewton, L., & Andrews, G. (2012). A clinical audit of changes in suicide ideas with internet treatment for depression. *BMJ Open, 2*(5), e001558.

Weissinger, G., Myhre, K., Ruan-Iu, L., Van Fossen, C., & Diamond, G. (2022). Adolescent suicide risk, firearm access, and family functioning: Screening in primary care. *Families, Systems, & Health.* Advance online publication. https://doi.org/10.1037/fsh0000680.

Westrin, Å., Ekman, R., & Träskman-Bendz, L. (1999). Alterations of corticotropin releasing hormone (CRH) and neuropeptide Y (NPY) plasma levels in mood disorder patients with a recent suicide attempt. *European Neuropsychopharmacology, 9*, 205–211.

West, J., Otte, C., Geher, K., Johnson, J., & Mohr, D.C. (2004). Effects of Hatha yoga and African dance on perceived stress, affect, and salivary cortisol. *Annals of Behavioral Medicine, 28,* 114–118.

White, J., Marsh, I., Kral, M.J., & Morris, J. (Eds.). (2015). *Critical suicidology: Transforming suicide research and prevention for the 21st century.* UBC Press.

WHO. (2012). *Public health action for the prevention of suicide: A framework.* https://apps.who.int/iris/bitstream/handle/10665/75166/?sequence=1.

WHO. (2014). *Preventing suicide: A global imperative.* www.who.int/publications/i/item/9789241564779.

WHO. (2019). *Suicide: One person dies every 40 seconds.* www.who.int/news/item/09-09-2019-suicide-one-person-dies-every-40-seconds

WHO. (2021). *Suicide worldwide in 2019: Global health estimates.* www.who.int/publications/i/item/9789240026643

Widom, C.S., Horan, J., & Brzustowicz, L., 2015. Childhood maltreatment predicts allostatic load in adulthood. *Child Abuse & Neglect, 47,* 59–69.

Wiglesworth, A., Clement, D.N., Wingate, L.R., & Klimes-Dougan, B. (2022). Understanding suicide risk for youth who are both Black and Native American: The role of intersectionality and multiple marginalization. *Suicide and Life-Threatening Behavior, 52*(4), 668–682.

Wilks, C.R., Lungu, A., Ang, S.Y., Matsumiya, B., Yin, Q., & Linehan, M.M. (2018). A randomized controlled trial of an Internet delivered dialectical behavior therapy skills training for suicidal and heavy episodic drinkers. *Journal of Affective Disorders, 232,* 219–228.

Williams, D.R., Smelser, N., Wilson, W.J., & Mitchell, F. (2001). Racial variations in adult health status: Patterns, paradoxes and prospects. In National Research Council. *America becoming: Racial trends and their consequences, Volume II* (pp. 371–410). Washington, DC: National Academy of Sciences Press.

Williams, D.Y., Wexler, L., & Mueller, A.S. (2022). Suicide postvention in schools: What evidence supports our current national recommendations?. *School Social Work Journal, 46*(2), 23–69.

Williams, J.M.G. (2001). *The cry of pain.* Penguin.

Wingate, L.R., Burns, A.B., Gordon, K.H., Perez, M., Walker, R.L., Williams, F.M., & Joiner Jr, T.E. (2006). Suicide and positive cognitions: Positive psychology applied to the understanding and treatment of suicidal behavior. In T.E. Ellis (Ed.), *Cognition and suicide: Theory, research, and therapy* (pp. 261–283). American Psychological Association.

Winger, J.G., Adams, R.N., & Mosher, C.E. (2016). Relations of meaning in life and sense of coherence to distress in cancer patients: A meta-analysis. *Psycho-oncology, 25*(1), 2–10.

Winter, J., Meyer, M., Berger, I., Royer, M., Bianchi, M., Kuffner, K., ... & Neumann, I.D. (2021). Chronic oxytocin-driven alternative splicing of Crfr2α induces anxiety. *Molecular Psychiatry,* 1–14.

Witt, K., Potts, J., Hubers, A., Grunebaum, M.F., Murrough, J.W., Loo, C., ... & Hawton, K. (2020). Ketamine for suicidal ideation in adults with psychiatric disorders: A systematic review and meta-analysis of treatment trials. *Australian & New Zealand Journal of Psychiatry, 54*(1), 29–45.

Witt, K., Spittal, M.J., Carter, G., Pirkis, J., Hetrick, S., Currier, D., ... & Milner, A. (2017). Effectiveness of online and mobile telephone applications ('apps') for the self-management of suicidal ideation and self-harm: A systematic review and meta-analysis. *BMC Psychiatry, 17*, 1–18.

Witt, K.G., Hetrick, S.E., Rajaram, G., Hazell, P., Taylor Salisbury, T.L., Townsend, E., Hawton, K. (2021). Psychosocial interventions for self-harm in adults. *Cochrane Database of Systematic Reviews, 4*(4), Art. No.: CD013668. DOI: 10.1002/14651858.CD013668.pub2.

Wolford-Clevenger, C., Vann, N.C., & Smith, P.N. (2016). The association of partner abuse types and suicidal ideation among men and women college students. *Violence and Victims, 31*(3), 471–485.

Wolfson, J.A., Azrael, D., & Miller, M. (2020). Gun ownership among US women. *Injury Prevention, 26*(1), 49–54.

Wu, H., Lu, L., Qian, Y., Jin, X.H., Yu, H.R., Du, L., ... & Zhu, B. (2022). The significance of cognitive-behavioral therapy on suicide: An umbrella review of systematic reviews and meta-analysis. *Journal of Affective Disorders, 317*, 142–148.

Wyder, M., Ray, M.K., Russell, S., Kinsella, K., Crompton, D., & van den Akker, J. (2021). Suicide risk assessment in a large public mental health service: Do suicide risk classifications identify those at risk? *Australasian Psychiatry, 29*(3), 322–325.

Wyder, M., Ward, P., & De Leo, D. (2009). Separation as a suicide risk factor. *Journal of Affective Disorders, 116*(3), 208–213.

Xavier, A., Otero, P., Blanco, V., & Vázquez, F.L. (2019). Efficacy of a problem-solving intervention for the indicated prevention of suicidal risk in young Brazilians: Randomized controlled trial. *Suicide and Life-Threatening Behavior, 49*(6), 1746–1761.

Xuan, Z., Naimi, T.S., Kaplan, M.S., Bagge, C.L., Few, L.R., Maisto, S., ... & Freeman, R. (2016). Alcohol policies and suicide: A review of the literature. *Alcoholism: Clinical and Experimental Research, 40*(10), 2043–2055.

Yang, H., Leaver, A.M., Siddarth, P., Paholpak, P., Ercoli, L., St Cyr, N.M., ... & Lavretsky, H. (2016). Neurochemical and neuroanatomical plasticity following memory training and yoga interventions in older adults with mild cognitive impairment. *Frontiers in Aging Neuroscience, 8*, 277.

Yang, L., Liu, X., Chen, W., & Li, L. (2019). A test of the three-step theory of suicide among Chinese people: A study based on the ideation-to-action framework. *Archives of Suicide Research, 23*(4), 648–661.

Yard, E., et al. (2021). Emergency department visits for suspected suicide attempts among persons aged 12-25 years before and during the COVID-19 pandemic – United States, January 2019-May 2021. *MMWR Morbidity and Mortality Weekly Report, 70*, 888–894.

Ye, Z.J., Qiu, H.Z., Liang, M.Z., Liu, M.L., Li, P.F., Chen, P., ... & Zhao, J.J. (2017). Effect of a mentor-based, supportive-expressive program, Be Resilient to Breast Cancer, on survival in metastatic breast cancer: A randomised, controlled intervention trial. *British Journal of Cancer, 117*(10), 1486–1494.

Yeager, D.S., & Dweck, C.S. (2012). Mindsets that promote resilience: When students believe that personal characteristics can be developed. *Educational Psychologist, 47*(4), 302–314.

Yehuda, R. (2005). Neuroendocrine aspects of PTSD. In *Anxiety and anxiolytic drugs* (pp. 371–403). Springer.

Yehuda, R. (2006). Advances in understanding neuroendocrine alterations in PTSD and their therapeutic implications. *Annals of the New York Academy of Sciences, 1071*, 137–166.

Yi, J.P., Vitaliano, P.P., Smith, R.E., Yi, J.C., & Weinger, K. (2008). The role of resilience on psychological adjustment and physical health in patients with diabetes. *British Journal of Health Psychology, 13*(2), 311–325.

Yip, P.S., Yousuf, S., Chan, C.H., Yung, T., & Wu, K.C.C. (2015). The roles of culture and gender in the relationship between divorce and suicide risk: A meta-analysis. *Social Science & Medicine, 128*, 87–94.

Yonemoto, N., Kawashima, Y., Endo, K., & Yamada, M. (2019). Gatekeeper training for suicidal behaviors: A systematic review. *Journal of Affective Disorders, 246*, 506–514.

You, S., Van Orden, K.A., & Conner, K.R. (2011). Social connections and suicidal thoughts and behavior. *Psychology of Addictive Behaviors, 25*(1), 180.

Youssef-Morgan, C.M., & Luthans, F. (2015). Psychological capital and well-being. *Stress and Health, 31*, 180–188.

Yuryev, A., Värnik, A., Värnik, P., Sisask, M., & Leppik, L. (2012). Role of social welfare in European suicide prevention. *International Journal of Social Welfare, 21*(1), 26–33.

Zalsman, G., Hawton, K., Wasserman, D., van Heeringen, K., Arensman, E., Sarchiapone, M., ... & Zohar, J. (2016). Suicide prevention strategies revisited: 10-year systematic review. *The Lancet Psychiatry, 3*(7), 646–659.

Zayas, L.H., & Gulbas, L.E. (2012). Are suicide attempts by young Latinas a cultural idiom of distress? *Transcultural Psychiatry, 49*(5), 718–734.

Zhang, J., Jia, C.X., & Wang, L.L. (2015). Testosterone differs between suicide attempters and community controls in men and women of China. *Physiology & Behavior, 141*, 40–45.

Zhang, X., Yin, G., Cui, R., Zhao, G., & Yang, W. (2018). Stress-induced functional alterations in amygdala: Implications for neuropsychiatric diseases. *Frontiers in Neuroscience, 12*, 367.

Zisook, S., Shear, M.K., Reynolds, C.F., Simon, N.M., Mauro, C., Skritskaya, N.A., ... & Qiu, X. (2018). Treatment of complicated grief in survivors of suicide loss: A HEAL report. *The Journal of Clinical Psychiatry, 79*(2), 17m11592.

Zivony, A., & Lobel, T. (2014). The invisible stereotypes of bisexual men. *Archives of Sexual Behavior, 43*, 1165–1176.

Zonana, J., Simberlund, J., & Christos, P. (2018). The impact of safety plans in an outpatient clinic. *Crisis, 39*(4), 304–309.

Index

optimism, 81, 95–100, 102, 103, 105
Oregon, 64
oxytocin, 40–43

paraventricular nucleus, 35–36
past attempts, 13–16, 61, 70, 71, 80, 105
Patient Health Questionnaire-9, 68–69
PCT. *See* Perceptual Control Theory
peer support, 44, 105
perceived burdensomeness, 61, 71, 104, 105
Perceptual Control Theory, 12
PHQ-9. *See* Patient Health Questionnaire-9
physical exercise. *See* exercise
poisons, 47, 89–90
positive organizations, 100
positive psychology, 97, 101, 102
positive suicidology, 98–99
post-traumatic stress disorder, 31, 33, 34, 37
postvention, 66, 75, 83–84
poverty. *See* financial problems
prefrontal cortex, 35, 40
pregnancy, 19, 57
premenstrual dysphoric disorder, 57
previous attempts, 60
primary prevention, 66, 92
problem-solving. *See* coping
problem-solving therapy, 75, 95
PST. *See* problem-solving therapy
PsyCap. *See* psychological capital
psychache, 9
psychodynamic theories, 8–9
psychological capital, 100–101
psychosis, 33, 36, 43, 73, 95
PTSD. *See* post-traumatic stress disorder
public health approach, 4, 88, 93, 102
purpose. *See* meaning in life

quarrying, 64

rates, United States, 4, 47, 48, 50, 52, 55–57, 91
reasons for living, 23, 25, 79, 81, 98, 105
relationship loss, 18, 19, 25, 71
religion, 22, 23, 25, 51, 63, 71
religiosity, 22–24, 54, 63
resilience, 40–42, 63, 95–100, 102, 104, 105
risk assessment, 67–72
risk stratification, 68, 69, 95
rural, 62–64, 92

safety contracts. *See* no suicide contracts
safety planning, 74, 80–84

Saint Augustine, 2
Schopenhauer, Arthur, 6–7
screening. *See* risk assessment
secondary prevention, 66, 92
self-efficacy, 86, 96, 97, 100, 106
seppuku, 1
sertraline, 99
sexual orientation. *See* LGBT
Shneidman, Edwin, 9
smartphone applications, 83–87
social isolation, 18, 35, 45, 50, 51, 55, 62, 98
social media, 103
social support, 11, 22, 25, 32, 54, 63, 70, 71, 93, 98, 105
social-ecological model, 66, 92, 100
societal-level interventions, 89–93
stigma, xi, 19–20, 52, 61, 62, 74, 84, 85, 91, 94, 103, 104
Stoics, 1–2
strengths, 98, 99, 101, 102, 104
substance use, 13, 16, 23, 43, 55, 60, 62, 63, 71, 79, 85, 90, 105
suicidal mode, 12
suicide capability, 10–12, 93
surveillance, 91
Systems Training for Emotional Predictability and Problem Solving, 75

Teachable Moment Brief Intervention, 75
technology-based interventions, 84–87
telehealth, 80, 84–86
telomeres, 36
tertiary prevention, 66
testosterone, 57, 58
Thanatos, 8
Three-Step Theory, 11–12
thwarted belongingness, 71, 104
training, 68, 69
trauma, xi, 44, 51, 53, 55, 57, 71

unemployment, 10, 17, 21, 25, 49
urban, 62–64

Veterans, 64

war, 21
welfare. *See* economic support
well-being, 98, 99, 101, 104
White, 25, 48, 50, 54–56, 58, 74
Wyoming, 64

young adults, 49, 51, 53, 54, 58, 60

Milton Keynes UK
Ingram Content Group UK Ltd.
UKHW020646011123
431708UK00022B/118